W9-ADP-589

YOUR CHEATIN' HEART

"THE DEFINITIVE BIOGRAPHY OF A MAJOR AMERICAN FOLK HERO."
—Austin *American-Statesman*

"Savvy reporting, raw social history, and fine writing . . . A tingling vision that will live in your head for quite a spell."
—Timothy White, author of the bestselling *Catch a Fire: The Life of Bob Marley*

"A superior piece of scholarship and writing."
—*Los Angeles Times*

"The explosive life story that deserves to be read by every urban cowboy in America."
—*Playboy*

"Hank's story has been told before, but . . . never better." —*Dallas Times-Herald*

"A vivid, moving picture of a remarkable man." —Nashville *Tennessean*

Music writer CHET FLIPPO is a veteran contributor to *Rolling Stone* magazine. He is the author of *Yesterday: The Unauthorized Biography of Paul McCartney* and *On the Road With the Rolling Stones.*

Your Cheatin' Heart

A BIOGRAPHY OF HANK WILLIAMS

CHET FLIPPO

ST. MARTIN'S PRESS/NEW YORK

Published by arrangement with the author

YOUR CHEATIN' HEART

Copyright © 1981 by Chet Flippo.

Library of Congress Catalog Card Number: 80-20582

ISBN: 0-312-91400-8   Can. ISBN: 0-312-91401-6

Printed in the United States of America

Simon and Schuster edition/June 1981
First St. Martin's Press mass market edition/February 1989

10 9 8 7 6 5 4 3 2 1

For
Herman P. Willis,
J. J. B. Flippo,
and
M. H. Flippo

Preface to the
Paperback Edition

In the years since this book was first published, a major and previously unknown event in Hank Williams's life has come to light. A woman claiming to be Hank's illegitimate daughter has stepped forward—along with conclusive evidence to support her case.

When I was researching *Your Cheatin' Heart*, I learned that in the last few months of his life Hank had carried on at least one half-way serious love affair, in spite of his precarious health. And I discovered that the object of his affections, after she had become pregnant by Hank, had moved into the Montgomery rooming house of Hank's mother, Lillian Skipper Williams Stone. So Hank spent his last days under the same roof with his second wife, his lover, and his mother. The pregnancy was a closely guarded secret, but Hank admitted in writing that he was responsible for it, and that he agreed to financially care for the child until he or she had gained her majority. I learned that this unidentified lover had given birth to a child just five days after Hank died.

But a veil of secrecy descended after that. Any traces of a Hank lover and a Hank love child vanished. I would not find out why for many years.

The person who claimed to be the love child came forward in a 1985 interview and announced her claim to the Hank Williams estate. (The story, which appeared in *Southern* magazine, was reported and written by Martha Hume, to whom I am fortunate to be married.)

What happened, this love child and her lawyer said, was this: Hank's lover had been a Nashville secretary named Bobbie Jett, who was no stranger to country music stars.

She met Hank and was swept up by his aura of danger and recklessness and living on the edge. They became lovers and, after she discovered she was pregnant, was taken in by Hank's mother Lilly, a very tough, no-nonsense woman who had seen just about all there was that life could throw at someone. Just who persuaded Hank to sign the paternity agreement has never been determined: it was out of character for him, but he did so.

After his death on New Year's Day of 1953 and after this child's birth soon after, Lilly shouldered an additional burden. She legally adopted the baby girl (who had been born as "Antha Belle Jett") and named her Catherine Yvonne Stone.

When Lilly died in 1955, her daughter Irene was appointed legal guardian of Hank Williams, Jr. on March 7. Three days later, she gave Catherine Yvonne Stone up for adoption. The Hank Williams estate, administered by Irene, provided $2,000 to be invested for Catherine Yvonne Stone, to be claimed on her 21st birthday. Once the child went into the foster care system, all legal records involving her were sealed.

The next year, she went to a foster family in Pine Level. Still later, Wayne and Louise Deupree of Mobile took her in and filed for adoption. The adoption became final in 1959. Catherine Yvonne Stone now became Catherine Louise Deupree. She grew up in Mobile as a typical teenager. She knew that she was adopted and pestered her parents about her origin. They were reluctant to say anything. They suspected that Hank was the father but did not know for sure. In a 1967 closed-hearing lawsuit, which pitted Hank Jr.'s mother Audrey against Irene and the publishing house of Acuff-Rose, the matter of the lost daughter was brought up, but apparently—the court records have not been released—it was ruled that the daughter was ineligible to inherit. Under Alabama law, even though the father admitted paternity, there had to be proof that the father had supported the child—or, at least, that his estate had supported the child. Catherine's adoptive parents, the Deuprees, declined to testify.

Time went on. Catherine was graduated from Bishop Toolen High School. She became a physical education major at the University of Alabama at Tuscaloosa. She pledged a sorority and did all the things Alabama college students do.

When she turned 21 in 1974, she was informed by the court in Montgomery County that some money was waiting for her. It turned out to be a check for $2,000 from the estate of a Mrs. Stone. (Obviously the money had never been invested.) Catherine became very curious about this Mrs. Stone, but was unable to learn anything. Meanwhile, she was graduated from the University in 1975, and married an Eastern Airlines pilot.

Five years later, apparently weighed down by years of speculation about Catherine's real identity and anguish about having never faced it, Catherine's adoptive father told her what he knew and suspected about her heritage. She started searching earnestly for her past, for her identity. She found her first foster family; she found a woman from Lilly's boarding house who remembered her; and she found out what had happened to her real mother—who had moved to California and died there in 1974. But Catherine could not get access to her adoption records.

Then she met a high-powered lawyer who said he could get things done. He was F. Keith Adkinson, a University of Virginia Law School graduate who had been operating on the fringes of national government for some time. He had been a special counsel and investigator for the United States Senate Permanent Subcommittee on Investigations until he had been invited to resign. He was later cleared of any wrongdoing. Nonetheless, Adkinson was a skillful investigator and was plugged into the ways of government. He successfully sued for possession of Catherine's adoption records. Along the way, Catherine was divorced from her airline pilot husband. She married Keith Adkinson and they are now suing for a share of Hank Williams' legacy. Should they win, the money awarded could be astronomical. They have some formidable adversaries, whom you will meet in these pages.

Still, all the evidence suggests that Catherine, who decided to call herself "Jett Williams" after she became sure of who she was, really is the daughter of Hank Williams. After she announced that she was Hank's flesh and blood, someone very close to her gave her a copy of this book, suggesting that it would explain her heritage in black and white. I spoke with her later and she agreed the book had helped. For my part, I have little doubt that she is indeed Jett Williams, and I wish her Godspeed.

Her tale only serves to heighten the drama of Hank's tortured life—and its lingering, intricate half-lives that threaten to outlive the very lawyers and litigants who will never let him rest.

Chet Flippo
New York City
May, 1988

Preface

I FIRST BECAME aware of Hank Williams sometime in the summer of 1951 as a kid in Fort Worth, Texas, riding around in the back seat of a 1949 Mercury convertible. It seemed, that summer, as though Hank Williams was about the only singer there was. His songs, especially his heart-rending love-sick laments, were seemingly all I heard on that Mercury's radio and on jukeboxes in cafes and drive-ins. Without being told, even then I knew that Hank Williams was somebody special.

When he died, just twenty-nine years old, on New Year's Day of 1953, he was mourned in Fort Worth on a scale that befitted the passing of a national hero. To this day, when you walk into most homes in the South and mention the name "Hank" in connection with music, everyone knows who you're talking about.

Hank Williams was the first country singer and songwriter whose songs consistently crossed over to the pop music audience, heartfelt songs like "Your Cheatin'

Heart" and "Cold, Cold Heart" and "I'm So Lonesome I Could Cry," with such undeniable emotional appeal that they transcend time and place and audience. Almost everybody, it seemed, could identify with the suffering that Hank Williams packed into a two-and-a-half-minute blues song. What everyone didn't know, as it turned out, was that Williams was privately suffering most of what he sang about so convincingly.

He was raised in the most abject poverty in Alabama; he had an absentee father and a domineering mother and an equally domineering first wife. He also had a crippling birth defect of the lower spine, which had never been treated and which eventually drove him to drugs and alcohol.

He was the first Cadillac cowboy. Yet he never believed he had earned the astonishing success that was his; he felt success had been forced upon him, a bitter pill to be choked down daily. The pull Hank felt between God and Satan showed in his recordings: he recorded Saturday night "sin" songs; his alter ego, "Luke the Drifter," recorded Sunday morning messages of hope. In the end, Saturday night won the battle, and Hank lost it on a combination of drugs and alcohol.

For years, I had collected Hank Williams records and memorabilia. In 1977, I began serious research for this book. I started with newspaper and magazine clips and was surprised at how little there was, until I remembered that in the late 1940s and early 1950s, hillbilly singers like Hank were not considered respectable by the media. Consequently, the clips show only two or three concert reviews, two or three interviews, an arrest record and accounts of domestic squabbles.

Unlike today's music superstars, Hank Williams had no press agent and did not want one. He distrusted the press and preferred direct contact with his audience, in the country tradition.

After the clips, I read the books—previous biographies of Hank and the histories of the South and of country music. There was still not a complete picture of Hank. A very private person, he seldom read anything but comic books and record charts and almost never wrote a letter.

It was not much to go on. I began interviewing dozens of people who had known and worked with Hank. But memories have a way of becoming highly selective after many years. Several different Hanks were emerging from the interviews. Many of Hank's Alabama friends and acquaintances swore that Hank never took a drink; many of those from Nashville said that he was not only a falling-down drunk but also the first country star to take amphetamines. I needed to find some balance.

I went through the files of the Country Music Foundation Library and Media Center in Nashville and of the John Edwards Memorial Foundation at UCLA in Los Angeles, the two leading country music archives. I found the few remaining tapes of Hank: his radio shows, his Grand Ole Opry appearances, his famous Sickbed Announcement. I found a tape of his funeral and kinescopes of his few television appearances. The filmmaker Paul Schrader gave me copies of Hank's home movies with Fred Rose, so I could study their mannerisms. I exchanged correspondence with many members of the large network of fiercely dedicated Hank Williams admirers. I bought every Hank Williams record ever made. I went through the entire history of the Grand Ole Opry. I placed discreet classified ads in newspapers around the country and received some very satisfying replies. I searched years of back issues of *Billboard* and *Country Song Roundup*. I was able to get my hands on some M-G-M royalty statements regarding Hank's records. I found copies of some of his travel records, of his divorce records. I poured over phone books, catalogs, and road maps from the 30s, 40s, and 50s. I obtained the Okla-

homa State Legislature's file on Horace "Dr. Toby" Marshall, the quack doctor whose prescriptions led to Hank's
death. I corresponded with friends of the late Paul Gilley,
who sold Hank some of his best-loved songs. I went
through Hank's medical records, especially those of his
enforced drying-out periods in sanitariums, and I studied
his autopsy report. Finally, I acquired a copy of Hank's
last written words, which had never been published before.

But this book might have been just another fan story
had it not been for the wonderful people in Nashville who
provided me with what had been a private collection of
the papers of Audrey Williams, Hank's first wife. Much
of this book is based on those papers, especially the reconstructions of Hank's thoughts and his conversations.

I am very grateful to Braxton Schuffert, who was in
Williams' first band and spent days recalling conversations with Hank; my reconstructions of Hank's walks
and talks are based on such recollections.

Once I had done the research, I decided that the narra-
tive approach would best accomplish my purpose: to
write an account of Hank Williams' life with the immedi-
acy and fire that I feel it deserves. This is not meant to be
a critical biography. Nor is it a music book. It is the story
of the Hank Williams who made the music.

Special thanks go to many: John Dodds, Erica Spellman,
Paul Schrader, Martha Hume, Delfina Rattazzi, Stu
Werbin, Jim Ramsay, Susanne Weil, Jeri Simon, Paula
Batson, Speed Vogel, Earl McGrath, M. B. Rose, Jann
Wenner, Sara B. Ware, Gloria Harris, Louis Dunn,
Dewey Gibbs, Margaret Stone, Taft and Erleen Skipper,
Braxton Schuffert, Chet Atkins, Owen Bradley, Mrs.
R. R. Young, Jim Owen, Charlie Walker, Doug Hanners,
Tyra H. Berry, Audrey Winters, Minnie Pearl, Jerry Riv-
ers, the Drifting Cowboys, Hank Williams, Jr., and
Becky, Vincent Virga, Bill Malone, Doug Sahm, Town-

send Miller, Kinky Friedman, Waylon Jennings, Howard Vokes, John Rumble, Curly Fox, Helen Price Stacy, the John Edwards Memorial Foundation at UCLA, Milo B. Howard and the Alabama Department of Archives and History; Bob Oermann, Bob Pinson and the staff of the Country Music Foundation Library and Media Center in Nashville, Bill MacEwen, Faron Young, the late Tootsie Bess, Tompall Glaser, the late Vic McAlpin, and the persons in Nashville who provided access to a large collection of Audrey Williams' private papers. The Hank Williams International Appreciation Society welcomes queries at its office: 32 Georges Vanier, Roxboro, Quebec, Canada HBY 253.

CHET FLIPPO

"WE LIVED in Georgiana and my children attended school in the year '16, '17. Papa persuaded Mr. and Mrs. John Skipper and their daughter Lilly to leave a small house on our place and to move into our home so they could keep house for him at the old place during our stay in town. It was a short move— about one hundred yards. One Sunday morning, during our stay in town, E.O. and Carl left our house on Palmer Avenue for the country. They stopped at the Bryant Drug Store for a soft drink and Mr. Lonnie Williams asked if he could ride out with them. According to E.O., Lonnie talked very little on the way to the country. When they arrived, Lonnie said that he might want them to carry him somewhere in a short while. They went into the house. E.O. and Carl went into Papa's side and Lonnie went into the Skippers' section. In a short time, Lonnie called E.O. and Carl to join him in the yard. They knew that he frequently called at the Skippers' and they

knew that he was interested in Lilly. But they were un-
aware of the seriousness of his attachment to her. In the
yard he told them he wanted them to carry him and Lilly
somewhere so they could marry. The four of them piled
into our T-model and headed for Starlington where Reverend F. M. Catcher was preaching the morning sermon.
He was still preaching when they arrived, so they waited.
Within minutes of their arrival, Reverend J. C. Dunlap
drove up and E.O. suggested that maybe he would perform the ceremony. Lonnie spoke to him and everything
was in readiness. So then and there on the church
ground, Sunday, November 12, 1916, as church services
went on inside, and at 11:50 AM, Elonzo H. Williams, age
26, and Jessie LillyBelle Skipper, age 21, were married as
E.O. and Carl were eyewitnesses to the event. The
records in marriage record book number four, page two
hundred and ninety-seven shows this couple did marry
on the date stated above and that J. C. Dunlap performed
the ceremony. They went back home. E.O. and Carl went
into the Mixon quarters and the newlyweds went to her
room. There, in a west room, a room that was added
when the one-room house was enlarged to five, the room
with the arched fireplace, they spent their honeymoon
and the first five months of their marriage. They lived
there until we moved back home in the latter part of May
1917. When we moved back in May 1917, they moved
three miles south to the Wally Kendrick home, in the
vicinity of the Mount Olive Community. In the Kendrick
home, September 17, 1923, a son was born to this couple
and he later became famous nationwide as a country music writer and singer. His name was Hank Williams."

—From the Mixon family diary

1

LILLY WILLIAMS looked, in the wavering orange glow cast by the single kerosene lamp in the clapboard house's kitchen-living room-dining room, like a giant she-bear protecting her little cub. Lilly was a big, strong, rawboned Southern woman who stood right at six feet barefoot and weighed in just over 200 pounds and had a steely gaze and a good right hook. She wasn't afraid of anything or anybody, least of all a current husband. She was developing a habit of marrying weak men and the present husband, her second one, had just weaved in from the front porch breathing bootleg hooch fumes stronger than those coming from the kerosene lamp. Lilly turned her large back on Lonnie Williams and went back to tenderly bathing her little cub, five-year-old Hiram Williams, in the galvanized tin washtub on the floor. He was the only thing she would ever love, in her own peculiar way of loving, this skin-and-bones little runt splashing around in the suds of the bar soap that Lilly made herself from hog fat and ashes from the kitchen stove. She also kept the family together and she daily reminded Lonnie of that. She and little Hiram and six-year-old Irene would have long ago gone to the poorhouse or worse, she told Lonnie with an affectionate roundhouse to his ear to get his attention, if she weren't working her fingers to the very bone raising strawberries for the kids to sell. Garland, Alabama, in 1928 was not a prosperous area. The timber and cotton economy of south-central Alabama proved to be a false prosperity and families like the Williamses, who were barely marginal components of that economy to begin with, were left to scratch whatever living they could out of the hard, red dirt. Sharecroppers were lucky to make ten cents a day.

"A two-mule nigger farmer is better off than this family," Lilly would hiss at Lonnie in her nightly lecture.

Among poor white families like the Williamses, malnutrition became the rule rather than the exception, and pellagra and rickets further ravaged an entire generation of children. Lilly did whatever she could to augment the common diet of cornbread and molasses and scrap food with the little truck garden out back where she grew collard greens and sweet potatoes and green onions. Although, Lord knows, it wasn't easy for her, what with Lonnie's drinking and his precarious physical condition. "Lon enjoys ill health," Lilly would sigh to her sister Alice. Her tone made it clear that she was getting sick and tired of Lonnie's being sick and tired. She was sick and tired of stooping in the blistering heat all day to raise enough strawberries to pay their rent of $80 a year and she was sick and tired of sewing and cooking. If she was going to have to function as the man of the house, by thunder, she was going to act like the man of the house.

When Hiram Williams was born in the double-pen cabin in Mount Olive West, Alabama, at one AM on Sep-

tember 17, 1923, Lilly delivered him herself, although a
country doctor and a black midwife were present. Con-
sidering that she was weighing about 225 at the time,
removing a five-pound child was an easy enough matter.
She didn't trust doctors, anyway, and halfway blamed
them for the stillbirth of her first child. Her sister took
care of Irene during the accouchement. Lonnie occupied
himself by tasting a mason jar of liquid fire out on the
porch. Lilly tied off the umbilical cord and saw—and
refused to see—and ignored the ugly red raised spot at
the base of the baby's spine. She wrapped him in cotton
and held him and went to sleep.

They decided to name him "Hiram," but misspelled it
on the birth certificate as "Hiriam." There was no middle
name or middle initial. The name was of biblical origin:
Lonnie was a Mason and Lilly belonged to Eastern Star
and they picked Hiram after King Hiram of Tyre. Little
Hiram hated the name and years later would start calling
himself Hank.

Young Hiram was an introspective child. Indeed, there
were those who thought he was a bit thick between the
ears. He was frail. Lilly, although she was big and full-
bosomed, did not breastfeed Hiram as she had Irene. She
fed him on Eagle brand canned milk, warmed up a little
bit on the stove, and left him alone as she worked.

Lonnie Williams lurched into the house where Lilly
was bathing little Hiram. He was looking for his pouch of
Bull Durham so he could roll himself a smoke but he
stopped to regard his only male offspring.

"What's wrong with Skeet's back?" he finally asked
Lilly, pointing uncertainly to an angry red spot on his
son's lower back, a raised sore at the base of the spine.

Lilly turned on him with a fury. *"Nothin'!* Now git!
Git *out!* Nothin's wrong with the boy!"

Lonnie knew better; he had seen that sore enough
times to know there was something wrong with the boy.

But he fled anyway. He was afraid of Lilly. It didn't pay to plague her with questions.

Little Hiram, brown hair plastered to his scalp and jug ears sticking out and protruding ribs the most prominent part of his thin body, began crying. "Mamma, mamma, is there somethin' wrong with me?"

Lilly cradled him, splashing soapy water down the front of her faded cotton apron, which still bore the dim imprint of its original function as a flour sack: "Martha White Mills."

"No, baby," she whispered. "Nothin's wrong with you. Mamma'll take care of her baby." She began crooning to him: "Bye oh baby bye oh baby bye."

Lonnie went back to contemplating the purple-tinged sunset through the tall pines. He sat down heavily in his cane-back chair on the porch and rolled a smoke. He struck a match against one of the big metal buttons of his Can't-Bust-Em overalls and inhaled deeply from the cigarette. He flicked the match at a toad frog. Lonnie took a sip from his ever-ready jar of cloudy hooch. He was worried. Lonnie was not a bad-looking man. He was as tall as Lillie and was part Choctaw Indian and had the high cheekbones that Hiram inherited. His future was not bright, though, and he knew it. He was thinking about the VA hospital. Lillie had threatened him with it a couple of times but the more he thought about it, the better it began to sound to him. It was true that his health was not good. (Though if he had known that he would outlive Lilly by fourteen years . . .) But life without Lilly was not a disturbing prospect. The VA was really the only way out. Lonnie had been forced to give up his job as engineer on the donkey engine for the W. T. Smith Lumber Company over in Chapman when he developed that problem with his nerves. He started drawing a little Army pension for disability from World War I, wherein he had been disabled while stationed in France with the 113th Engineer Regiment of the 42nd Division. Lilly

thought he was suffering from shell shock and from being
gassed by the Krauts. It had been hell over there in the
trenches, he'd told Lilly, hand-to-hand combat with the
filthy Huns. He was lucky to escape with just his nerves
shot all to hell.

What was really bothering Lonnie at the moment was
his jaw. And his nerve. While he was in France, he once
got into a fist-fight with another G.I. over a French girl
that both of them wanted. The other soldier had knocked
Lonnie down with one blow with a wine bottle and then
kicked him unconscious while he was down. His jaw,
where he had been kicked, was still bothering him and he
had started having trouble talking. Although, praise
God, he was still able to ingest liquids. He took another
sip of hooch to calm his nerves and he regarded the sunset and thought awhile. Lilly. What a prize she had
seemed. A proud Skipper from the respected—if poor—
Butler County Skippers. Lonnie was only a Lowndes
County Williams. Lilly the tall and desirable. Lilly the
strong. How quickly she had turned on him after the
courtship and marriage! She had wanted so much, expected so much. It wasn't his fault he wasn't rich. His
nerves weren't right. She was too impatient, she wouldn't
give him a chance. Just like the foreman at the lumber
company. Lonnie just needed time to work things out.
People pushed him too much. He heard footsteps inside
the house. Heavy footsteps heading toward the front
door. Lonnie grabbed up his jar and his sack of Bull
Durham and slipped off the porch into the woods.

After Lilly had finally dried little Hiram's tears and his
slender body following his weekly bath, she dressed him
in his faded blue overalls—and nothing else—and sent
him out into the backyard to catch lightning bugs with
Irene. Instead, Hiram melted into the shadows by the
well and ran and ran and ran until he got to the little
cemetery by the Mount Olive Baptist Church. He felt
safe there. No one ever came there. It was peaceful.

Lilly dried her hands after Hiram's bath and headed for the front porch. It was time to have it out with Lonnie, once and for all. He had to straighten out and make something of himself and get off the bottle and take care of his family and . . . Lilly swung the screen door open and got ready to tell Lonnie a thing or two. His chair was empty. Lilly set her mouth into a thin, hard line. Lonnie was going to regret running away from her. She went to the back door and called Irene and Hiram. Only Irene came. So . . . Hiram had run off, too. He would learn to stay at home, he'd learn to mind his mamma. Like father, like . . . the thought formed in her mind.

"Irene, where's Skeets at?" "He run off, Mamma." "He's gonna get a good hidin'. Go cut me a switch."

Hiram, lying on his back between two grayish-white Skipper tombstones in the moonlight, knew that he should go home but knew that he would get a good whipping from Lilly when he got there. He shut his eyes and pretended he was somewhere else. Not far away, Lonnie did the same. Lilly waited patiently. She knew they would both come home. They had no place else to go.

Lilly caught them separately as they tried to slip into the house. Hiram went to bed weeping, without supper, and with welts where Lilly had whipped his bare bottom from a switch from a pine branch. Lonnie snored on the wooden plank floor just inside the door where Lilly had decked him when he staggered in. She went through his pockets to make sure he wasn't hoarding money to throw away on more of the devil's whiskey.

Lonnie was dreaming that he was back in France, chasing a mam'selle from Dardanelles or somewhere, it didn't matter where. Hiram dreamt that it was a year and a half ago and he had gone to work with Lonnie one day and was proud he was an engineer's son. Lonnie had introduced him to all the men and the foreman had given Hiram a Tom's Peanut Patty and he could still taste it; all crystalline pink and syrupy and crunchy. Lilly lay awake pondering ways to make it out of the strawberry patch.

Lonnie and Lilly Williams were, though they would never have admitted it, tough Southern white trash, absolute bottom rung of the ladder peckerwoods. It must be remembered that in the Twenties white trash was more of an economic designation than a moral one. They could not help being white trash. Given their ancestry, their surroundings, and the general state of the South, there was nothing else they could have been. They were ill-educated, poor, suspicious, and accustomed to being all of those things. Their parents were scrabbling out a living from poor soil at a time when the South was turning toward urbanization and industrialization, and it didn't surprise them that their lot in life would be the same. It took money to make money then—either via the textile mills or by running a large farm—and the Williamses had no money. Anyway, much of the best land had been burned out by overplanting of King Cotton. Had the Williamses not had Lilly's wits, they would have gone on growing and selling strawberries till they worked their fingers down to the nubs. The Williamses were barely removed from the absolute bottom—the "dirt eaters," who were so poor and witless and ill-nourished that they literally did eat dirt—but were still uncomfortably close to being niggers, which would leave them no one to look down on. They had to keep some pride, after all.

Their only immediate possible consolation was fundamentalist religion, with its teaching that a hard life on earth would be compensated by paradise in heaven. It was a valuable emotional outlet and pressure valve with its almost orgiastic church services and revivals. Their only economic hope was to move to one of the proliferating towns or cities and hope for something better than being cheap, unskilled labor or going onto the relief rolls. There was little chance that their children would ever be any better off than they, given the South's woeful economic situation and its generally abysmal public schools. After the South's economic collapse in the wake of the Great Depression, about all that could be hoped for was mere survival. Lilly Williams would have none of that. Hopelessness was for weaklings, like Lonnie. The church had served Lilly well, but she was not content to eat dirt on earth while waiting for pie in the sky after death.

Lonnie left when Hiram was seven. He didn't know why his daddy disappeared, unless it was because he drank out of his medicine jar too much. Lilly had harangued Lonnie day and night for years. Then one day Hiram came home from playing with his cousin Gordon Skipper and his daddy was gone and his mamma told him his daddy was sick and had gone off to the hospital. Hiram and Gordon had gotten a good whipping that day for hiding in the woods and throwing dirt clods at the postman, L. G. Sellers, as he walked down the dirt road. Hiram had been worried that his mamma had found out about it and would give him another hiding. She was very calm, though, and fed him and Irene their supper of biscuits and greens and syrup and put them to bed. She just said "I don't know" when Hiram asked her when his daddy was coming back home.

Hiram worried that if his daddy could disappear so quickly, be there one day and be gone the next, that it might happen to him, too. He was afraid to say anything about it, since his mamma might decide to send him away for being bad. He missed his daddy, though. Daddy was the only one who ever smiled around the house, although that was usually when he was sipping from his jar and Lilly wasn't there. But his daddy used to tell him stories and take him fishing and sometimes in the evenings, when Lilly was toiling away over the washtub and frowning, a halo of fumes from lye soap and boiling water

forming around her head, Lonnie would take out his
jew's harp and play little jigs for Hiram to dance to.

Lilly countermanded this quasi-sinful bit of pleasure
by hauling Hiram and Irene regularly to the Mount Olive
Baptist Church. From the time he was three years old,
she sat him down on a little stool beside her. While she
sawed and pumped away on the church organ, Hiram
tried to sing in his frail little voice: "I will cherish the old
rugged cross and exchange it some day for a crown." He
would rather have been outside with his Skipper cousins,
playing hide-and-go-seek and blind-man's bluff and
catching June bugs and grasshoppers and pulling the legs
off them or shooting marbles. But Lilly kept Hiram right
by her. The hellfire and brimstone sermons he sat
through terrified him greatly and he never forgot the central lesson: the wages of sin is eternal damnation and
terrible suffering in the bottomless pit. The soul, he
learned, was imperishable and would either ascend to
Heaven—there to be reunited with Mother and all the
other loved ones—or would be thrown straight down to
hell to burn for eternity while a cackling Satan stoked the
flames with his pitchfork and the damned cried out
pleading for death. But they would burn and suffer forever.

Living a good life was no passport to Heaven; Hiram
and everyone else was born with Original Sin and had to
be cleansed in the blood of the Lamb, had to be saved by
precious Jesus, had to race down to the little wooden
altar under Lilly's stern, judging gaze and cry out for
salvation and weep and wail and pray through till salvation came.

And all around the altar the women in their gingham
dresses (most of their husbands, like Lonnie, went pretty
light on church, especially when the sermons got around
to drinking and smoking—two of the fastest lanes
straight to hell) were caught up in the Holy Ghost and
speaking in tongues and flailing around with unseeing

eyes, chanting in an unknown language—kumbli-kumbli-li-die!—their bodies snapping back and forth as though caught in the throes of some terrible whiplash until they would collapse on the plank floor. And then one of them would rise and stretch her arms heavenward and interpret the unknown tongue, which was of course a message from God. It came to seem to Hiram that the message was directed right to him and his sinful heart (for hadn't he already discovered masturbation out in the woods with the other boys and didn't they sometimes smoke grapevine?): "Behold, I say unto you, there is a sinner here tonight who has hardened his heart unto Me. Tarry not, O sinner, lest I harden my heart unto thee."

And then came the invitational, which Hiram grew to fear. Usually he would stand beside his mother and sing it, so as to try to feel exempt from the final altar call: "Softly and tenderly, Jesus is calling, calling for you and for me."

That mournful hymn, with its awful stamp of finality —choose salvation tonight or go to the pit—never left him. Technically, the church's doctrine was elastic enough to leave children out of the salvation business until they had reached the "age of accountability"—a vague and unsure age, usually put at about twelve years, suggesting the onset of puberty. But no one ever told Hiram that.

One Sunday night, he and Lilly and Irene got home from a particularly intense revival meeting. Two sinful men had been saved while the congregation softly sang "Why Not Tonight" and the preacher thundered on about the pit: "Dear sinner, don't leave this church tonight without getting right with God. Oh, it may be your last chance. It happens every night—the terrible car wrecks and the bodies broken and bleeding beside the highway. Jesus saith, I come in the twinkling of an eye. Listen to Him, hear your precious, sweet wife and your loved ones praying, O sinner, listen to them, heed the call." The men collapsed, sobbing in the sawdust, hiding their tears with their calloused and roughened working-man's hands and the loved ones gathered around them and sang hosannas that their drunkard truck-driving worthless skirt-crazy husbands had vowed to stop chasing after painted women and vowed to shun the devil's whiskey and give up their wild, wild ways and settle down to take care of their dear, sweet wives and precious children. One of the men even tore his pack of Camels in half and scattered the devil's tobacco in the sawdust.

The scene greatly affected Hiram. He crawled onto his little iron cot and tried to sleep but the awful reality of hell and damnation began to weigh upon him. The terrible knowledge that he would burn forever was too much for him to bear. He felt as though he were suffocating. He crept out of bed and tiptoed out to the front porch. Even the crickets in the weeds seemed to be talking to him, God was speaking through them. "Damn-*nation,* damn-*nation!*" He was sure he was going to die that very night and go to hell. His heartbeat felt to him like a waning flutter, like that he once felt of a dying rabbit that he held in his hands. He sat in the cold darkness until dawn, weeping silently and praying for Jesus to touch him. Finally, in his exhaustion, he felt the great burden being lifted from his chest, although he heard no message from Heaven. It would have to do. He slipped back into bed as the sun came up and slept a troubled sleep. His little face was pinched and drawn. He awoke with a start, still worried.

With his father disappearing from his life when Hiram was only seven, Hiram never really had an example of how a man ought to be and act. Instead, he had the massive Lilly as both mother and father, a person to be more feared than loved. Increasingly—especially after Lilly began running boarding houses where the clientele consisted mostly of young women—Hiram knew only a matriarchal circle. He would never really have a man as an intimate friend, as a true confidant. Lilly would later allow him to marry but would never let go of him. She was determined not to let him grow up and therefore grow away from her. Irene was another story—she was female and therefore her lot in life was to marry as well as possible. But Hiram was Lilly's only manchild and she would gradually develop designs for him.

In 1930, with Lonnie packed off to the VA hospital in Alexandria, Louisiana, Lilly moved her little brood from the country into Georgiana, on the L&N railroad line. They lived in a rented shack that was near the imposing home of Herman Pride and his family. The Prides were an "old" family and the Pride children did not let young Hiram forget that he was poor and fatherless. They called him "Two-Gun Pete" because he liked to play with toy pistols. He didn't like the "Pete" part and would never forget Herman Pride and the humiliation that he felt was visited upon him.

The Williams house burned down one night and they salvaged only Hiram's pajama top, Irene's pajama bottom, and Lilly's nightgown. He was further humiliated. The next day, they found a furnished room and scrounged clothing from charity. That day, Hiram became a working man. Irene roasted a pound of peanuts and Hiram went out to sell them on the streets. He made thirty cents and dragged home at sunset with ten cents worth of stew meat, ten cents of rice, five cents of potatoes, and five cents of tomatoes. He handed the goods over to Lilly and said, "Mamma, we'll eat tonight!" He began working every day, selling peanuts and shining shoes for a nickel a shine. One day a kindly man named Oscar Vickery bought a nickel's worth of peanuts from Hiram and made a suggestion to him: if he were to hold out one peanut per bag, he could save them up and buy himself a Coke with the extra money and, best of all,

Lilly wouldn't know about the extra income. He didn't need to be told twice. Lilly caught up with his business acumen when she discovered firecrackers and a cap pistol and caps in his back pocket one night. She bragged years later that she started to whip him when she discovered that he'd bought playpretties instead of food but that her first lash across his backside ignited the firecrackers.

Lilly located a big house for her family and decided to open a boarding house. She was a good cook and there were enough young single men and women moving to town to support such a venture. The house, on Rose Street, about a hundred yards from the railroad tracks, was big. It sat up on red brick pillars with a crawl space underneath. The house was dark yellow with a shingled roof, a big, banistered front veranda, fourteen-foot ceilings and four fireplaces. Hiram had the little bedroom nearest the railroad tracks and the sound of the Pan American chugging by became a welcome sound. It was headed for the city, for Montgomery and for adventure. Hiram had heard on the radio down at Durham's Shoe Shop the lonesome train songs that Jimmie Rogers was singing and the sound of the train whistle thrilled him.

Mr. Rose was letting Lilly have the house rent-free, but she never told her children that. Hiram, in particular, as he earned money was determined not to take charity and told his mother that. She told him she was proud of her boy.

Hiram continued selling peanuts and shining shoes and selling seed packets from the Lancaster Seed Company. He started first grade, where he was so undistinguished as to be virtually invisible. He was thin and withdrawn and pale and kept to himself and still confided in no one. He and Irene had taken a few music lessons at a singing school in Avant, out in the country, but he didn't show any great musical aptitude. Indeed, he was reprimanded at school for beating on a tin piepan in music class. One of his cousins would step forward years later to recall that Hiram replied to the teacher who reprimanded him: "I ain't going to school always. I'll sing my songs and make more money than any of you."

Firelight flashed on Hiram's face and his eyes were even brighter than the flames. The sight before him reminded him of church, but this was *fun*. These flames weren't hellfire, they were bright and cheerful and beckoned to him. He and his cousin J. C. McNeil edged closer to the bonfire. They were in a large clearing at the fringes of a logging camp near Fountain, Alabama. Five or six men were roasting a pig in the fire and were trading swigs from a bottle and telling jokes. On the other side of the fire, a three-piece hillbilly band was playing jigs and reels and couples were dancing and laughing. Saturday night at the logging camp was like nothing Hiram had ever seen. The women were beautiful as they whirled and laughed and twirled their dresses.

A week earlier, when Lilly had told him he was going to the country for a year to live with the McNeils—so the McNeil's eldest girl could move in with Lilly and finish high school in Georgiana—he hadn't cared one way or another. At least he wouldn't have to shine shoes and sell peanuts every day after school and keep turning the money over to Lilly. He moved into the McNeils' railroad car—which is what they called home—and went to the little country school at Fountain and played in the woods every night with J.C. To tell the truth, after a few days he didn't really miss his mother at all. Mrs. McNeil was nice to him and nobody looked down at him because he was poor. Everybody here was poor.

"C'mon, Harm," J.C. said to him, "ain't no sense hidin' in the bushes." Hiram held back a little but finally followed his cousin up to the fire. He was surprised when the men didn't run them off. "You boys get you a Coke-Cola," one of the men said. "Maybe we'll give ye a little surprise." He laughed coarsely. Hiram ran back with their Cokes. The man poured some hooch into each Coke bottle. "Drank up, kids. Make a man out of ye!" The men whooped as Hiram choked and gagged at the first taste of cheap whiskey. They finally swallowed some of it and Hiram started to feel like he had never felt before. He felt a warm flush spread through his body and he suddenly felt bigger and everything around him took on a hard glow. He no longer felt tense and his head felt light. The flames were dancing and the music was louder and he suddenly seemed to . . . *understand* a lot of things. He and J.C. started dancing, skipping back and forth while the men laughed and egged them on. Hiram got dizzy and fell over on his back in the red dust. He was laughing, though, and felt wonderful. He didn't feel ordinary anymore. He didn't hear the loggers laughing at the drunk kid. He felt *special.*

If Lilly noticed a change in Hiram when he moved back to Georgiana, she didn't let on that she had. She put him back to work on the peanut and shoe-shine trail, but Hiram started staying out later and started hanging out with a black street singer who visited Georgiana often. People called him Tee-Tot. He seemed to be ageless and he walked the streets with his battered old guitar and sang his songs for pennies and nickels.

Lilly was getting her family ready for another move, when she and Hiram had their first real argument. It was the first time he stood up to her and it amazed her. He had found out that Mr. Rose had not been charging Lilly any rent for the house and he had heard talk around town. There was nothing concrete but there was just enough talk to make him feel ashamed of something. "Mamma, I told you we didn't have to take no charity, I'd make us money." She slapped him, hard enough to knock him down, and told him not to put his nose where it didn't belong. He ran out of the house and didn't come home till dawn but he didn't say anything else. Lilly moved him and Irene to Greenville, a bustling four-cotton-gin town further north on the L&N railroad line. She set up another boarding house.

Hiram kept up the shoe-shine and peanut business but Greenville was where Tee-Tot lived, in a shack by the train tracks, and he followed Tee-Tot around. And on nis shoe-shine rounds, he made it a point to pass through the edges of niggertown and he loved to listen to the syncopated rhythms wafting out of the piccolo joints. The songs were gut-bucket blues and down and dirty dozens and Hiram remembered many of them.

Hank had learned what he knew of traditional country music—ballads and reels transplanted to the South from England and Scotland—from the fiddlers who would sit around Cade Durham's Shoe Shop. Durham and Jimmie Warren and O. P. Curry taught him "Soldier's Joy" and "Sally Goodin' " and the like but they seemed tame once he had heard the raw power of black blues. He started showing a real interest in music.

He had already badgered Lilly into getting him a guitar. He announced to her that he was going to buy one, one way or another. Lilly was surprised by the sudden determination in her little runt but decided to turn it to her advantage.

"If you make good grades in school," she told him, "I'll give you a guitar." He promised and she put fifty cents down on a second-hand Silvertone acoustic guitar and paid it off at fifty cents a month. He still had to turn over his shoe-shine and peanut money to her, but at least he got a guitar. When Lilly brought it home, he was, for once, demonstrably happy. He ran through the front yard, swung the gate open and grabbed and twisted the tail of a calf that happened to be loitering there. The calf knocked him down and broke his arm. Lilly predicted that the guitar would be bad luck for him. As soon as he could wriggle his fingers, he started practicing on the guitar.

In Greenville, Hiram spent more and more time with Tee-Tot. His real name was Rufus Payne. Tee-Tot was slightly hunchbacked and his hands hung down nearly to his knees. He did odd jobs at Peagler's Drug Store and was known thereabouts as a good nigger—one who still knew the benefits of Uncle Tomming the whites, even the poor white trash who needed someone to look down on. He was quite a good entertainer, though, and people sometimes invited him into their houses to perform. He wore a tin drinking cup attached to his belt, which itself was fastened with a wooden matchstick because the buckle was broken. He sipped out of the cup all day and insisted that it was just tea that he drank. But Hiram soon found that Tee-Tot's tea was as potent as the hooch he had discovered when he was living with the McNeils out by the logging camp, and he started sharing Tee-Tot's whiskey. They were an odd-looking pair: the grinning, shuffling, white-haired negro with his flat feet that over-ran his torn shoes and the rail-thin, pale-faced kid who never smiled.

Even though Hiram with his shoe-shine kit was lower than Tee-Tot on the economic scale, he was still a white man, even if he was only twelve years old. So he de-manded that Tee-Tot teach him guitar. Tee-Tot was de-lighted with the skinny white boy's newly found impertinence and soon became his only real friend in Greenville. He shared his teacup and his musical knowl-edge with his little friend "Harm" and they fished to-gether and sang together on Greenville's streets and on the courthouse lawn on Saturdays when the farmers came to town to shop. People started calling them the "Greenville Troubadors."

Greenville's merchants even encouraged them to per-form in front of their stores, for what a heartening sign of harmonious racial relations it was to see a grinning nigger and a shy cracker kid playing together. Sometimes Tee-Tot and Hiram would fish an afternoon away. There was nothing Hiram liked better than going fishing, unless it was going fishing and drinking beer.

Hiram found that Tee-Tot, despite his shucking and jiving for the white folks, was a pretty shrewd man and an instinctive entertainer. Besides teaching Hiram the songs he knew, he gave him very valuable lessons in how to work a crowd.

"First, Harm, you smiles at 'em. Folks wants to know that you're friendly. Then you tells 'em a little joke. Folks likes to laugh. 'Say, colonel,' you says to a man what's smokin' a pipe, 'has you gots Prince Albert in a can?' He says, 'Yes, I have' and you says, 'Well, sir, you had oughter let him out, 'cause I reckon he cain't breathe in ther.' "

Hiram didn't laugh. "That ain't funny, Rufe."

"Folks likes jokes like that. Homey *jokes*. Don't never act like you knows more than they knows. And look 'em direct in the eye, speshly the womens. They likes that. Play like they ain't nothin' in this world you rather be doin' than makin' 'em happy."

"Gimme some tea, Rufe," Hiram ordered him. "That sounds hard. People make me jumpy. They stare."

"Hear me out, Harm. I knows people. Ain't nothin' they likes better than if you makes 'em laugh and you makes 'em dance. Smile and wink and you be foxin' 'em."

Hiram had written one song by then, and Tee-Tot helped him find a melody to the words:

> *I had an old goat*
> *She eat tin cans*
> *When the little goats came*
> *They were Ford sedans.*

One day, when Tee-Tot could tell that his pupil was
progressing well, he sat him down and taught him his
"bestest" song, one that had been passed down to him,
one called "My Bucket's Got a Hole in It." It was to be
one day copyrighted by Hank Williams and to become
another of the little gold mines that were Hank Williams
songs in the Acuff-Rose publishing catalog.

"That's a good 'n, Harm. You learn it."

As his musical knowledge grew, Hiram's self-confidence increased and he acted more and more like an individual. He stayed out all night sometimes, sleeping at
Tee-Tot's if he was drunk. Sometimes he went down to
the jail after a big fight with Lilly and the cops would let
him sleep over there. Lilly, ever the white-trash aristo-
crat, was at first furious to hear that her son was being
seen regularly all over town with a nigger. She tried to
make Hiram quit seeing Tee-Tot if she would pay for
guitar lessons. He stood up to her and refused. "I'm doin'
what I want to, Mamma." She gave in to him for once.
She told her friends, though, that Tee-Tot always addressed her boy as "Little White Boss" and that she herself rewarded Tee-Tot with "food from my kitchen."

Lilly and her boy argued more and more often and the
arguments became bitter as it became apparent that Hiram was not going to automatically give in to her. They
fought over everything: Tee-Tot, Hiram's drinking and
late hours and bad grades, money. He kept throwing it up
to her that she had taken his daddy away from him. Lilly
was thirty-eight years old and in the prime of life and her
sexuality made Hiram ashamed. Men visited the women
who lived in Lilly's boarding house and men called on
Lilly. She refused to mention Lonnie, who was still in a
VA hospital.

Status and money were what Lilly was concerned
about, and her boy was not helping much with either. He
was wasting his time lollygagging around town with that

guitar and that nigger and was woolgathering around the house listening to hillbilly singers on the radio from Montgomery and Nashville. He would never make anything of himself that way, she told him. He had better straighten up and pay attention in school or he'd end up being a worthless hillbilly, a no-good-for-nothing drunk.

He got pretty hot about that and said that maybe he had already decided to become a hillbilly singer and there wasn't a gol-durned thing wrong with that. Hillbilly singers got to be on the radio and travel and own fine big cars and fancy suits.

Well, if he wanted to throw his life away after all his mother had done for him, had worked her fingers to the bone, had done without so her boy could have food on the table and clothes on his back, had sacrificed to put him through school; if he didn't know no better than that, then he deserved to be a hillbilly and . . .

He ran out the door and she knew she wouldn't see him till morning. Well, no mind. Lilly was planning on packing up and moving the family to the City, up to Montgomery. Things in Greenville were not all that they could be for her, and her kids would be better off there. The schools would be better and Irene might have a better pick of men when it came time for her to be married off and maybe the schools in Montgomery would be stricter on Harm. Lilly herself was getting a little tired of the strictures of small towns and the way that people talked about a woman who didn't have a husband at home. Lilly was quite independent-minded and if things didn't suit her, she'd either change things or leave them. It didn't look as though she was going to turn Greenville around, so it was time to head 'em up and move 'em out. She didn't waste much time on decision-making and once she had made up her mind, that was it: there was no time to wishy-washy around or cry over spilled milk. Once you decided to do something, you went on and did it. She got out her red Indian Chief tablet that she used for bookkeeping and sat down at the kitchen table and started making a list of things to do. "Irene! Come hep your mother."

At least her daughter minded her. That boy was out runnin' wild in the streets, gettin' drunk with that nigger. Well, she'd fix that right quick.

2

W HEN THEY got off the train in Montgomery on July 10, 1937, Hank—for that was what he had decided to start calling himself as soon as they made the move from Greenville to Montgomery—tried not to be impressed by the bustling crowds of people and the cars and the tall buildings. Lilly and Irene didn't know where Hiram had come up with this "Hank" business but he was insistent on it so they told him he could call himself anything he wanted. When Lilly had told him that she intended to pack the family up and move from sleepy Greenville to Montgomery with its 75,000 people, Hiram decided—on his own, certainly, for he still did not confide in anyone—that he would start a new life in the big city. He knew that he was beginning to make progress with his music, and his self-confidence was also growing.

As the three of them with their cheap luggage got off the L&N train in Union Station and started walking

down Lee Street towards Lilly's new boarding house on
Perry Street, Hank couldn't help but be impressed by the
magnitude of everything. The courthouse square in
Greenville seemed like hillbilly central by comparison
with downtown Montgomery. Hank lagged two or three
steps behind his mother and sister so that bystanders,
who were surely struck by his manly presence, would
know that he wasn't with those two dowdy creatures,
who were obviously just off the farm in their ill-fitting
dresses. Hank stopped and took the pillowcase off his old
guitar so that everyone would know that he was probably
some visiting hillbilly star, down from Nashville to pick
and sing on station WSFA or WCOV. Although Hank
was only thirteen, he was already just over six feet tall.
He was stick-thin and lean-jawed and jug-eared and had
a big brown cowlick sticking up in back, even though he
had slicked his hair down with Brilliantine until it fairly
shone in the sunlight. With his solemn air and his steel-
rimmed glasses and his jutting jawbone, he did look
much older than thirteen. But his exaggerated swagger
gave his age away. He blushed and swore under his
breath as Lilly turned, impatient at his dawdling, and
yelled at him like he was some kind of barefoot rube. He
might as well have been, he thought bitterly. He was
wearing an old pair of Lonnie's work boots and they were
at least two sizes too big. With his too-short overalls that
ended at mid-ankle, he was flapping along like a scare-
crow wearing shoeboxes. He knew that people were staring.

"Where's the house at, Mamma? I'll run on ahead and
open the door."

"All right, son," Lilly said. She fished around in the
pocket of her jacket for the key. "It's at Number 114, on
South Perry. Be careful you don't get run over. This isn't
Greenville, you know—"

"I *know*, Mamma." Hank flapped off ahead, guitar in
right hand and his cheap cardboard suitcase in left hand.

He almost broke his leg at the corner of Lee and Church. Weeds had grown up around the street sign, which was a low cement post, about a foot and a half high, and he wasn't used to suchlike and stripped all the skin off his right shinbone when he ran into it. He hopped down the narrow sidewalk, cursing. "Sumbitch buttwipe turd!" His vocabulary was still in the building stage.

He stopped in his tracks when he passed the stately Jefferson Davis Hotel, but it wasn't the sight of the long touring cars parked out front or the elegant doorman and his uniform that had more epaulets and trim than a four-star general. What caught Hank up short was a little sign that told him that radio station WSFA was located in the hotel. WSFA he knew. He should: he'd been listening to the station and its country music shows ever since Lilly had broken down and bought a cheap little second-hand Philco radio for the kids to listen to. WSFA's 3,000 watts poured over young Hiram Williams in Georgiana and Greenville and told him—even more so than did the whistle of the L&N chugging by—that there were worlds beyond the one bounded by Lilly. On days when Hiram went to school, he'd get up at six in the morning to listen to the singing cowboy shows on WSFA.

So that's where Radioland came from, Hank said to himself as he stared at the hotel and laughed inwardly at the person he had been two years before, who was so backwoods that he had thought Radioland was a foreign country or at least some Yankee state he didn't know about. Radioland. He mouthed the words: "Howdy folks, this is Hank Williams the Singing Cowboy comin' to all you folks out there in Radioland on radio station double-yew ess eff ay!" He would have stood there forever maybe, but all of a sudden he heard Lilly's booming voice coming at him from half a block away. He ran and found the rooming house and opened it up and ran back and helped Lilly and Irene carry their things in.

That night he dreamed of Radioland again as he often

did, but this time his dream was all mixed up with the exotic sounds of powerful motorcars cruising down South Perry after dark. It was a long way from Greenville.

At dawn, Lilly was up and set to clean and straighten her new boarding house. First, though, she got her kids ready to hit the pavement and earn their keep. Irene was sent out with sandwiches to sell to the town's workingmen. Hank shouldered his familiar old shoe-shine kit and carried a paper bag full of roasted peanuts. But not without a fight.

"Mamma, that's kid's work."

Lilly landed a roundhouse right on the side of his head.

"Oh? OH? And just what does his highness want to do? Lollygag around niggertown all day?"

"I can play gi-tar," he began and he regretted having answered. She cuffed him again and propelled him through the door with his shine kit and bags of peanuts trailing after him. "When his highness makes some money he can twiddle around with his music box."

He hit the streets. It was already warm and sticky and humid and as the sun rose overhead his well-worn cotton shirt stuck to him and sweat ran into his eyes. He hadn't made any money yet. But he had to. The first thing he had done that morning after Lilly pitched him out was to run to the Jefferson Davis Hotel and finally mount enough courage to walk in, past the doorman and his splendid uniform and past the fine-dressed gentlemen and gentlewomen. He found his way to WSFA's studios and was disappointed at what he saw. He had imagined a kind of castle of the air for Radioland central, but all he found was an ordinary office and a secretary who asked him if he thought he intended to sell shoe shines over the air. He vowed that the next time he went there it would be with his guitar and they would by durn know who he was. He belonged in Radioland.

Meanwhile, he drifted in front of Union Station's cathedrallike entrance on Water Street and had to be drawn out of his reverie by a businessman who called to him rudely, "Oh bootblack, over here!" Hank was taller than the man but he kneeled down obligingly in front of him and began to buff his shoes. He had to make some money. What was it Tee-Tot had told him? Hank was beginning to suspect what the word "nigger" really meant, that it was a code word that had nothing to do really with the color of a man's skin. He began humming a scrap of a tune as he shined those shoes and he danced a little bit of a shuffle as he popped the cloth. The man tipped him a nickel and Hank gave him a mock salute: "Thank you, Colonel. Shine! Getcha shine!!"

He learned soon how to make his money in the morning so he could spend the afternoons drifting through niggertown and learning music. He still heard Roy Acuff and Ernest Tubb on the radio but they were nothing like those nigger singers who could just raise the hair on the back of your neck. When they had the blues they were so blue they were black, they liked to say, and Hank took them seriously. When they hurt, Lord they *suffered*. And they put it into songs: "Want you to write my sweet mother, please tell her the shape I'm in. Won't you write my dear mother, tell her the fix I'm in. Won't you please ask her, Lord, to forgive me all my sins." It was nothing fancy, none of this ballroom singing Hank sometimes heard on the radio from Chicago and sneered at. This was just a man feeling bad and singing about it.

Singing to sweet Jesus and dear Mother and 'fessin' 'bout the liquor and the wimmens and the runnin' 'round and low-down sinnin'. Don't wanna be treated this away. Hank heard Jimmie Rodgers in their songs and he knew that old Jimmie, the "singing brakeman," had put in his time in niggertown. He had sung the blues, ole Jimmie had, before the TB blues carried him away back in '33, and there wasn't many white folks could sing the blues, not the way the niggers did. Hank listened close to them, listened to the way they could make their voices break and almost cry in the middle of a note, and listened to how the best songs were the simple songs, the songs that took a single emotion—like *Mother's gone*—and worked it and worked it till anybody could understand it and want to cry and weep over it. One simple emotion: my baby's gone, my mother's gone, I'm no good, I need Jesus, I got to put the bottle down, my woman's slippin' 'round, what am I gonna do? It was hard to be that simple in music and it took Hank years of writing songs to get down to those stripped-down basics, thus yielding a lean and supercharged song that could appeal to the basic common denominator in an audience.

Thus far, he couldn't even appeal to the basic common denominator in his own mother. The summer of '37 Lilly left him alone as long as he brought home a pocketful of nickels every night and stayed sober and closed his eyes to any goings-on at the boarding house that didn't necessarily concern a young boy, strange noises in the night, moans and groans and bed springs creaking, long hot nights when even the bed clothes clung to you as you tossed in your bed and you heard the sucking sound of wet, hot flesh sticking to and popping loose from and sticking to wet, hot flesh. Hank coaxed the family radio away from Lilly's kitchen and to his little room and he lay on his iron cot and tried to ignore the sounds of the house while he listened to music. That summer he started hanging around the studios at WSFA and at WCOV, which was in the Exchange Hotel. He still didn't dare take his battered old guitar up to the stations, so they just knew him as the kid with the shine kit. Some of the singers befriended him. One in particular was himself a teenager. Braxton Schuffert was an eighteen-year-old cowboy singer who had had his own radio shows on both stations and seemed like a real old-timer to Hank. They became good friends, though, after Hank played stage-door-Johnny to Schuffert one August morning and stopped him as he left the station.

"Pardon me, sir, aren't you Braxton Schuffert, the singer?"

"Wal, now, I'm Brack Schuffert. Whether I can sing or not is sometimes up in the air."

"No sir! I listen to your show ever' mornin'!"

"Wal. What's your name, boy?"

"Hank. Hank Williams and I'm a singer too."

"Wal. Okay, singer. Come and get a cup a coffee."

They sat down in the coffee shop of the Jefferson Davis Hotel. Schuffert took off his white felt cowboy hat, ordered two coffees like a man of the world and studied the skinny youth sitting across from him.

"So you a singer, huh?"

"Yessir," Hank answered seriously. "I—"

Schuffert laughed. "How old are you?"

"Sixteen," Hank lied. "And I got my own band—"

"Sure. Drink your coffee. You wanna get on the radio, I expect?"

"Yessir."

"Do you know how?"

"Nossir. How—"

"I expect you wanna start out right on WSFA?"

"Yessir, to start with—"

Schuffert laughed. "Son, they's a dozen singers right ahead a you. I better hear you sing before I tell you what to do. I got a little band, we play here and there. Come sing with us tonight." He got up and awed Hank by leaving a fifteen-cent tip.

That night, Hank grabbed his old guitar and ran out of the house right after supper without even telling Lilly where he was going. At the Schufferts', Braxton was impressed when he heard Hank sing.

There was something . . . something very basic about Hank's sincerity that reached Schuffert. He taught Hank a couple of songs, never imagining that he himself would soon be a member of Hank Williams' first band.

"Tell you what you do if I was you, Hank."

"What's that, Brack?"

"Wal, ever Sat'day night, 'SFA has their Sat'day Night Jamboree. I was you, I'd go down there Sat'day night 'n' audition. Now, they don't pay, it's a free program, but you get to play."

"Well, Brack, that sounds okay to me. How soon do I get my own show?"

Schuffert just laughed. It didn't take Hank long, though.

Summer crept by and Lilly was busy enough with her boarding house business to leave Hank alone, other than to accept his shoe-shine and peanut money every night and to make sure he enrolled in September in seventh grade at Baldwin Junior High school, a fortress of a gray and moldy building on South McDonough Street. As was the case with elementary school, Hank was undistinguished enough as to render himself almost invisible. Some of the time, he was literally unseeable, since he'd rather go to the matinee at the Empire Theater on Montgomery Street to watch Tom Mix or Hoot Gibson movies instead of going to school.

Lilly didn't care and there was no one else to care.

Towards Christmas, Hank was down at the Empire for a Red Ryder double feature when he noticed a little flyer for a Christmas talent show. First prize of fifteen dollars. He held his breath and crossed his bony fingers and made a wish when he saw the flyer and didn't tell anyone that he intended to win that gol-durn talent show himself. And of course he did, with an original song entitled "WPA Blues":

> *I got a home in Montgomery*
> *A place I like to stay*
> *But I have to work for the WPA*
> *And I'm dissatisfied, I'm dissatisfied.*

It was not a song he would repeat and indeed he may not have even written all of it himself. It may have been an old rhyme that Tee-Tot taught him. Lilly long hinted that she was responsible: she said, after all, that she'd moved her family to Georgiana in 1930 so she could work for the WPA Cannery there. The only problem was that the WPA wasn't formed until 1935.

In the wake of Hank's first public triumph, Lilly did something unexpected: she said she was proud of Hank and she expressed interest in his singing career. She got him a new Gibson guitar for Christmas and she encouraged him. It made him very uneasy, but after he noticed that Lilly quit ragging him for shoe-shine money he didn't care what she thought.

Hank's "brand new life" that he had promised himself with the move to Montgomery wasn't quite so brand new after all. He was managing to attract attention with his music and he was showing his independence from Lilly. He was also flunking school and drinking too much. Those were things he didn't think too much about, though.

"Hey, Brack."

"Ho, Hank. How you?"

"Awright. How 'bout a beer?"

"Naw, I got to get to work."

"That's right. You drivin' that meat truck for the Hormel now, ain't that right? Why don't you come work for me?"

"Wal, Hank, what do you mean? Hadn't you oughter be in school?"

"Whyn't you ask Hezzy that?" Braxton knew the answer to that. Hezzy, whose real name was Smith Adair, had been Braxton's musical partner until Hank suddenly lured him away to be half of the musical team of "Hezzy and Hank." After a few weeks, the name was changed to "Hank and Hezzy" and Braxton wondered just how long

the "and" part would remain in there. Hank did have a
bit of an ego.

He was also fourteen. It was three in the afternoon and
Hank was yawning and thirsty for a beer. Braxton looked
at him closely. "Hank, what happened to your glasses?"

"Why, Brack, what do you mean?"

"It done looks to me like there ain't no glass in 'em."

Hank looked confused for a moment, then reached up
and felt his steel-rimmed eyeglasses. "Oh. When I go to
school, I take the glass out. That way, the teachers think
I can't see and they leave me alone."

"Hank, you really can't see without those lenses, can
you?"

"Aw, hell, Brack, come on and let's get us a beer. You
know I can't set up and play dances till three and then
get up and go to school. I know all I need to know,
nohow. Ain't nothin' those teachers can teach old Hank.
Come and work for me, Brack."

"Well, what you got in mind, Hank?"

"Come work and you'll see."

Hezzy, who was an orphan, had not only left Braxton's
band to join Hank, he had also moved out of the Schufferts' home—where he had been welcomed almost as a
long-lost son—into Lilly's boarding house—where he
was barely noticed. Braxton, who knew that next to
Hank he had practically no ambition at all, decided to
join him. The next afternoon, they assembled in the parking lot behind the Jeff Davis Hotel for the first group
portrait of "Hank and Hezzy's Driftin' Cowboys." Hank
was the youngest member of the band but appeared the
most self-assured. They posed in front of a little silver
bullet house trailer, and in the foreground was a saddle
Hank had borrowed from the fire department. The band
was Smith "Hezzy" Adair on bass, Braxton Schuffert on
guitar and vocals, Irene Williams as vocalist and ticket-
taker, Hank Williams on guitar and vocals, and Freddy
Beech on fiddle. The instrumental lineup was similar to

that of most string bands; some of the more rural bands added a banjo. Two guitars were not unusual, especially since Hank never really learned to play lead and depended on his guitar as more of a stage prop. He liked to have Freddy's fiddle playing out front, anyway, for the fiddle's mournful sound was more suited to the country blues. Hank could play a little fiddle himself, just enough so that he could tell good fiddling and bad fiddling and he was proud of Beech's playing. When he'd hired Schuffert, Braxton had protested, "Hank, I don't know but three chords on the guitar."

Hank said, "Well, you're the very player I want then, 'cause I got a three-chord fiddle player. Come on."

Beech was unusual in that he was left-handed and could never afford a left-handed fiddle. He had learned to play his daddy's fiddle by playing it upside down and backwards, bowing over the bass strings and he certainly got a different sound out of the fiddle.

Beech was also the oldest in the band, at nineteen, and was married and had two children. He was obviously a professional musician and it pleased Hank that he, a mere presumptuous kid, was attracting professional musicians. Hank had beat on the doors of the radio stations in Montgomery until they let him in. He first got on WSFA's Saturday Night Jamboree, singing Roy Acuff's "Wabash Cannonball," and then got a twice-weekly show on WCOV. He auditioned at WSFA and landed a singing spot on Dad Crysell's show, where they dubbed him "The Singing Kid." Once he got his own show on WSFA and was making fifteen dollars a week, he decided it was time to form a band and start playing show dates on weekends. He was still not all that good but he knew he was better than most. When he started getting fan mail at the radio station, letters from Greenville and Fort Deposit and Georgiana and other postmarks in Radioland, Hank knew he was an entertainer. School was just something to be tolerated or to sleep through.

Schuffert was the only one in the band with a car—
Lilly hadn't yet got her first automobile—so they would
slide Adair's big standup bass down the middle of the
passenger compartment of his 1935 Ford and pile in
around it and head south on Highway 31 to play dances
and parties. Hank's first booking—and he was proud of it
—was at the Georgiana High School on a Wednesday
night. They all bought black cowboy outfits, including
black leather belts and holsters and Hank hit town like he
was the prodigal son returning home. He made sure everyone in Georgiana got an opportunity to take a look at
him. He and Schuffert even stopped in at the Baptist
church in their cowboy outfits to impress the girls. Hank
picked out the prettiest girl in church and walked her
home before he and his band bedded down on pallets on
the floor at his Uncle Ed Skipper's house. That weekend
the Drifting Cowboys played the Grable Theater in
Georgiana and the Pigeon Creek Schoolhouse, out in the
country near Georgiana. Hank couldn't get enough bookings in his old stomping grounds to suit him: he wanted
everyone to know what he was becoming.

The dances did not pay all that well—admission was
usually twenty-five cents per person—but there were
plenty of them and there were other engagements the
better-known bands would pass up. The Drifting Cowboys were always glad to play a birthday party at someone's house or a sweet sixteen party, for a young girl's
coming out at age sixteen. Those were generally pretty
sedate affairs, with the girl's father watching over things
very carefully.

The Drifting Cowboys, though, soon graduated to the
honky-tonk circuit and found themselves in a very adult
world. They started out playing dances at Thigpen's Log
Cabin, just north of Georgiana. It was run by Fred Thigpen, the Georgiana Ford dealer, who would in later years
claim that it was he and not Lilly who had bought Hank
his first guitar. Thigpen's Log Cabin was fairly typical of

the honky-tonks that were becoming the social clubs of
the South. They were not for family entertainment; the
barn dances were for families. The honky-tonks were
where the workingman went to drink, to blow off steam,
to fight, and to pick up women. Bands that provided music for this tableau had to play loud, sing loud, and be
ready to take care of themselves in a fight. Honky-tonks
changed the direction of country music. A honky-tonk
crowd didn't want to hear maudlin songs about mother
and church or one of Roy Acuff's weepers about a little
boy dying and going to heaven. They wanted raucous
dance music: songs like "Honky Tonk Blues" and
"Headin' Down the Wrong Highway." Singers had to
develop a voice that could be heard above the din, often
without the benefit of a public address system. Bands
began adopting electric instruments and Hank himself
would soon add an electric steel guitar to his lineup.

Butler County was dry, so Thigpen's sold ice and set-
ups and the customers carried "spot whiskey," the cheap-
est form of bootleg whiskey, identified by a spot on the
label. Hank had favored beer before, especially in Montgomery where it was easy for him to get. At Thigpen's,
he learned all about whiskey, or thought he did, and he
began educating himself seriously about women.

Thigpen's was out in the pines just off Highway 31
between Georgiana and Chapman. It was nothing but a
ramshackle barn with a low stage less than ten feet
across, rough chairs and tables and a dance floor. The
parking lot was the real center of action. That was where
the heavy fighting, drinking and romancing went on.
Thigpen kept a bouncer inside but the parking lot was a
kind of free zone and the boys in the parking lot sometimes liked to lay in wait for the musicians and make
them run the gauntlet. They liked to pick on the musicians, especially the ones who attracted women. "Pretty
boys," they called them; that and "queers." The boys in
the parking lot, ill-educated poor whites, were usually the

same ones who put on bedsheets and went out to terror-
ize the niggers but they had an even stronger tradition of
sudden and senseless violence against each other. The
wrong word uttered, a quick glance at the wrong woman,
and there was an inevitable fight. For honor. If a man
backed down in the face of a challenge, he was not a man.
And if he failed to lay down a challenge to someone who
was obviously impugning his honor, he lost face. That
tradition of machismo and rugged individualism and
stubborn ignorance was at the core of Hank's behavior
and was really part of his stage presence. He did not so
much get on a stage as occupy it. He came loping out on
those long bony legs and coiled himself into a crouch
over his guitar and shot a defiant gaze out of those snapping black eyes and all but verbally dared anyone to challenge his right to be there. Slight as he was, he never
backed down in the face of a fight, and he attracted many
fights and even provoked some himself as an entertainer
who excited women. He was one of the first country musicians to notice that women didn't necessarily want their
singers to be like Roy Acuff, who looked and acted as if
he'd been sixty years old the day he was born. Hillbilly
women liked Hank to hit 'em with that pelvic chord, they
liked the hint of sex and danger and Hank seemed to offer
both.

Hank learned the usual short cuts to self-preservation
in barroom brawling: the sucker punch, the bottle upside
the head, the blackjack, the metal leg off a steel guitar,
and—the ultimate—guns. Early on, though, when he was
just starting in the honky-tonks and learning about the
knock-down, drag-out clientele of the bloody buckets, his
big weapon was his new manager, driver and ticket-taker.
None other than Lilly. She could smell money the way
some women could smell a future full of perfume and
she'd taken quick notice when Hank gave up his shoe-
shine kit and still had money on him. When it became
apparent that her boy actually had some talent and might

even become successful in music, there was never a quicker change in attitude than took place in Lilly's treatment of Hank. She had moved to a bigger boarding house on Catoma Street and all of a sudden Hank's band members were staying there and she was feeding them. To her way of thinking it was a wise investment in the future. At a time when laborers might make only thirty cents a day, she could see young Hank making real dollars just by singing. She quit mocking his attempts at music and appointed herself caretaker of the boy's career and his protector. Lilly was rougher than many men and she lost only one honky-tonk fight. That was the night they were playing a really rough dance down at Fort Deposit and the place was overrun with crazy drunks who fought each other and then joined forces to charge the bandstand. One of them sliced Hank's new fiddler, Mexican Charlie Mays, from his left ribs all the way around behind his right ribs and his guts popped out and they thought he was dying right there on the pine dance floor. Lilly had been distracted by that and took a sucker punch to the jaw. This was before Lilly took to regularly belting Hank around when he was drunk or pilled-up, and that night Hank was unusually vocal in his pride of his mother. As they drove back from Fort Deposit to Montgomery after Mexican Charlie got stitched up and they knew he'd pull through, Hank piped up: "There ain't nobody in this here world that I'd rather have standin' next to me in a beer joint brawl than my Maw with a broken bottle in her hand." Lilly just laughed and hugged him. Hank would often repeat that, especially to an acquaintance who seemed to him to be sissy-like and who got nervous in the face of an obvious impending free-for-all. Shit, by the time he was sixteen, Hank had knocked grown men unconscious, had drunk straight whiskey, and had screwed grown women. There was nothin' in the world he was afraid of. He would challenge policemen, he welcomed taking on the Yankee bastid fly-boys stationed at Maxwell Air Force Base in Montgomery, he would bait any heckler. "Hey," he would yell, "why don't somebody get a shovel and cover that up." He was outwardly quiet but inside he was a coiled spring and, for such a skinny guy, his intensity and fierceness surprised many opponents. Nossir, old Hank was ready for any comers and he wasn't afraid of nobody or nothing. Except his mother.

But Montgomery in the late Thirties and early Forties was his kind of town and it didn't take him long to realize that. He was cocky, he was good, and he wasn't scared. Men respected that and women were impressed by that. He would swagger down the street like he owned the town, like Johnny Mack Brown in the movies. Except Johnny Mack Brown didn't have a mother like Lilly who would charge down to the WSFA studios like a mad bull and haul Hank off the air because he was drunk and march him home and knock him around. Other than little scenes like that, Hank thought he had the world by the balls. He was soon disabused of that notion, but life for the time being seemed to be giving him an even break for once.

He still did not have what could be called a real friend. The turnover in the Drifting Cowboys was high. They were not paid especially well; Hank regarded them as less than equals, and Lilly treated them like chattel. They were just ornaments to surround her son. She had started rolling Hank to get his money when he had had a drink too many. And she started pushing him hard to make more money. Lilly could never do anything halfway. Hank started drinking more; Lilly rode his back to make him work more. He was eighteen years old and in the eighth grade when World War II broke out. He was not surprised when the Selective Service doctor took one look at his back and rejected him out of hand as being unfit for military service. Hank's lower back troubled him off and on and he had already started walking a bit hunched over and started sitting slumped down like he was trying to sit on his very shoulderblades. He had once told Smith "Hezzy" Adair when he'd been drinking that he was sure that he had TB of the spine and wasn't long for this world. Hezzy laughed uncomfortably at first but Hank was serious about his disability. His intensity frightened Adair: Hank knew just how mortal he was and how frail life was and he mocked life. Then he would get drunk and forget his blasphemy. He began to feel that Lilly was suffocating him and that he was stuck on a treadmill. He had secretly hoped the army would take him so he could get away and start over. Throughout the first part of 1942, he continued things as before: going to school now and then, playing the honky-tonks and dances and handing over his money to Lilly and trying to hold out enough to get drunk and get a woman. He knew that he had gained a reputation in the music business as a good draw but a dangerous one because of his drinking. He was nineteen years old and in the ninth grade at Sidney Lanier High School when he decided to pack it in and head on out. He and Lilly had a terrible fight and he knew it was a serious mistake to tell Lilly he wanted to leave. First, she wept and told him he was no better than Lonnie, just a weak drunk who was ready to desert her in her hour of need. He was selfish and weak and didn't care about his poor old mother. He tried to argue, which he knew he shouldn't even try. She raged at him and then knocked him down. He ran out into the night and drank and slept in an alleyway. At sunrise, he sneaked back into the boarding house to get the few dollars he'd hidden away in a hollow leg of his iron bedstead, and he headed for the Greyhound bus station. "Mobile, one way," he told the ticket agent.

Mobile, where six rivers empty into the Gulf of Mexico to form Mobile Bay, was a bustling port city in late 1942 as its shipyards geared up for war. It was not so bustling

however that it was waiting with open arms for an unskilled nineteen-year-old high school dropout. Hank
walked the streets for three days, sleeping in a quarter-a-
night flophouse. His fantasies of going to sea were dashed
pretty quickly when it was obvious, in the first shape-up
he went to at the docks, that he would never be an able-
bodied seaman. He couldn't even stand fully erect, because of his back trouble. "Sorry, kid, maybe you can try
the shipyards. They're hirin' anybody."

He settled into the warm afternoon darkness of the
first bar he found and tried to drink away the frustration
of rejection. What was he to do? He couldn't go back and
face Lilly. Well, he could, but it would just mean misery
and ridicule. He hadn't even brought his guitar with him
to Mobile, he'd been so sure that he'd be at sea by now.

"What'll it be, mister? You drinkin' or prayin'?"

Hank reddened at the barmaid's words and looked up.
" 'Nother Falstaff, please, ma'am." He dug into his worn
wallet and pulled out a crumpled dollar bill.

He started to tuck his wallet away when several folded-
up pieces of paper fell out. He spread them out on the
bar. They were the scraps of songs that he was writing.
There were at least half a dozen that he had almost finished and felt pretty good about. He picked one piece of
paper up and laughed at the words he saw. He had
started writing this one when he'd decided to join the
army and go off and win the war and be a hero. He had
called this one "Granddad's Musket" because he'd been
thinking about his Granddaddy Skipper and the stories
he'd told little Hiram about the Spanish-American War.
Hank had written several verses but he needed a hook, a
catchy line that he could repeat. His lips moved as he
read the words: "Granddad with his musket in the days
of yore, could knock off a squirrel at a hundred yards or
more, so give me granddad's musket and I'll march to
war, to da da da da something something and even up the
score. Grandma with her knitting is doing the best she

can, Sis is buying savings stamps, but I've a better plan, just give me granddad's musket and I'll march off to war, and da da da da something the score. The boys up in the mountains have closed down their stills, they've moved into the city and are making leaden pills, while me and granddad's musket when we are off to war da da. If you haven't bought a bond or stamp now is the time, join up with the million more who are falling in line, let's all grab granddad's musket and march right on to war and join up with da da da and even up the score." He thought for awhile about the last line. He ordered another Falstaff. " 'Scuse me, ma'am, what's the name of some famous gen'rals?" She just looked at him. The war had sure brought some squirrelly bastards to Mobile but this one had the weakest line she had ever heard. Maybe he was some kind of fruit.

Finally, the man on the barstool next to Hank spoke up. "General Douglas MacArthur, what a leader—"

Hank cut him off: "Thank you, sir. That's perfect." He scribbled the last line he needed: "We'll join up with MacArthur and even up the score." He felt better. It wouldn't win the war or get him in the army but he felt he'd gotten himself a pretty damn good little war song there. People liked patriotic songs. Maybe he'd crank a few of them out. His beer-induced euphoria soon passed and he was just tired and depressed again. He went back to the flophouse and slept.

The next morning, he made up his mind pretty quickly. He couldn't go to war or go to sea and he couldn't go back to Lilly. What he needed was cheering up and that meant a woman and there was only one who had been on his mind of late so he decided to go see her. He rode the Greyhound all day, chain-smoking Camels, and thought about Audrey. She was the first girl he'd been to bed with more than once and, to tell the truth about it, she had taught him a thing or two and he smiled at the memory. Built like a brick shithouse and fucked like a snake, oh my, Miss Audrey! Hair like spun gold and flashing eyes and those soft, full lips and magic hands. . . . He got a hard-on right there on the bus and took off his hat and put it on his lap. He looked at his Timex: with a little luck he'd be dipping into Audrey's soft flesh in another two hours. He leaned back, as far as the seat would let him, to take the pressure off his spine and stroked himself under his hat and thought about Audrey.

She came on like a house afire and that's what had attracted him to her. At the same time she scared him a bit with her strength: she was, although he wouldn't admit it to himself, remarkably like Lilly in that regard. She was one independent-minded woman. If you told her the sun set in the west, she'd stand up to you just for the sake of arguing. A feisty little piece.

She was the same age as Hank and they'd met in the spring of '42, just a few months back, when he was playing a medicine show in Banks, over in Pike County. He was bored with it and there wasn't much of a crowd. This was really out in the bow-jacks, the boondocks, and Hank was taking a few nips of spot to ease the boredom when he saw Audrey in the crowd. He liked what he saw and he introduced himself. She was a little standoffish and that just attracted him more.

Her name was Audrey Mae Sheppard Guy and she was living at home with her parents in Enon, a few miles out of Banks. Her parents, Artie Mae Harden Sheppard and Charles Shelton Sheppard, farmed cotton and peanuts as best they could. Audrey wanted out of that kind of life as soon as she could get out, and for a poor farm girl the only way out was marriage. She'd dropped out of high school to marry Erskine Guy and they immediately had a daughter, named Lycrecia. Erskine went into the army when the war started and was shipped overseas so Audrey had to move back in with her folks in Enon. She was, however, getting Erskine's monthly allotment check of $80 and she got a job working in the drugstore over in Brundidge and she didn't intend to let marriage tie her down too closely. In point of fact, she had a pretty fast reputation in that part of the state. "She's a real hellcat," people would say knowingly, or "Audrey's always got her pilot light turned up." She was on the prowl the night she met Hank and they sparred for a while before she appeared to give in and go out with him that night. They had an argument right away about his drinking. "You gonna have to let whiskey alone if you go out with me," she had told Hank and, to his own surprise, he agreed. He didn't even blink when Audrey told him that she, too, was a country singer. He was crazy about her and she ran just fast enough to let him catch her. They argued from the first, but the sex more than made up for the fighting and, indeed, sometimes the fighting turned them on. By the time he'd told her a dozen times that he loved her, Audrey was believing it. She had no trouble at all in talking him into letting her sing with the Drifting Cowboys although her voice was at best tuneless and talentless. She kind of sounded like a rusty fence gate on a windy night, but Hank was so pussy-crazy he pretended not to notice. The Drifting Cowboys joked that she was such a bad singer that she had to sneak up on a song before she could sing it and even then it would sometimes get away from her. Of course, they didn't let Hank hear them.

They had a bit of a falling-out when Hank had taken her home to Montgomery to meet Lilly. Somehow, through Lilly's mental powers or her network of informers, she'd known immediately that Audrey was married, and she lit into Hank right away: "Where'd you pick up this whore?" Audrey cowered in a dark bedroom while Hank and Lilly slugged it out. As usual, Lilly won. Audrey surrendered that battle but would not concede the war. Hank was easy pickings and he was a good horse to ride out of rural Alabama. Plus, he would let her sing.

She had already decided to divorce Erskine as soon as—
or if—he returned from the army and was able to sign the
papers.

She hadn't planned on Hank's abrupt decision to quit
music and try to enter the war, any more than Lilly had
planned on it.

Hank still confided in no one, let alone in a woman,
but he had dropped a broad hint to Hezzy Adair that his
"spinal TB" had returned and worsened and that Hank
had therefore decided to get into the war and if he died,
why, that's the way it was. Lilly and Audrey later explained that Hank was just depressed because he hadn't
yet hit the big time in music. He really needed their help,
they said, before he could do that. Meanwhile, the silly
child, he had to run off and try things on his own for a
while. Well, let him, they said, he'll come to his senses
soon enough and realize what's good for him.

Hank awoke with a start as the Greyhound pulled into
Troy, the county seat of Pike County, shortly before twi-
light. He had a headache from not eating and from smoking all day and for being cramped up in the bus. He got
down off the bus and fished a cold bottle of Coke out of
the cooler box inside the bus station. He let his hand trail
in the ice water inside the cooler box and splashed water
across his face. He went into the men's room, closed the
door on a stall, and sat down heavily on the commode.
He drained a third of the Coke in one swig and reached
inside his jacket pocket for the flask there. A little taste of
spot—ah, how it burned going down—and then a little
chaser of Coke. Hank felt better. He finished off the
Coke, washed up, and hiked out to the edge of town to
hitch-hike out towards Banks on Highway 26. He soon
caught a ride with a farmer, told the farmer that he was a
soldier on furlough, and got out of the farmer's truck at
least a half a mile from the Sheppard farm. Old man
Sheppard hated Hank and knew he was a good-for-noth-
ing hillbilly singer drunk who was just after his daughter

—his *married* daughter—for one thing and one thing only. He forbade Audrey to see Hank and thereby did Hank a big favor. Audrey could not have had a better endorsement of Hank.

The sun was going down as Hank limped down the dirt lane in his cowboy boots. He sat down in a shadow of a large honeysuckle bush and smoked a cigarette as he waited for darkness. He wanted to make sure old man Sheppard didn't catch him. Lights winked on the Sheppards' white clapboard frame house. Hank tiptoed towards the window of Audrey's bedroom and tapped the windowpane lightly with his fingernail. "Shh! It's me, it's ole Hank," he whispered when Audrey's face appeared. "Meet me at the barn in half an hour," she mouthed the words and then disappeared. Obviously, old C.S. was home. Hank slipped down to the barn, keeping in the shadows, and helped himself to another taste of spot as he waited for Audrey. He checked his wallet to make sure he had a rubber. He got out a Lifesaver mint he'd been saving to make his breath fresh and unalcoholic for Audrey and he sat and waited. She was upon him without a sound and surprised him. She was barefoot and wearing a loose dress without a thing under it.

She grabbed him with both hands and thrust her tongue down his throat and he didn't come up for air until they were stretched out naked in the straw and he was inside her and they were both moaning and thrashing around. She wrapped her legs and arms around his bony frame and he thought she was going to break him in half. She half-screamed and shuddered and dug her nails in his back. "Ohh, baby, baby!" They lay together silently for two or three minutes. "Hank, you got a cigarette?" She sat up and patted her hair back into place. After he lit the cigarettes for both of them, she exhaled lazily. "By the way," she asked, "how come you ain't in the army like you wrote me you was gonna do?"

He tensed and gathered his courage. "Marry me, Ordrey. I love you."

She laughed. "Oh, Hank, I love you, too. But I'm married. You know that. Besides, if you ain't in the army, what are you doin'?"

He had planned and rehearsed a long speech to be delivered straight from the heart, one that only she could understand for only she knew how sensitive he was, how different he was. And he knew how special she was. Weren't they the only ones who understood each other? "Ordrey," he was gonna say, "I need you baby, I'm hurtin' and only you can make it right. The world don't know what I'm really like. Let me tell you . . ."

But he realized that she could never understand. If he tried to even tell her about his back she would leave, he knew that. There was nothing he could say to her except "I love you" which he repeated over and over.

"Hank," she said impatiently. "Now I love you *too*. But we got to be practical. What are you gonna *do*? Now I am perfectly ready to divorce Erskine but I must know just exactly what you plan to *do*. Now are you workin' or just exactly what are you *doin'*? You know how my daddy feels."

Despite the chill of the evening, Hank began sweating, and he reached for his clothes. "I . . . I got a *defense* job, Ordrey," he finally said. He pronounced it *dee*-fense. "I'm gonna be in Mobile. I'll be in touch." He got to his feet and reached down for his boots but Audrey grabbed him and pulled him down on top of her, and she smelled of straw and sweat and woman and Hank shucked his clothes again right quickly. "Hank, you *are* gonna keep a band together and all once ever' thin's settled, ain't you?" She ran a fingernail down the length of his spine and he shivered. "Yes, baby, baby," he whispered.

He awoke alone in the morning but he felt good. He hustled out of the barn before old C.S. could find him and put a load of double-ought buckshot in his skinny ass. He hitched a ride right quick into Troy and downright enjoyed the breakfast he had of Coca-Cola and Tom's Peanuts while waiting for the bus to Mobile. He smiled a lot for once. When he got to Mobile he rented a furnished room to save money and hit the streets looking for work until he finally signed on as a laborer with the Alabama Drydock and Shipbuilding Company. He eventually became a welder and bought a guitar and played infrequently around Mobile. And continued to see Audrey now and then. Lilly he tried to do without. Even though Hank stayed in Mobile almost two years, Lilly later recalled that he was there only three weeks and that she herself, Lilly the unselfish, had rescued him from mundane workaday existence and restored him to show business. This is what she recalled: "Hank was nineteen when he once gave up hopes of ever making the big time as a singer. He even went so far as to quit playing at all. He got a job in the shipyards and left for Mobile. But I believed in Hank. I knew he had what it took with his singing. So I rented a car and went to every schoolhouse and nightclub in the Montgomery area. I booked Hank solid for sixty days. Then the third week he had been 'out of the music business,' I went to Mobile and got him and put him back in it. When Hank saw the datebook for those shows, he gave me the sweetest smile I've ever seen and said, 'Thank God, Mother. You have made me the happiest boy in the world.' "

In August of 1944, Hank gave up whatever pretense he had of a separate life and crawled back home to Lilly's boarding house in Montgomery. His time away had not been entirely wasted. He had a walletful of songs he had written, he had kept in very close touch with Audrey, and he was ready to get serious about his career. She and Lilly were not close and never would be, but they understood each other. That did not mean things were pleasant in the boarding house. Lonnie came to Montgomery once to visit, long after Lilly had divorced him and after he

finally got out of the VA hospitals in 1940. Lilly refused
to see Lonnie, and Lonnie found young Hank in a bar.
Getting drunk. Hank called Lonnie a deserting drunk
and Lonnie, stung badly, went back home to McWilliams
where he was living. Hank went back to pursuing Audrey.

He also quickly reassembled a Drifting Cowboys band,
which included Audrey. He went back on WSFA as
though he had never left, and things seemed better than
ever. Audrey had briefly been a competitor: when Don
Helms joined the Drifting Cowboy's on steel guitar,
Hank told him, "They's a cunt on the other station
[WCOV] that's buttin' heads with me." Only a woman
could compete; there wasn't a male singer around who
was a serious threat to Hank. Hank himself was finally
serious; he seldom if ever smiled, and he was down to
business all the time.

Oddly, he seemed to spend as much time with the bottle as he did with his career: he worked hard at everything, as if there weren't enough time left for any of it. He
had in fact been deceptively lazy during his time away
from Montgomery. One day country comedienne Minnie
Pearl and country singing star Pee Wee King had walked
into the radio station in Dothan, in southeastern Alabama, and found waiting for them a young man who
looked old beyond his years. He was waiting to sell a
song to Pee Wee King. The song was a good one, Hank's
second composition about World War II. Nobody had
been interested in "Granddad's Musket" but "I'm Praying for the Day Peace Will Come" seemed a little bit
more commercial and Pee Wee King gave him two bottles of Southern Comfort for it. Hank's family preferred
to recall that King gave him ten dollars for the copyright
to the song. Buying and selling songs was very common-
place then and Hank bought as many as he sold and that
was a practice he continued up to the very end.

He was suddenly working double-time at everything.

Audrey gave way quickly before his resolve and agreed to get married. They were wed on December 15, 1944, while on the road in Andalusia, in Covington County in south Alabama. Audrey had filed for divorce from Erskine Guy only ten days earlier, and under Alabama law she should have waited sixty days before marrying again.

Audrey and Hank were ultimately legally wed only because they lived together long enough to satisfy Alabama's requirement for a couple to be considered wed by common law. Even though their marriage service was a "filling station" wedding, performed by a Justice of the Peace in his service station, Hank and Audrey did take it seriously. They went before an examining doctor, L. L. Parker, who wrote that he believed they were free from any venereal diseases and then they got Justice of the Peace M. A. Boyett to marry them. Hank wrote "band leader" as his occupation on the marriage license. Lilly raised ungodly hell about it. She finally let Hank and Audrey move into Hank's bedroom in the boarding house but she never let up. She continued as the Drifting Cowboys' driver and manager, and she still would not even let a blood relative into a Drifting Cowboys dance for free. It was cash money or else see you later! Lilly and Audrey began to give each other the fish eye. Each knew that the other was out to control the income generated by Hank Williams. They were generally civil toward each other. They managed to arrive at and leave Hank's shows separately. They had no argument with each other the first time Hank was committed to a hospital for treatment of alcoholism, when he was sent to the Prattville, Alabama, hospital in early 1945. They both had their own ambitions, though. Audrey, the "cunt" on the other radio station whom Hank had married, was no longer a direct competitor but she had her own road map for Hank to follow. Lilly—well Lilly had had it all figured out for years and had invested too much time and energy in this little project to allow some blonde hussy, some Audrey-

come-lately to come along and tell her how to run Hank.
As Lilly settled into middle age, she became even more
prepossessing and formidable in appearance and manner.
No boarding house was ever run with a firmer hand. Life
at Lilly's was pretty well regimented, especially for Hank.
By mid-1945 he had never been doing so well with his
career and had never been more miserable. He and Audrey fought often and she was more and more insistent
on getting equal stage time. She even wanted to cowrite
songs with him and did so, songs like "My Darling Baby
Girl," which Hank ultimately managed to forget about.
It was written about Audrey's daughter Lycrecia, whom
Hank never got close to or wanted to get close to. Audrey
wrote most of the words: "When my days are sad and
dreary, and there's so much trouble in this world, then I
thank God in Heaven for my darling baby girl. Her eyes
are big and blue, her hair in golden curls, to me she's an
angel, my darling baby girl." It got stickier and sweeter
but Hank preferred to forget about it. He would sit out
on the front porch and drink openly, which he had never
used to do around Lilly, and sing "My Darling Pain in
the Ass" and write songs and drink till he was knee-
crawling drunk. He could always write, though, no matter how drunk he got. He would end up passed out in the
rocking chair with scraps of paper at his feet with
scrawled lyrics on them. Audrey was already the subject
of some of his mournful songs, as in "You Always Seem
to Go the Other Way."

> When I pass you on the street
> Sweetheart, you hardly even speak.
> No matter where my footsteps stray,
> You always seem to go the other way.
>
> Why must I always be alone?
> Why must I cry from dusk to dawn?

> *No matter how hard I pray*
> *You always seem to go the other way.*
>
> *What a shame we ever met*
> *Why can't my lonely heart forget?*
> *I go on grieving day by day*
> *You always seem to go the other way.*

That was no masterpiece, and he knew it, but he kept writing on the same theme for years until he did produce masterpieces of the broken heart, all generously inspired by Audrey. "Your Cheatin' Heart," "I Can't Help It"—he could crank 'em out all day.

Hank was drinking more and more. He had never been a bigger draw on the honky-tonk circuit but it gave him no rest. He was up at dawn for his first show on WSFA. Sometimes he'd do three shows a day and then drive out of Montgomery that afternoon for the night's honky-tonk dance in Andalusia, Opp, Fort Deposit, Evergreen, Dothan—all the stops in south Alabama. As his popularity grew, more and more wise-asses were waiting to fight him. He was beaten up as many times as he beat up the challengers or laid them low with a blackjack. He had a piece of one eyebrow bitten out one night by a drunken psycho and it scared him. Sometimes now he would get drunk before they got to the dance and pass out in the car. Lilly and Audrey collaborated in keeping him sober till he had been on stage long enough to satisfy the paying customers and then they'd start letting him drink. Lilly started rolling him regularly and when she didn't Audrey didn't mind doing so; someone had to take care of the money so that he didn't waste it. At least that was the way they figured it.

Audrey started drinking and that was like a dam bursting. If Hank often seemed like he was in a fog, that's because he was. His interests were drinking, writing songs, and buying guns. Hank discovered early on that

often the biggest country music fans were local policemen. They always were able to find pistols for sale and—
conveniently—knew which local women were willing and
ready. With police sanction. That was one trade secret
the women country singers never learned about.

The better Hank became, the less he seemed to care
about his career. Lilly and Audrey both tried lecturing
him and they both received hostile stares for their trouble. They resolved that it was their duty to stoke the
career along, since Hank wasn't responsible enough to do
so. Audrey, too, still had designs of making it big as a
singer herself.

Hank spent more time out on the front porch with a
paper and pencil and a flask. He was writing some of the
songs that would later keep his career afloat; songs like
"When God Comes and Gathers His Jewels," "Six More
Miles," "Calling You," and "Wealth Won't Save Your
Soul." Mournful and maudlin were they all, but he was
sincere about them. He had not been to church since they
had moved to Montgomery, but Hank still remembered
the hellfire sermons he'd heard as a child and he feared
eternal damnation. Writing gospel songs seemed to be the
best way to keep the devil from the door.

At the same time he was writing honky-tonk songs. He
never really got it straightened out in his mind whether
he was writing for Saturday night—the full-tilt drunken
blow-out that the workingman supposedly deserved every
Saturday night as a reward for working hard all week
long—or whether he was writing for Sunday morning,
when the sun shone down on happy couples and their
fawning parents and children as they marched into a
spotless white church. He kept writing both kinds of
songs and could never get it entirely straight in his own
mind just where he belonged. He wanted to have Saturday night every night, drink it up and have a good time
but then he'd start to feel guilty and want to go back to
Sunday morning and the sunlight and the white church

and innocence. That was one thing Audrey just didn't understand and never could, and Hank just gave up trying to explain it to her.

He still had a little touch of whimsy that Lilly and Audrey hadn't beaten out of him yet, and he would now and then let it show, like in his song "Backache Blues."

> *I went to dance, stayed out all night*
> *Woke up this morning, wasn't feeling right.*
> *I had the backache blues,*
> *I had the backache blues,*
> *O, I'm suffering with the backache, Oh, Oh Lord.*
>
> *I went to see my baby and we drank some gin,*
> *Boy, that's when all the fun began.*
> *I've got the backache blues [etc.]*
>
> *My gal's long, man, my gal's tall,*
> *But let me tell you something boy, that ain't all.*
> *I've got the backache blues [etc.]*
>
> *Me and my gal sitting on the porch,*
> *I said, 'Look here baby don't hold me so close.'*
> *I've got the backache blues [etc.]*

Oh Lord. He had the backache blues and plenty more blues besides. His hair was falling out in bunches and he started wearing a hat all the time. His stomach was acting up and it was all he could do to keep a little liquor down. His back hurt badly but everyone was tired of him crying wolf and was sick and tired of hearing Hank complain about his back.

He used to go out and drive around and pick up black men and go to niggertown with them and listen to nigger singers there. It was better than listening to Audrey or Lilly drone on and on. It got to where he kind of liked hearing himself bitch and moan for a change about how

bad things were and he some days wouldn't bitch and
moan if it were only Audrey or Lilly listening. He'd
rather be his own audience. He had better taste than Lilly
or Audrey did. He began to draw a select kind of audience, an elite crowd for Montgomery and environs. Even
his Nashville idols, Ernest Tubb and Roy Acuff, seemed
to want to come and listen to Hank Williams. They actually did. Tubb was so impressed that he took the unprece-
dented step of advising Grand Ole Opry manager Jim
Denny that the Opry should get Hank soonest. The Opry
management crowd knew all about Hank; knew that he
was the only candidate from the minor leagues who was a
shoo-in for the country music major league. The Opry
management suspected, however, that Hank might be
difficult and therefore recommended that he not be
brought up to the major leagues just yet. Frankly, they
thought that he was a binger, and the Opry didn't really
need any more drunks just yet. It already had more than
enough drunks, although none of them were really identified as such. As long as they managed to stand up on
stage at Ryman Auditorium every Saturday night and
could belt out a song or two without falling over—well,
they were good country-music citizens, weren't they?
Hank couldn't even be counted on to stand up, no matter
how good he was. Showing up was certainly preferable to
falling down in the alley outside; still, Hank's name was
spelled no-show in Nashville.

The Opry was Hank's only real ambition. Ever since
he had first, as a kid, sat listening on Saturday night to
WSM and its 50,000-watt clear-channel beam out of
Nashville and heard the Opry, he knew that was where
he belonged. The Opry was the true cathedral of the
South. People drove hundreds of miles to get to Ryman
Auditorium on Saturday nights just to see the Opry. The
Opry stars played for scale, although Hank didn't yet
know that, just for the exposure. And it didn't hurt once
you were an Opry regular to have the Opry booking ser-

vice behind you and to go out on the road booked as coming direct from the Grand Ole Opry. The Opry was a select club and Hank, although he was more and more the loner, wanted in that club and knew that he deserved to be in that club. He just didn't know how in the hell you got in. He had thought that if you were good and you worked hard, why, they came and got you and asked you to join the club. It didn't seem to be working that way. He knew he was good. Hadn't Ernest Tubb himself, the best honky-tonk singer around, told him that? He worked hard, worked his ass off, worked harder than any two country singers and nothing was happening except the constant grind of the honky-tonks and the nagging and harping and bitching and moaning and lectures and tears and fights and all the other crap he took from Lilly and Audrey. Jesus. No wonder he had to take a drink every now and then—mostly now to be sure, but Hank did not have an easy life. No sir. He had to be the resident musical genius, the songwriter, the lead singer, the front man, the draw and he wasn't getting a hell of a lot out of it but grief. It did occur to him one day that he was virtually a small industry supporting several people. He was sick of the honky-tonks but he didn't know any other life and could not envision any other way of life. It just seemed that maybe if he could get on the Opry and maybe get a record contract, maybe he wouldn't have to spend half his life driving to beer joints, playing in beer joints for people who just wanted to get drunk and screw or fight, for people who by and large did not give one damn for him unless it was a drunk man who wanted to fight him or a drunk woman who wanted to screw him. It just sucked, all the way around. He talked to Audrey about it, which was hard for him. It was hard for him to talk to anybody and he never did really carry on a conversation with anyone for more than ten minutes or so. But he had to get this crap off his chest and Audrey was really the only one he could tell. He and Audrey did get along at times, after all. Audrey surprised him. She heard him out, heard his blurting, unhappy story and agreed with him. "You damn right, honey," she said. "You are too good to play these beer joints all your life." He felt better, even if nothing had been settled.

Audrey, of course, had really meant "*We* are too good to play these beer joints," for she had high ambitions of a singing career for herself and was still plaguing Hank for equal billing with him and equal stage time. Audrey was smart enough, however, to realize that Hank was a fool, nothing but a damn silly fool if he thought that he could just stand around and wait for lightning to strike him. Maybe he entertained the silly delusion that if he was halfway good that he would be discovered. Crapola. The world was full of talented people who withered away on the vine. Audrey read magazines, she kept her eyes and ears open, she listened to network radio—not just hillbilly crap. She sensed that success was about thirty percent talent and the rest was just pure drive. She liked to say that there was no such thing in the world as luck. "You make your own luck," she would say. Hank didn't understand that. He still thought that talent was automatically rewarded and he grew increasingly bitter when his obvious talent was not rewarded while other, less talented musicians became rich and famous. All he knew was that he was breaking his balls and getting nothing but a hard time in return. The bottle became his solace and he sometimes spent the first half of a dance passed out. Then he might lurch onto the stage, playing an open E chord—he only felt comfortable with G, C and D—and trying to sing "New Moon Over My Shoulder" while the Drifting Cowboys, this week's version of them, played "Blue Steel Blues" or something to drown him out. He was only twenty-two. He looked and acted ten years older.

Hank smiled once or twice a year. Onstage, he would turn to steel guitarist Don Helms and tell him, "Shag, take it on the turnaround [i.e., repeat the last verse]. They ain't enough people cryin' yet. I wanta see at least half of 'em cryin'." He drank more and more, it was true, but he was such an easy drunk that it wasn't funny. Twenty minutes left alone and he would be falling down drunk. If ever someone could not handle alcohol, Hank was the guy: four drinks and he was gone for the night. Even Audrey could outdrink him. Sometimes that was their entertainment on the rare night when they weren't working: sit in their little bedroom at Lilly's and silently drink till sleep came. Things were getting to a desperate stage by 1946. Audrey wanted her ambitions fulfilled; she wanted to be a star and, if it were also possible, she wanted to be married to a star. One thing was for sure: she wanted to be rich. She had been through Hank's pockets enough and shared honky-tonk stages with him enough to know that bouncing the joints in south Alabama forever was gonna do nothing but ruin their livers. Audrey wanted some positive action.

Lilly didn't want to run a boarding house and cook and clean forever like some menial. She had worked her fingers to the very bone—just ask her—and sacrificed for her only son, had given herself up to his career, had bought a Chevrolet and driven Hank and his band to dances and physically fought for and defended her little boy, and tried to protect him from grasping women who only wanted to exploit his success and talent and virility. She had tried her best to run Audrey off, the scheming blonde hussy. But if her boy insisted on living with that woman at least they would live under Lilly's roof where she herself could keep an eye on her boy and watch after his fortunes since no one else was capable of doing so. Audrey was just using him to get a singing career herself; Lilly had explained that to Hank and he wouldn't listen, skirt-crazy man that he was. Women were a bad influence that led him to drink, and he no longer honored his mother. He needed disciplining; he had no self-discipline

and threw his money away on liquor. He was lucky he
had Lilly to take care of him and look after him. Audrey
would steal his money if Lilly didn't watch after things.
Audrey was a whore; Lilly watched her as no one was
ever watched and Lilly herself was no stranger to men
and Audrey watched her and the poison that flowed back
and forth was quite remarkable. Neither woman was an
angel, they hated each other, they pretended that taking
care of Hank was their only mission in life and knew that
the other was mistreating Hank and lying to him about
the other woman. The lying bitch. Hank was aware of the
bad blood between Lilly and Audrey—how could he not
have noticed it?—but he tried to let it simmer along without his active participation. Besides, there wasn't no way
he was gonna get caught in the middle of a fight between
those two women. Might as well step into a nest of rattle-
snakes. He wasn't that dumb and . . . he just preferred
to not be aware of it, that's all. He played his honky-
tonks when he could, wrote his songs when he could, and
drank when he could. If he could have had his way, he
would have been long gone, but he had no control over
his life anymore. If Lilly had managed to get total control
of his life, he would still be playing honky-tonks in south
Alabama to this day and handing over the proceeds to
Lilly. Lilly had limited ambitions and didn't look much
past the day after tomorrow. Audrey, though, Miss Audrey wanted to make something out of herself and if that
first required whipping her husband into shape, well, that
was what she had to do then. She knew that for her to
make it as a singer, she would have to ride Hank's coattails and before she could do that he had to have some
coattails worth riding and that was obviously her task.
She had to make sure he was hot stuff. So that meant
nursing him along to blood-bucket performances
throughout south Alabama and the long drive back to
Montgomery at two in the morning with Hank drunk
and then pouring him into bed at Lilly's and hauling his

ass out of bed at the goddamn crack of dawn and marching him down to the studios at WSFA for his radio shows. And was he grateful for all she did? Goddamn, don't even ask Audrey about that or she'd claw your goddamn eyeballs out, she was that put out about her lot in life right along there in 1945 and 1946 or so. What she'd married for—the life of a singing star—just was not happening and besides that she was living in a goddamn furnished room in her goddamn mother-in-law's goddamn boarding house and paying good goddamn money for that privilege and her the mother of a little daughter trying to live there also. It was just getting to be a bit goddamn much, thank you very much Lilly, and whatever the hell happened to Lonnie anyway?, and Lilly, you got a moustache anyway. Audrey got quite carried away when she had had a drink or two and started thinking about Lilly. Doyle and Bernice Taylor, a nice young married couple from over in Memphis who'd become Drifting Cowboys—turnover in the band had become quite high—were living at Lilly's like the rest of the Drifting Cowboys and paying Lilly $57 a week and they had gotten upset. Bernice had come to Audrey—a quiet woman-to-woman talk—and mentioned how Hank's drinking was really kind of . . . like spoiling everything for everyone else and couldn't Audrey speak to him about it? and meanwhile being a Drifting Cowboy was kinda like indentured servitude and having to kiss Lilly's ass was the worst part but Bernice was damned if she was gonna have to also kowtow to Miss Audrey. . . . Oh, it got messy. More than one night, Hank laid up drunk in the back bedroom while the women argued about him. Sometimes they would sit on the bed while he snored and argue back and forth across his somnambulant body. His libido was not terrific, as Audrey reminded him, but he was usually drunk. He did dare to tell her that women could still drink and screw since liquor did not hinder their ability to get a wide-on. Audrey did not smile or laugh at that. She whopped the shit out of him. She was only doing it for his own good, as she reminded him. Who, after all, would even take the trouble for a worthless drunk like him? Thanks a lot, Audrey. He said that to himself, but never to her. At least she didn't weigh as much as Lilly and couldn't hit as hard.

Lilly would march forth every morning like a goddamn Roman legion; the woman was awesome. She was obviously afraid of no one; she carried her 200 pounds with the grace of an athlete and her cold stare could wither Satan's own glare. Lilly was hell on wheels, to start with. Then, if you got her mad, you could really look out.

Maturity had brought her a stony gaze, a rugged handsomeness of the statue sort, and an improved right hook. Most people that Lilly met feared her on sight. W. W. Stone, who was now married to her and was her last husband, was no exception. Somehow, he could not recall how he and Lilly had met, it was all kinda hazy and all of a sudden he was hitched up and was taking orders from Lilly and helping run the boarding house. W. W. Stone put on an apron at Lilly's order and did not dare say anything about it. W.W. didn't know Hank from any other so-called star. "Listen, boy," he'd told Hank once, "I was you, I wouldn't mouth off so much. Lilly don't like it." Well, Hank sure as hell knew that. He didn't like W.W., though, and once put one of his Trojan rubbers in W.W.'s wallet when W.W. wasn't looking while he was bathing. Hank figured that Lilly beat W.W.'s ass every which way when she was rifling through W.W.'s wallet that night—just routine, she checked out all her men every night—but Hank figured grimly that every man was entitled to go through what he went through. He was a masochist, no doubt about it. Audrey, who took her punching lessons from Lilly, was initially concerned about Lilly bouncing Hank around. Lilly popped her on the jaw when she spoke up and then lectured her: "Well,

Miss Whore." It took them years to get to understand each other. "Well, Miss Whore. My son listens to *me*. I don't know what *your* problem is. Hank listens to his mother." Bad blood there.

Audrey understood just how fierce Lilly was and she vowed to be just as fierce or whatever the hell it took to win Hank away from Lilly. Hank claimed that he was standing on his own two feet. He cited the latest fight in a showdown in Andalusia. Some asshole in the crowd had yelled to Hank that "Ever' mornin' when my wife gets up, she's listenin' to you on the radio. If she's listenin' tomorrow mornin', I'm a gonna beat her up." Hank had actually stared the man down before answering, "Well, friend, why don't you just turn *off* the radio? That's why they put knobs on it." The guy went berserk and it took half an hour to get things under way again. Hank finally had a tight grin; the asshole had been beaten up by impatient men in the crowd and Hank could act triumphant. "Hey! Did that jackass finally get hitched back to his wagon?" Hank would fight if he had to but he rarely felt that he had to and he depended on boozed-up supporters to defend his honor for him. If not, he would pull his pistol. He never pulled the trigger. The sight of the pistol was the jackass-to-wagon signal. He only pulled the pistol on jackasses and they always kissed his ass when they saw the .38. He wouldn't have shot them, anyway.

That scared Audrey and really set her to thinking. She could tolerate Hank's drinking but guns scared her. It seemed to her that the honky-tonks were changing Hank and she didn't like what he was becoming. She didn't like honky-tonks and the kind of people they attracted and she sure didn't like the rough men who were sucking up to Hank and got guns for him. She didn't like the direction life was taking for her and Hank. A future set entirely in the honky-tonks did not appeal to her. Characteristically, she decided to change things. Hank didn't want to talk about it, so she began plotting action on her own. Obviously, she reasoned, Hank had considerable talent and should be able to make a lot of money and do better than play honky-tonks forever. What he lacked was ambition and any kind of business sense. Audrey had ambition enough for both of them and wisely realized that Hank's career needed to be put into the hands of someone with good business sense. She started looking for that someone. Everyone she asked gave the same answer: Acuff-Rose, in Nashville. So she grabbed Hank by the arm and they rode the Greyhound to Nashville.

3

FRED ROSE and his son Wesley decided at noon on September 14, 1946, to play a fast game of ping-pong before going out to lunch. Fred was beating Wesley when the door opened and in walked a blonde in a tight dress. Behind her, kind of backing shyly into the room was a tall, thin man in a tan, western-cut suit, white hat, and flashy two-tone boots.

"Excuse me," said Audrey Williams. "Which one of you is Fred Rose?"

"I am," Fred said, without even stopping the game. Fred, as usual was wearing a long-sleeved shirt buttoned up to the neck, no jacket, and elastic suspenders to hold up his trousers. He was balding and nearsighted and squinted through thick glasses. Wesley was portly and always looked a bit pompous with his thin moustache.

Hank was about ready to bolt; he had thought this

whole thing was one wild goose chase. But Audrey forged
ahead.

"I'm Audrey Williams and this is my husband Hank
Williams, the singer. My husband would like to sing you
some songs."

"Well," Wesley said, "do you have an appointment?
That's the way it's usually done."

Fred interrupted him: "Do we have time to listen to
him?"

"Sure, why not?" Wesley said.

They went into an empty studio there in the WSM
building and Hank, who still hadn't spoken, sat down
and started singing.

He hadn't really expected this to happen and hadn't
planned what to sing, so he just did the first songs that
came to mind. He did "My Love for You (Has Turned to
Hate)" and "Six More Miles to the Graveyard" and
"When God Comes and Gathers His Jewels." It was just
the sort of stuff Fred liked, but he kept a poker face.

Hank finished. The silence was deafening. Finally,
Fred spoke up. "You write those songs?"

"Yessir."

"Well, son, those are nice songs. I'll give you ten dollars apiece for them."

Hank laughed. He couldn't believe what he was hearing.

Fred Rose, Roy Acuff's partner, liked his songs.

"I'll tell you what," Fred said. "I'm looking for material for Molly O'Day to sing and I think your songs
might be right for her. If you want to sign a contract with
me, then every time you come to Nashville, we'll work on
some more songs." They shook hands and signed a publishing contract.

Hank was jubilant on the bus ride back to Montgomery, but Audrey was strangely quiet. "What's the matter,
honey?" he asked. "Ain't this a lucky day?"

"Well," she finally answered. "I had hoped they'd give you a recording contract."

He laughed. "That'll come, honey. We cain't rush things."

"Well, I don't know." Audrey knew they weren't out of those honky-tonks yet.

Hank went back to reading his contract: he got three cents for every copy of sheet music sold and fifty per cent of royalties for records. It seemed to him like finding money on the street. He had been writing songs for years anyway and now somebody was going to pay him cash money for doing so.

When he told Lilly the good news, she refused to allow Audrey any credit and in fact preserved a garbled account of Hank's meeting with Fred Rose that would persist for years. She said that Hank once said that if Audrey locked him out he would "go out and tell that little dog to move it on over in the doghouse." From that, Lilly said, Hank wrote the song "Move It on Over" and that, somehow, Fred Rose heard about the song and summoned Hank to Nashville. There, Rose supposedly said, "It's good, but how do I know you wrote it? Here, I'll give you a test. Take this situation: there's a poor boy in the valley in love with a rich girl on a hill. Go in the room there and see if you can make a song out of that." Well, said Lilly, Hank cranked out "A Mansion on the Hill" in thirty minutes. That would certainly have surprised Fred Rose, who was a master songwriter himself.

The more Fred Rose thought about Hank's songs, the better he liked them. Fred was an unlikely man to end up as Hank's benefactor and, ultimately, collaborator. He saw true sincerity and emotion in Hank's compositions and he rightly sensed that they had immense potential appeal to audiences. He didn't sense that Hank as performer had that same appeal and potential.

Fred had gotten into country music via a very unconventional route. He was born, of Scottish-Irish parents, in

Evansville, Indiana, on August 24, 1897, and grew up in
St. Louis. When he was eighteen, he decided to see the
world and hopped a freight train for Chicago. There he
worked as a pianist in bars and recorded barrel-house
piano tunes for Brunswick and QRS Records. He joined
Paul Whiteman's band for a spell and later formed a duo
with Elmo Tanner. He got his own radio show, Fred
Rose's Song Shop, on which he would write songs on the
spot based on titles suggested by listeners. He was a pro-
lific writer and was elected to ASCAP (American Society
of Composers, Authors and Publishers), which collected
royalties for composers, in 1938. He wrote "Red Hot
Mamma," "Deed I Do," and "Honest and Truly" for
Sophie Tucker. In 1940, Gene Autry hired Fred to write
for him and Fred turned out sixteen songs for him, including "Be Honest With Me" and "Yesterday's Roses."
He ended up in Nashville literally as the result of a wrong
turn one day, when he was touring as part of a trio called
the Vagabonds, and landed a job at station WSM. "I believe in just letting things happen," he said. It was odd
that he would end up as one of the founders of Nashville's country music industry: he was a slick songwriter
who wrote with his head, rather than with his heart,
which is the traditional country music mode and reason
for its appeal. He was also a reformed alcoholic (while
living in New York, he once went down to the East River
to throw himself in but decided against it) and a Christian Scientist. He initially hated country music but once
he was in Nashville he decided, with his usual pragma-
tism, to study it and discover what made it popular. He
actually went out into the country and knocked on doors
to ask people about country music. He finally decided
that it was music that came from the heart and that
sincerity could sell a lot of records.

His partnership with Roy Acuff, in forming Nashville's
first publishing company in 1942, was also unusual. Acuff
was as rural as Rose was urban and wrote straight from

the heart. He was the reigning king of country music, no doubt about that. When Japanese troops attacked U.S. marines on Okinawa in World War II, their battle cry was "To hell with Roosevelt, to hell with Babe Ruth, to hell with Roy Acuff."

Fred grasped the secret at the core of country music's appeal one night when he was standing backstage at the Grand Ole Opry. Acuff was singing "Don't Make Me Go to Bed, and I'll Be Good," a real weeper of a song about a little boy who was dying and Acuff himself was sobbing as he sang it. Fred was deeply impressed.

When Acuff and Rose formed their partnership, Acuff-Rose publications, it was partly a result of politics within the music industry. ASCAP allowed few country song-writers to join and, as a result, country writers literally had no organization to protect their compositions. When the National Association of Broadcasters formed a rival licensing firm, Broadcast Music Incorporated (BMI) in 1939, country writers rallied to it. Acuff-Rose signed with BMI. Rose himself kept one publishing company (Milene Music) with ASCAP but the Acuff-Rose catalog went to BMI and greatly strengthened that organization. Acuff-Rose itself, as the only all-country publishing house, quickly became an empire. Roy was a silent partner and let Fred run the company. Fred himself, once things were running smoothly, let his son Wesley run the company and occupied himself by working with song-writers. No song became an Acuff-Rose song until Fred had studied it and, in many cases, had improved it. He seldom took credit for reworking a song and preferred to stay in the background. "I have found my happiness in helping others to help themselves," he said. He would soon devote all his energies to Hank, but that didn't happen immediately.

Hank went back to the honky-tonk grind. Molly O'Day recorded "Six More Miles" and "When God

Comes and Gathers His Jewels." Hank didn't get rich from the royalties but his reputation grew.

Allen Rankin, a columnist at the Alabama *Journal,* heard Hank's program, liked it and decided to go and talk to Hank up at WSFA. Hank was suspicious—he had not yet been asked for an interview—but he finally got along well enough with Rankin to talk. "I got the popularist daytime program on this station," he said. "Fans? There's a mob of 'em up here every mornin' and every afternoon! Some come from fifty miles! A lady from Opelika wrote me just this mornin'—here, read it. She says, 'Say, Hank, how much do it cost to come up there and hear you sing. If it don't cost too much, we may come up there.' If anybody in my business knew as much about their business as the public did, they'd be all right! Just lately, somebody got the idea nobody didn't listen to my kind a music. I told everybody on the radio that this was my last program. 'If anybody's enjoyed it,' I said, 'I'd like to hear from 'em.' I got four hundred cards and letters that afternoon and the next mornin' . . . they decided they wanted to hear my kind of music."

In early December 1946, Fred got a phone call from Sterling Records in New York. Sterling wanted to record a western band and a country singer, and did Acuff-Rose know of anyone? Fred had seen a band called the Oklahoma Wranglers at the Purina Checkerboard Jamboree radio broadcast down at the Princess Theater and thought they'd be good, but he couldn't think of a country singer offhand. He asked Wesley and Wesley thought for a minute and said, "Hey, what about that guy from Alabama?"

"Sure," Fred said, so they called Hank and he climbed aboard the Greyhound with his guitar, on December 11.

Fred had already told the Wranglers—three brothers named Vic, Guy and Skeeter Willis—that he wanted them to play on Hank's recording session, since Hank couldn't afford to bring his own band with him. "This fellow writes his own songs," Fred told them, "but he sings a little bit out of meter." Fred said that Hank aped Roy Acuff's singing style a bit too much but that he did write pretty well.

The Willis brothers had moved to Nashville from Chicago and before that had been regulars on the Brush Creek Follies in Kansas City and thought that they were pretty slick. When Hank showed up there in Studio D at the WSM offices in his cheap overcoat and dirty cowboy hat that he kept on all the time, they wondered, Who was this hick? They recorded their four songs quickly, while Hank stood around nervously, and then they all went down the street to have lunch at the Clarkston Hotel. Vic, who remembered meeting Hank one night at the Princess when Hank was trying to pitch a song to Ernest Tubb, took pity on the nervous kid and asked him if he'd like a beer with his sandwich. "No," Hank replied seriously. "You don't know ole Hank. Ole Hank don't have just one." He drank black coffee and they went back to the studio to cut his songs. Hank had decided on "Wealth Won't Save Your Soul," "When God Comes and Gathers His Jewels," "Never Again (Will I Knock on Your Door)," and "Calling You." The Willis brothers were snickering: Hank sounded like a real hayseed and those songs were so morbid and maudlin that nobody would ever buy them. Fred, who was producing the session, got into a shouting match with the Willises when Hank was cutting "Wealth Won't Save Your Soul." He wanted them to sing backing vocals and they were screwing up. Hank sang the word "poor" as "purr"—he couldn't pronounce it any other way and the Willises kept singing it as "poor." "Damn it," Fred said, "sing it the same way he does." So they had to sing "purr."

Billboard, the music trade publication, ran a brief review of "Wealth Won't Save Your Soul" and "When God Comes and Gathers His Jewels" and said that "It's the backwoods gospel singing—way back in the woods—that

Hank Williams sings out for both of these country songs
taken at a slow waltz tempo. Both the singing and the
songs [sound] entirely funereal." The review also said the
songs were not suited for jukebox play. Even so, Sterling
was pleased with the results and asked Fred to cut four
more songs with Hank. One of them—"Honky Tonkin' "
—was far removed from Hank's earlier Acuff posture,
was not funereal, and was quite daring in its description
of hitting the honky-tonks. Fred and Wesley were impressed by it. Fred decided that Hank might actually sell
a few records and he thought about trying to put Hank
on a major record label—the Sterling sessions had earned
Hank only $500 and were a nonroyalty deal. After Paul
Cohen at Decca turned him down, Fred called Frank
Walker, whom he knew from the days when Walker had
been president of RCA-Victor Records and Columbia
Records. Walker was just launching the M-G-M Records
label and Fred told him, "You're starting a record company and I've got a country artist I want to record."
Fred's word was good enough for Walker. He gave Fred
carte blanche with Hank. Fred could record Hank any
way he wanted to and send the results to M-G-M in New
York. It was quite an unusual deal but it was not acciden-
tal. Fred had spent quite a bit of time thinking about
Hank and had spent hours talking to Wesley about him.
Fred finally reached the decision that Hank could be a
major star, with the right direction and coaching, and
Fred decided to mold him into a star. Fred and Wesley
drew up a virtual blueprint for his career, and step-by-
step progression. First was a recording contract, then a
power base—which meant the Grand Ole Opry, but since
the Opry was still wary about Hank they might start him
off on a smaller barn dance. It would be like a farm team
for the Opry. Then Fred would work closely with Hank
on his songwriting. No man ever got closer writing super-
vision than did Hank from Fred, whom he began to call
"Pappy." And then would come the crossover into pop

music sales, which was where the big money was. The country record market was small fish compared with the millions of records sold by the pop stars. Fred knew that market. There was no reason why Hank's songs couldn't be recorded by pop stars. Hank himself was too raw and country to cross over but others could do it for him. And then there was Las Vegas and movies . . . there was no limit to what they could do with Hank. Hank had no idea that his future was being plotted out for him. He was still bouncing around the honky-tonks in Alabama, trying to keep Audrey placated and trying to keep Lilly off his back. He had already started zipping up to Nashville to see Fred, whenever he could get the time. Fred— "Pappy"—was the first person who really appreciated his songwriting. They could talk. Fred knew songwriting, knew how tough it was, and he praised Hank and also helped him. It was okay if Fred changed a few words here and there . . . the result was probably what Hank intended in the first place. Fred filled in the blanks in Hank's mind. Fred was like Hank's long-lost father, although he would never say so in so many soppy words. Hank would drop in with a few words scribbled on a scrap of paper and hand it to Pappy and ask, "Ya think there's anything there?" Fred would read the words and move over to his piano and noodle out a tune and invent a verse and change a few words here and there and before long Hank would have written one hell of a good song. It was a nice process. Hank never told Pappy that he himself sometimes bought some of those words that he brought to Pappy, bought them from struggling young songwriters, just as Hank himself had sold songs when he was hurting. What the hell, everyone did it.

When Pappy called him in Montgomery and told him of the M-G-M recording contract, it was the happiest day he knew. He finally felt vindication for all the deprivation, the humiliations he had known, for all the crap he had had to swallow. He drank openly from a flask of

whiskey and Lilly and Audrey just stared at him. He even
offered W. W. Stone a drink and W.W. slipped into the
hall closet and knocked back a taste. It was quite a day,
all in all. Lilly's and Audrey's uncharacteristic silence
seemed to spring from the dollar signs in their eyes. It
was high damn time that Hank made some real money to
compensate them for all the sacrifices they had made to
advance Hank's career. God alone knew how those
women had suffered in silence while putting him ahead of
everything else, even their own precarious health, it
seemed.

Hank's first record for M-G-M was "Move It on
Over," his old novelty song about being in the doghouse,
and the other side was "Last Night I Heard You Crying
in Your Sleep." "Move It on Over" did quite well in 1947
and Hank was clearly on his way. Frank Walker told
Fred to pull out all the stops with Hank: he was a big part
of M-G-M's future. Fred and Wesley talked all day and
decided it was time to get Hank on the Louisiana Hayride in Shreveport and start grooming him to get him
ready for the Grand Ole Opry, which was just a matter of
time. Fred had already put two Acuff-Rose acts, Johnny
and Jack as well as the Bailes Brothers, on the Hayride.
All he had to do was call up Henry Clay, who ran station
KWKH, which broadcast the Hayride every Saturday
night. "Henry? Fred Rose here. Fine. Listen, Henry, I've
got a young fellow who's ready for you. Fine. I'll send
him over and he can do a guest shot this Saturday night.
See what you think."

KWKH, the CBS outlet in Shreveport, was a powerful
50,000-watt clear-channel station that blanketed the
southeast. Like most of the big Southern stations,
KWKH had a series of live early morning country music
shows. They were so well received that Henry Clay decided to emulate the Grand Ole Opry. He started the
Louisiana Hayride on April 3, 1948.

Fred Rose called Hank in Montgomery on May 26 to

tell him the glad news about the Hayride agreeing to try
him out. Lilly answered the phone. "No, Mr. Rose, I'm
sorry. Hank isn't here. No, I don't know where he is. He
ain't been home in three days." She sounded bitter. "I'll
tell him." Fred wasn't too worried. He knew Hank sometimes went off on a binge, but he didn't think it was too
serious. Fred's theory, which he talked about now and
then, was that if a person's personal life was stable, then
his talent and his professional life would straighten itself
out. He knew, from Hank's hints, that all was not what it
could have been between Hank and Audrey, but Fred
thought it was just the usual troubles married people
sometimes had. Fred didn't ask too many questions. He
really didn't want to know.

Hank woke up at about four in the afternoon. At first
he didn't know where he was. He heard birds singing and
he could see honeysuckle vines outside the window of the
little bedroom. His mouth tasted like dogshit. There was
an empty whiskey bottle on the floor and he kicked it on
his way to the bathroom. He threw up and it was just
liquid and foam. He had not eaten in two days or was it
three? He couldn't remember. He sat back down on the
bed, dressed in just his dirty BVDs. His bony legs were
the color of a fish's belly. They had rarely been exposed
to sunlight. He started to remember things, in bits and
pieces. He was at Lonnie's house, at his daddy's house in
McWilliams. He remembered crying on Lonnie's shoulder: "Daddy, she left me. I don't know what I'm a gonna
do." It was a fact: Hank had the legal paper in his coat
pocket. It was all very legal, signed by Eugene W. Carter,
judge of the fifteenth judicial circuit in Montgomery. Audrey, after threatening it almost daily, had divorced him.
On May 26, 1948, he no longer had a wife. Audrey had
moved out February 7 and filed for divorce that very day.
They had had a terrible fight and he was drinking and
blacked out and didn't remember much, but he thought
for sure she'd come back. Then he got the legal paper. It

said: "Complainant avers that the respondent has committed actual violence on her person attended with danger to her life or health. Complainant further avers that from respondent's conduct there is reasonable apprehension of such violence in the future."

Lonnie had looked the paper over. "Hell, son. You hadn't oughtta beat her up if you love her."

"I don't remember, Daddy. She hit me all the time, anyhow."

Lonnie puffed on a Camel and his eyes took on a faraway look. "She puts me in mind of your mother, son. Those two women must be a lot alike." Lonnie had not met Audrey but he didn't have to. Life with Lilly had taught him a thing or two about women.

"Well, son, what are you gonna do about it?"

Hank took another belt of whiskey and chased it with a sip of lukewarm Coke. "I don't know, Daddy. I got this contract with the M-G-M people. Maybe I'll head on up to Nashville. I need Ordrey, though, Daddy, I love her."

"Well, son, if you want her, you got to go get her."

That's what he finally did when he sobered up. He still didn't know about the Louisiana Hayride offer. Audrey wouldn't see him. He went to Banks, where she had run home to her mamma and daddy. She wouldn't talk to him. He crawled back to Lilly's in Montgomery and she finally told him about Fred's phone call. He talked to Fred, who didn't understand why Hank wasn't jumping up and down with joy about the good news. Hank just said, "I'll be there," and he hung up. He never told Fred about the divorce. He called Audrey's house and pleaded his case to her mother. Audrey finally got on the phone. "Honey," he pleaded. "I'm sorry. Now, I'm gonna be on the Louisiana Hayride over in Shreveport. Come with me there. We'll start over. Please honey. You know I can't stand it when you treat me this way."

"Will you stop drinking, Hank?"

"Yes, baby, I'll do anything. Come back to me." He was crying.

"Will you let me sing with you?"

"Anything. *Anything.*"

"Well, okay. I'll give you one more chance. In Shreveport. I ain't livin' under the same roof with your mamma no more."

He was weeping when he hung up and Lilly looked at him with undisguised scorn.

Hank and Audrey and Lycrecia moved to Shreveport and first took a tiny garage apartment. Oddly, they did not remarry but lived together as common-law man and wife.

Hank passed the audition at the Hayride with no problems. As soon as he ambled out onto that stage at Municipal Auditorium, in front of the big Jax Beer sign, and coiled himself around the microphone and lit into "Move It on Over," he had that crowd with him. Henry Clay called Fred to tell him they had a winner here.

Hank didn't touch a drop for months. He knew, finally, he was getting the breaks and the big chance was there. He worked hard. Henry Clay decided to put him on the air every morning. His show was sponsored by the Johnny Fair Syrup Company and Hank decided that if he had to sell syrup, by God he would be the best syrup seller there ever was. He was down at the KWKH studios on the second floor of the Commercial Building at the corner of Texas and Market Streets at six in the morning. He started the show off by singing the Johnny Fair theme song: "When I die, bury me deep, in a bucket of Johnny Fair, from my head to my feet. Put a cold biscuit in each of my hands, and I'll sop my way to the promised land. Hi, there, it's the ole syrup sopper, Hank Williams. Friends, you know you gotta have something good for breakfast each and ever' day. How 'bout somethin' that will stick to your ribs and you can be sure it'll send the kids off to school feelin' good. Johnny Fair Syrup."

The fifteen-minute show passed quickly. Hank, accompanying himself on his guitar, sang three or four songs, plugged Johnny Fair Syrup and told corny jokes. "Say, Frank," he called out to his announcer, Frank Page. "Did you know what Eve told Adam when he was kindly complaining to her a little about her cookin'?"

"No, Hank, I sure don't. What did Eve say?"

"Well sir, she up and said, 'At least you cain't compare my cookin' to your mother's!' "

"Ha, ha. Pretty good, Hank."

"Well, friends and neighbors, old clock on the wall says it time to get it on outta here. This is Hank Williams, the ole syrup sopper, sayin' so long till tomorrow, same time, same station."

Hank turned off his smile the minute his microphone went off, and he started out of the studio.

"Some joke, Hank," Frank Page said to him.

"Fuck you," Hank muttered without a backward glance as he left.

"Nice guy," the engineer said to Page. "A real asshole."

Hank didn't care what those assholes thought of him. He had been in Shreveport four months and he knew the audiences loved him. That's all that mattered. He didn't have to be a nice guy. He didn't get paid for being a nice guy. He got paid to entertain. What he did the rest of the time was his damn business.

He went out onto Texas Street and winced as the bright sunlight hit him. He and Audrey had been at each other again last night and he hadn't slept. He got into his big blue Packard and laid his head back on the seat and closed his eyes for a minute before starting the car up. He ran his right hand over the steering wheel in what was almost a caress. He loved that car. His first big car. It was a big touring car, twenty feet long with four doors and

jump seats in the back. He had had big speakers mounted
fore and aft on a rack on the roof and a microphone on
the dashboard so that when he and the Drifting Cowboys
hit town during a tour, they could cruise up and down
Main Street and ballyhoo the show set for that night.
"Tonight only, ladies and gentlemen, direct from Shreveport, Louisiana, and the Louisiana Hayride, Hank Williams and His Drifting Cowboys! They'll be performin'
all their hits at eight o'clock PM tonight at the high
school auditorium. Come one, come all. M-G-M recording artist Hank Williams!"

Hank rubbed his eyes, lit up a Camel and started the
Packard. He drove slowly to the small white frame house
on St. Charles Street in Bossier City, where he and Audrey and Lycrecia had moved to from their first small
apartment. He drove slowly because he was not a good
driver and all the police in Shreveport recognized the car
on sight. They knew he took a drink now and then, and
he did not want to be run in. He was tempted, as he
pulled into the driveway, to turn on his public address
system, turn it up all the way, and pick up that microphone and let her have it: "WAKE UP, YOU WHORE
ORDREY, YOU BITCH WHORE." He thought about
doing it. Wouldn't the neighbors love that? He finally
decided not to. Three years ago, he knew, he would have
done it. Now he was twenty-five years old and a star on
the Louisiana Hayride. Maybe some night he'd try
it. . . .

He walked slowly into the house, half expecting to
have to dodge a flying ashtray or plate if she was still
mad. She was gone and Lycrecia with her. He ran to the
closet. Her suitcases were still there. His tense face relaxed. He might fight her but he needed her. He went into
the kitchen, fished a bottle of Jax out of the little Kelvina-
tor refrigerator. He found a Superman funny book he
hadn't read too many times and lay down on the worn
sofa. He didn't really want to drink, but he knew he

would drink till there was no more beer left or till it made him pass out. It was the only way he could get to sleep and he needed sleep so bad. He drank the beers as fast as he could; on an empty stomach they would hit him pretty fast. Six bottles later, he finally slept.

Hank awoke with a start. The light had faded. It must have been late afternoon. He didn't know what had awakened him. It hadn't been a loud noise. The room was so quiet he could hear his stomach rumbling. He could feel a presence, though, could feel eyes locked on him, intense eyes. Someone had *willed* him to wake up, he thought with a little chill of fear. "Who's there? Who is it?" He couldn't remember if he had locked the door or not when he'd come in that morning. Probably hadn't. Audrey would've already woke him up if she was there, she'd be slamming around the place; she couldn't stand to see him sleep in the daytime. It was too dark to see anything: the Venetian blinds were drawn in the tiny living room, no lights were on in the house. He sat up, very quietly—favoring his back—and swung his feet to the floor. His pistol was behind the radio, the big console Philco that stood right by the door to the kitchen. He felt carefully around on the floor by his feet till he found his Zippo lighter, gripped it in his left hand and rose slowly and cat-footed over to about where he figured the radio was. Hank was no coward but he *knew* somebody was there and the silence unnerved him. He found his .32 pistol and the feel of the hard steel gave him courage. He held the Zippo well away from his body, snapped it open and struck it. He was in a crouch and had the .32 at waist level, ready to pivot toward wherever the intruder might be. The Zippo's sudden yellow flame was reflected by a pair of eyes. He humped back, frightened. He could see Audrey, sitting motionless in the armchair, the ratty green velvet armchair that he hated and that had come with the place. What was wrong? She wasn't moving.

Just staring at him. She finally turned on the lamp by her chair. He lowered his gun, unsure of what to do.

"Ordrey . . . what're you *doin'?*"

"Just lookin' at you, Hank. I've been lookin' at you all afternoon." Her voice was flat, emotionless.

He got more agitated. "Well . . . *why?*"

"I went to the doctor this mornin', Hank. I called a taxicab and went to see the doctor."

"Now, I didn't hit you last night. . . ."

"That'd be easier . . . no. No, I'm pregnant, Hank. I'm gonna have a kid."

"You're kiddin'."

"No."

He was incredulous. "I'll—*we'll* have our own kid. That's *great*—"

She cut him off, still speaking without emotion. "No. It ain't great. I was gonna leave." She was almost speaking to herself. "Now I got to stay with you. You're a drunk. You don't love nobody but yourself. You don't care nothin' about my career. When I left you last year, I shoulda stayed gone. You lied to me. You said you'd change. Now I'm stuck . . . stuck with *you."* She raised her voice. "Now, you *better* change, you better give me some consideration, you better. . . ." She got up and walked slowly into the bedroom and closed the door behind her. Hank tossed the gun and the lighter onto the sofa and just stood there, looking confused. Then he went into the kitchen to see if there was another bottle of beer.

Hank sat on the couch in the dark, drinking and toying with his pistol and chain-smoking. He could hear Audrey on the phone in the bedroom: "I don't know what's got into him. He's drinkin' again. He won't talk to me, he won't talk to nobody. He don't trade three words with his band; he never has. Well, I will not put up with it if I'm gonna stay here and have this baby. He's gotta change or I'm a gonna leave." Hank smiled when he heard that sentence. He knew a potential song line when he heard one. He didn't know who Audrey was talking to and he didn't care. He had a comfortable alcohol glow working and he found his little spiral notebook and a pencil and he started working with Audrey's line. "You're gonna change or I'm a gonna leave," he sang softly. He started writing.

Hank slept on the couch. He awoke before dawn, dressed without washing or shaving—he would have had to go through the bedroom to get to the bathroom—and left quietly for the radio station. When he got back from doing the Johnny Fair Syrup Show, he slipped off his boots just inside the front door and tiptoed into the bedroom.

Audrey was there, asleep as he knew she'd be. Her fits didn't last long. He looked down at her fondly and his lean, too-lean, face relaxed. She looked child-like in her sleep, blond hair tousled, face soft and smooth. He sat down on the edge of the bed and kissed her. She stirred, then awakened. "What?" she murmured.

He reached down to the floor where he'd laid a grocery sack full of things. First he pulled out a big, heart-shaped, red-velvet box of chocolate covered cherries and handed it to her. It was wrapped in cellophane but she hugged it anyway. Then he produced a dozen red roses, kind of on the skinny side but red roses nonetheless. "Those are for you, honey," he said. Then he held up a big brown-and-white teddy bear. "This's for our son." He kissed her and she responded. "Oh, Hank, I *do* love you." Now, he thought, as he shucked his pants to dive into bed, there ain't gonna be no changin' *or* no leavin'. Things are fine. "Now just when are we gonna look for Hank Junior?"

Randall Hank Williams, a ten-pound, two-ounce baby was born in Shreveport on May 26, 1949, a year to the day from when Audrey's divorce had been granted. Things could not have been better for Hank, and he sometimes worried about that. Everything had been going right for once. Audrey had calmed down during the pregnancy and had quit nagging him about her singing career. He himself could not have been more popular at the Hayride. He had even started attracting a big contingent of black fans, which surprised the Hayride management but didn't raise Hank's eyebrows: he remembered Tee-Tot and could sing the blues with any colored man alive. With his Hayride-sponsored tours, he had a solid following in the Southeast and throughout Texas. He had run into a fallow period, true, with his records after "Move It on Over." Pappy told him not to worry; the break would come.

Pappy was surprised and not a little upset that the break, when it came, was not a Hank Williams song and therefore not an Acuff-Rose song. "Lovesick Blues" had been cowritten by Cliff Friend, from Cincinnati, and by Irving Mills, a Russian immigrant, and copyrighted in New York by Jack Mills Inc. in 1922. It was recorded twice in the 1920s by Emmett Miller, who introduced the yodeling style to country music. An Alabama singer named Rex Griffin recorded it in 1939 for Decca. Hank had sung it off and on for years and decided to record it for M-G-M. Pappy was not enthusiastic about it—he put "Never Again (Will I Knock on Your Door)," the first side Hank had cut for Sterling, on the other side of "Lovesick Blues" so that true Hank fans would have something to latch onto. Hank knew exactly what he was doing with "Lovesick Blues," though. His voice was not big but it was expressive and he could yodel the word "blues" and could put a sob into a song convincingly.

M-G-M released "Lovesick Blues" on February 25, 1949. It was amazing. It shot right up past George Morgan's "Candy Kisses" and Eddy Arnold's "Don't Rob Another Man's Castle" and Vaughn Monroe's "Riders in the Sky" to the number one spot on Billboard's "Folk Record Chart," which traced sales of "hillbilly records that sold best in stores." It stayed on the charts for forty-

two weeks. Hank carried around in the hip pocket of his
pants a creased and well-worn copy of Billboard; the first
time in years he had bought something to read besides a
comic book. By the time little Hank was born, big Hank
had already fired his current crop of Drifting Cowboys in
Shreveport. Pappy had tipped him off that the Grand Ole
Opry, the top of the mountain for country singers, could
refuse him no longer after the way "Lovesick Blues" was
going. He was now a power in himself and could demand, rather than ask. Pappy knew that radio station
WSM's general manager Harry Stone and its artists' service director Jim Denny—who in effect ran the Opry—
had been adamant against having Hank on the Opry because of his reputation as a drunk, a trouble-maker, and a
no-show. Pappy also knew that the Opry, despite its considerable facade of purity as country music's and indeed
the South's pinnacle of family entertainment, was in fact
heavily infested with singers who were drunks and worse.
And Pappy knew that Stone and Denny could not hold
out forever against a singer who had become in effect a
people's favorite. Pappy had quickly learned and Stone
and Denny surely knew—they would be utter and complete damn fools if they didn't—that the country music
fan was unlike any other music fan or for that matter any
celebrity fan that the United States had produced. The
country music fan asked few things of his hero, or her
hero—for women were the backbone of the country audience—but those few things had to be delivered. The
country star had to be from humble beginnings, just like
the audience, and had to gratefully acknowledge those
beginnings and never deny them. The star had to sing
about those beginnings and the other things he shared
with people from those beginnings: simple, everyday
problems of life and frustration and mainly miseries of
the heart and the troubles that that caused. Heartbreak
led directly to alcoholism, fighting, burglary, car theft,
estrangement from parents, spouses, children and other

loved ones; Godlessness, disrespect for the flag, jail terms and all the other such day-to-day afflictions that plagued lower-class white Southerners. The biggest problem, though, was slipping around. When the honky-tonks came in you couldn't trust anyone anymore. Everybody was looking for some strange stuff every night. The country star had to sing a bit about that as titillation and a bit as suffering; it was, after all, a forbidden pleasure that was not to be welcomed.

Above all, the country star had to remain loyal to his fans. He could earn a hundred thousand dollars a year and wear rhinestone suits and drive Cadillacs—those were commodities admired and envied by the country music fan. The country star could divorce and remarry countless times and be an adulterer for that matter and a drunk—but he had to publicly confess and apologize for his sins and weaknesses. Hank could be two hours late to a show and be staggering drunk and be forgiven for it. Country music fans would be forever loyal to their stars unless their stars committed the one total and unredeemable sin: turning on their followers, refusing to sign autographs. If they, in short, quit being just a singing representative of their peers and started putting on airs. Then, by God, they would be dropped so fast their pants'd be sucking wind before they hit the ground.

Now, Pappy Rose had learned all that and he knew he didn't have to prod Harry Stone and Jim Denny too much to remind them that the Opry had an obligation to present the best in country music. At the moment, Hank Williams was the best in country music. Case closed. Next argument. Hank would go on the Opry. They decided to put him on the Saturday night of June 11, 1949. "Lovesick Blues" was still number one, and, Hank's "Wedding Bells" was number nine that week.

The baby would be only sixteen days old on June 11 and Audrey was not in any shape yet to go to Nashville. She told Hank to go without her; she, of all people, knew the value of getting on the Opry. Finally getting to Nashville certainly wouldn't hurt her singing career, either. "Go ahead on, Hank. You can't pass up this chance."

He had no band, but that was not terribly important, he knew. His main appeal was his presence and his voice and he could do quite well with the Opry house band, as many Opry regulars did. At least, that's what Pappy told him. Pappy knew best. Hank was still twenty-five years old. Whenever he let himself think about what was happening, he started getting too tense and just too much . . . wound up like a top. He had fantasized for years that this would happen to him—*should* happen to him, because he was just so damned good—but when it did he wasn't ready. "Pappy, I'm gonna be on the same stage with *Roy Acuff*? Ohh—" He was at once arrogant and awestruck—maybe he should just put it off for a while, but if he did it might never happen—and finally he was defiant in seizing his moment when it came.

He had vowed to himself that he wouldn't drink before the Opry. This was no time to short-circuit his career, no time for weak weaknesses, no time to admit to being a weakling. He kept the vow. He couldn't sleep but he didn't drink.

On the afternoon of June 11, a fine balmy Saturday afternoon in Nashville, he left the Hermitage Hotel where he was staying. He was going to go for a walk; maybe it could calm him down a bit. He stood on the sidewalk for a moment, rocking back and forth on his heels, hands shoved into the pockets of his tan western suit.

He set off in his loping stride toward Broadway. No one recognized him here yet, the way they did in Montgomery and Shreveport, and the people who stared at him did so only because he cut quite a striking figure: a lean and hard-looking cowboy with a real no-nonsense air about him.

As he approached the corner of Broadway and Fifth

Avenue he could see crowds of people. Entire families were strolling up and down Broadway or stopping in at the Ernest Tubb Record Shop or just milling around or sitting on the hoods and fenders of their cars. Most of the cars had out-of-state license plates. Hank saw Alabama, Mississippi, Florida, Georgia, Louisiana, Indiana. People had driven to Nashville just to see the Grand Ole Opry and made a big weekend of it. None of them were really well-dressed. They were the country music audience and a trip to the Opry was a kind of pilgrimage for them. Some of them planned their vacations around an Opry trip and wrote a year ahead of time to get tickets.

Hank turned left on Fifth Avenue North and stopped in his tracks at the scene. The narrow street was choked with thousands of people, all waiting around in front of Ryman Auditorium, the huge, red brick former tabernacle that was home to the Opry. Ryman Auditorium had been built in 1885 by a riverboat captain named Thomas Ryman. He ran a fleet of floating casinos and bars on the Cumberland River. A crusading Nashville preacher named Sam Jones fought against the floating sin palaces and issued a public challenge to Captain Ryman to come and sit through one of his sermons. Jones eventually converted Ryman and the born-again captain built the tabernacle. It did not become the home of the Opry until 1941.

The Opry was born as the WSM Barn Dance on November 28, 1925. WSM itself was begun earlier that year by the National Life and Accident Insurance Company and the call letters stood for "We Shield Millions," the insurance company's motto. They hired as station director George D. Hay, well-known in radio as the "Solemn Old Judge," away from radio station WLS in Chicago (WLS was owned by the Sears, Roebuck Company and WLS stood for "World's Largest Store"). At WLS, Hay had started the WLS Barn Dance, which was not the first such hillbilly show, but it got immediate national recognition. It included "uptown" musicians as well as hillbil-

lies. When Hay got to Nashville and got to know his
audience, he decided that a strictly hillbilly barn dance
was what was needed. The first WSM Barn Dance consisted of Uncle Jimmy Thompson playing fiddle tunes for
an hour, accompanied by his niece, Mrs. Eva Thompson
Jones, on the piano. Public response to the show, which
was then only a radio broadcast, was tremendous and
musicians started showing up at WSM to audition for the
show and listeners called to ask if they could attend.
String bands were a tradition in the rural south and the
WSM Barn Dance became a tradition overnight.

The name of the show was changed to the Grand Ole
Opry in 1927 strictly by whimsy. Network radio had begun, with the formation of the National Broadcasting
Company, and WSM was one of NBC's first affiliate stations. The Barn Dance came on at eight PM and followed
the network's Musical Appreciation Hour. Dr. Walter
Damrosch, the composer and conductor, was that program's announcer and one night introduced a perfor-
mance thusly: "While most artists realize that there is no
place in the classics for realism, I am going to break one
of my rules and present a composition by a young composer from Iowa. This young man has sent us his latest
number, which depicts the onrush of a locomotive."

George D. Hay was of course listening and he thought
Dr. Damrosch was being a trifle patronizing if not pompous. At eight o'clock, Hay stood up in front of his big
carbon microphone to introduce the Barn Dance:
"Friends, the program which just came to a close was
devoted to the classics. Dr. Damrosch told us it was generally agreed that there is no place in the classics for
realism. However, from here on out for the next three
hours, we will present nothing but realism. It will be
down to earth for the earthy. In respectful contrast to Dr.
Damrosch's presentation of the number which depicts
the onrush of the locomotive, we will call on one of our

performers, Deford Bailey with his harmonica, to give us the country version of his 'Pan American Blues.' "

Bailey, who was the program's first black performer, played the song and he could make his harmonica sound remarkably like the onrush of a locomotive.

Hay got back on the air: "For the past hour we have been listening to music taken largely from Grand Opera, but from now on we will present the grand ole opry." The name caught on immediately and country listeners felt a certain pride in their own "opry," separate and distinct from the high-faluting "opera." Hay was very on target when he was talking about the realism of country music. He knew that was its appeal. That had been obvious to Hank Williams since the first Jimmie Rodgers song he heard when he was a kid. The one time Hank dropped his guard against interviewers, he tried hard to articulate what he liked about country music: "It can be explained in just one word. Sincerity. When a hillbilly sings a crazy song, he feels crazy. When he sings 'I laid my mother away,' he sees her a layin' right there in her coffin. He sings more sincere than most entertainers because the hillbilly was raised rougher than most entertainers. You got to know a lot about hard work. You got to have smelt a lot of mule manure [he said "muleshit," of course, but it was changed to "mule manure" in *Nation's Business*] before you can sing like a hillbilly. The people who has been raised something like the way the hillbilly has knows what he is singing about and appreciates it."

Hank had listened enough to the big Opry stars to know about sincerity: about Roy Acuff weeping onstage while singing about dying children and saintly old mothers, about Ernest Tubb writing a song, "Our Baby's Book," about his child who died and then having hundreds of strangers over the years come up to him and tell him that they had named their own child after his because the song had affected them so. History Hank did not know or care about; songs he did know instinctively and care about deeply.

He stood there on Fifth Avenue North across from the Ryman and smoked a cigarette. That's a damn nice building, he thought, looking at the massive, white-frame arched windows, and ole Hank's finally welcome in there. He was suddenly no longer nervous about playing there that night. He flipped his cigarette butt away and turned back toward Broadway. He was stopped by a kid, a boy maybe twelve or thirteen.

"Say, mister, are you on the Opry?"

"Oh, I might be. Who's your fav'rite singer, son?"

"I like Little Jimmie Dickens."

"Well, that's all right. You keep a eye out for Hank Williams, you hear?"

Hank walked back down to Broadway. He looked in at Tootsie's Orchid Lounge, with its dingy walls full of autographs and old Opry programs. Tootsie's back door opened right on the alleyway beside the Ryman and it was opened a lot by Opry regulars who got thirsty. Hank was tempted to go in but knew better. There would be time enough that night, after he played, to have a beer. Instead, he walked across Broadway to Linebaugh's and sat for a while over a cup of black coffee and a sugar doughnut and looked out the windows at the people who would be watching him on stage in a few hours. It was not such a big deal, after all. He went back to the hotel and took a nap.

4

THREE THOUSAND, five hundred and seventy-four people, having paid their sixty cents each for reserved seats and thirty cents each for unreserved tickets, filed into Ryman Auditorium the evening of June 11, 1949, sat down on the hard oak pews and waited for the Grand Ole Opry to start at 7:30. The men were in shirtsleeves and the women wore short-sleeved summer dresses. Ventilation in the Ryman was all but nonexistent and it seemed that everyone, especially those in the semi-circular balcony, was fanning himself with a cardboard fan mounted on a little wooden stick handle. There was still a line of people outside, lined up on Fifth Avenue North all the way down past the Hazelwood Motor Company's car lot. The Opry ran from 7:30 until midnight and the regulars usually performed twice—doing no more than two songs—so that the show was roughly divided into two portions. Some of the audience would leave after the first portion, after ten PM, and some people out on the street would get lucky and get to go in. There was a carnival atmosphere outside: hawkers sold cardboard fans, programs, pennants, ice cream, anything. One policeman stood down at the intersection of Broadway and Fifth to direct traffic.

On the broad wooden stage, musicians and stagehands wandered back and forth. Thirty or so persons were seated on the benches that were right in front of the huge canvas drops that bannered each segment of the program. The Opry was primarily a radio show—the audience had been added as filler—and the show was sold in fifteen- and thirty-minute portions to advertisers who literally stood in line to buy a piece of the Opry, such was the magnitude of its radio audience. Prince Albert Tobacco owned the central thirty minutes, which went out over the NBC network. Every fifteen or thirty minutes, depending on the sponsor, a different canvas banner was unfurled as stage backdrop to present the sponsor's name. Royal Crown Cola, Warren Paint, Martha White Flour, Jefferson Island Salt, General Shoe Corporation, O'Bryan Brothers Clothing, Harvey's Department Store. Advertisers loved the Opry. Royal Crown Cola itself was delighted when it got into an Opry song: "Give Me an RC Cola, a Moon Pie, and Play Maple on the Hill." The Royal-Barry Carter Mills, which ground Martha White Flour, adopted as its company slogan: "Early to bed and early to rise, work like hell and advertise on the Grand Ole Opry." Otis Carter sold baby chicks by mail order and he owned a half-hour of the Opry and wasn't about to give it up. He decided to sell his cattle once and got rid of $51,592 of beef after two Opry programs. "Anyone can sell a farmer anything he needs over WSM," he said. To test the drawing power of their sponsorship, the Jefferson Island Salt Company once bought a one-minute spot on WSM in the middle of the week and offered a picture of Little Jimmy Dickens to listeners who wrote in. They got 24,984 letters in a week, they said. The all-time champion advertising campaign would of course go to Hank Williams. In May of 1951, the Pops-Rite Popcorn Company, which was sponsoring Hank's portion of the Opry, offered to send photographs of Hank and the Drifting Cowboys to listeners who wrote in. Pops-Rite claimed it received 208,000 requests for pictures.

On June 11, 1948, Hank didn't yet have any advertisers scrambling to get his portion of the Opry. He would just have to be shoehorned in somewhere.

He stood backstage, holding his guitar by the neck. Pappy had already shook his hand and wished him luck. Hank started thinking they had forgotten about him. There were at least fifty people drifting around backstage. Little Jimmy Dickens, four feet, eleven inches, introduced himself to Hank and wished him luck. Hank remembered only that Dickens's cowboy boots had sterling silver toes and he thought he should get some like that. He was standing alone when stage manager Vito Pallettieri appeared beside Hank with his clipboard. "Williams? You're up now."

The Opry announcer, Cousin Louie Buck, a portly man dressed in slacks and an open sports shirt, was standing at a podium at the left side of the stage. "Give a big hand, if you will, ladies and gentlemen, to a boy who is making his first appearance on the Grand Ole Opry. Hank Williams and his Lovesick Blues." Buck motioned for applause from the audience and Hank drew a good hand. "Lovesick Blues" was well-known, if he wasn't. He dipped into his familiar crouch over the microphone, started tapping his right toe, and sang it. The photograph hounds broke from their seats and raced down to the lip of the stage and zeroed in with their Brownie Hawkeyes. Two dozen Sylvania Blue-Dot flashbulbs sizzled as they lit him up. Hank knew he had that crowd—it was so easy, why had he had to wait so long to get a chance at the Opry crowd when they were so easy?—had them

right there in his hip pocket and he really stretched out
his yodel on the word "blues" and hit them with a little
of that piston-like pelvic action and looked those women
in the first rows right square in the eye and gave them a
half-smile that was also defiant half-sneer. The Opry had
never seen anything like it. There was a real aura of sex
steaming up the front rows there. The photograph
hounds, instead of going back to their seat, leaned into
the stage and Hank teased them with a little hip action
and taunting glances. The cardboard-fan action in the
crowd speeded up. The temperature was going up, all
right, but it had nothing to do with the fact that it was a
summer night. Country music had just opened a door it
hadn't known was there and stepped through into . . .
what? New territory that wasn't defined yet. Hank was
obviously not some comfortable old shoe of a musical act
like Roy Acuff or Red Foley. Hank was lighting fuses
throughout that crowd and as they ignited, the country
sensibility was forever changed. Opry performers had
been as predictable—and as sexless—as Cousin Louie
Buck's silver pocket watch.

Nobody had ever gotten starry eyes or moist panties
over a country singer. It wasn't Hank's song. The song
was nothing new. But Hank's presence was electric. The
women wanted him and the men had to admire him. He
was nothing if not all man. He wasn't like other country
singers who came on all dewy-eyed and pleading and
weak and puppylike. Hank projected an ironlike resolve;
he was what he was and wasn't about to change for any
damn body, but if the women responded to his challenge
they might find rewards they hadn't dreamed about. He
finished "Lovesick Blues," grabbed the guitar by the
neck, waved goodbye, and started offstage. He had a tight
grin on his face; he knew he had just shown this tight-
assed Opry clique what was what and what a real star
was. All the singers and musicians who were on the stage
benches and standing backstage had stopped their con-

versations and their milling around to watch him: they'd
known he had just pulled off something magical. They
seemed to him to be frozen in midmovement. He would
always remember all those faces, the faces of the country
stars, locked in place, all eyes stuck on him. Cousin Louie
Buck looked poleaxed by the waves of applause and
whistling from the crowd, most of which was standing.
He grabbed Hank by the shoulder and pointed at the
microphone. If he'd spoken, Hank wouldn't have been
able to hear him above the crowd. Hank walked, slowly
so as to savor the applause, back to the microphone and
raised his right hand to ask for silence. He jumped into
the middle of "Lovesick Blues." The stage band struggled
to catch up with him. He finished and was called back
time and again by the waves of applause. It was incredible, unheard of. *Six* encores at the Opry. Never happened
before. Backstage, Harry Stone and Jim Denny just
looked at each other. There was no need to talk. They
knew who was the new star of the Grand Ole Opry. It
didn't matter if he drank antifreeze. He had the number
one record and he had just busted the Opry wide open.
He had gone over their heads and gotten the public to tell
them what to do. That didn't mean, though, that they
had to invite him home with them. If it was good business to put Hank on the Opry, well, they'd put him on
the Opry. And see if he sinks or swims. Either way, the
Opry would endure. It was ageless.

Hank had stood around backstage, accepting congratulations. It seemed that everyone was really proud of him.
It was like he was being welcomed into the Opry family.
A new life was waiting in the ranks of the country stars.
Mr. Denny had shook his hand. Everyone had wanted to
get together with him—"sometime"—to have a drink or
eat some fried chicken or go fishing. The crowd backstage
slowly thinned out, as people had to leave. Hank found
himself alone, suddenly very alone under the glare of
those bare light bulbs. Some things never change. He

wanted a drink very badly. He found his guitar and
stomped down the concrete steps that led from backstage
to the alleyway. He stopped in the alley to light a cigarette. Jukebox music came from Tootsie's back door, a
few feet away. He couldn't make out the song, could just
hear the bass line. He thought it might be George Morgan's "Candy Kisses." He and Morgan had disliked each
other on sight backstage earlier. "Candy Kisses" was
only number five in *Billboard* while "Lovesick Blues"
was number one but that was only part of it. Hank didn't
like the way Morgan had slapped him on the back—he
was obviously overdoing the congratulations business—
and he just plain didn't like Morgan, the cross-eyed bastard. That was that. "Candy Kisses" was a stupid song,
too. He took a deep drag off his Camel, squared his
shoulders and started for Tootsie's. He was ready for
them if they liked him and he was equally ready for them
if they didn't like him. Fuck them. Who were they, anyway? They couldn't stand alone in front of a crowd, a
crowd that might turn on him, you never knew, and win
over that crowd, those thousands of strangers who
thought they owned you anyway if they'd paid even
thirty cents to get in, who demanded that you bust your
nuts for them. Like you were a trained nigger. Tee-Tot
had told him that once in Greenville and he hadn't really
understood it until he had started working the white
trash honky-tonks across the South. "They be makin' you
so mad you want to take and kill 'em," Tee-Tot had told
Hank when he was just a kid and Hank had laughed:
Tee-Tot was a nigger. Of course white folks would tell
him what to do.

Now Hank wished he could apologize to Tee-Tot. Tee-
Tot had tried to tell him that race, that color had nothing
to do with it: if you made your living by holding out your
hand to the public, half the time the public is gonna take
a pee on your hand. Hank had laughed at Tee-Tot. He
laughed no more. Now he had captured the public—the

number one record, he had the chart from *Billboard* in his pocket—and the Opry, the damn Grand Ole Opry *belonged* to him now, after tonight. The public had voted and he had won. It was a hollow victory. The cream of the country music ruling class had made it apparent— Hank was no fool when it came to judging people and their real messages—that he would be tolerated because of his public acceptance but that he should expect no sudden membership in the country club. Other white trash had voted him lower white trash, he sensed. Well, he had always sailed his own ship and there was no reason he couldn't keep on doing so. He knew better than to accept or expect favors from anybody else. They just wanted something in return. Lilly had trained him well, so well, in fact, that on this night of his triumph he could not and would not call anyone to tell them about the Opry. Not Lilly, not Audrey, not anybody. They would just want something out of him.

He was standing stock-still in the alley by Tootsie's back door. His cigarette had burned down and he tossed it away. He listened to the drunken laughter inside and, as badly as he wanted a drink, he did not want to have to face a gallery of people looking at him. Waiting for him to talk. Or sing. Expecting him to perform like a trained nigger. Beads of sweat stood out on his brow. Things could not have been better or worse. He had everything and felt nothing. He sensed that all he had done was jump from one treadmill to a much faster one. He needed to get away. . . .

There was no way he could walk into that bar. He turned in the alley and walked toward Fifth. Before he reached the spill of light from the street lamp, he glimpsed movement at the Ryman's brick wall to his right. He stopped, dead still.

"Hank?" It was a woman's voice, one he didn't know. Snuff queen time, if he knew anything about women and country music. He had been surprised that Opry didn't

attract more of them, until he found out that the Opry
management, ever conscious of the family-oriented audience, had its guards chase off the painted-woman element. He wouldn't mind temporary blotto with a gash;
would welcome it, in fact. It had been a while. . . .

"Yeah, darlin'?" He spoke in his experienced-but-kind-
and-reassuring Hank voice. He had layers of instinct that
were astonishing. Sometimes even he was surprised by
the way he would react in a situation—he had at least
twice in honky-tonk fights disabled mean-drunk attackers
who outweighed him by fifty pounds or more. He was not
always right but he was fast, and that was more important. He also listened more than he talked and he had
long ago learned how valuable that was. He waited for
the woman to approach him in the alley. She was young,
she looked so young in the alley's dim light that he was
afraid she was illegal quail, was jailbait.

"Old enough to bleed, old enough to butcher," he murmured to himself. This night, he didn't care how young
she was. "Hank?" she said, softly. "I really, really like
your music and I write songs and I got some songs I'd
like to show you—" She had obviously rehearsed a little
speech and Hank was impatient. He put his arm around
her waist and started out in search of a taxicab and a
bottle and his hotel room, in that order. He should call
Audrey; she was home with the baby, with his little son.
He was too tired to talk, though. He could call Audrey
tomorrow. Tonight was tonight. He found a taxi on
Broadway and when he and the girl got into the back seat
he began to feel a little more awake. He had reason to
celebrate, didn't he? The Opry crowd had loved him. Nobody could stop him now. He leaned forward and whispered to the taxi driver that the first thing he ought to do
if he wanted a twenty-dollar tip was to drive to a bootleg-
ger's—any self-respecting taxicab driver would know
where to get a bottle after hours—and get a bottle of
bourbon. And the second thing he should do after that

was follow directions and not pay too much attention to what was going on in the back seat. Hank was in a sweat: he wanted to bury himself in a bottle or in a woman or both, it didn't matter which. He just wanted to be canceled out for a while. He was tired of holding up his corner of the world and wanted to let somebody else take over for him.

She was gone when he woke up. That was good. He hated small talk when he was drunk; sober, it was all he could do to get enough words out to order breakfast. He felt no guilt about last night. Women were one of the few benefits of being on the road. They were there and they offered themselves and you took them. That was that. No one gave it a second thought. A man's wife closed her eyes when it came to that. When you were on the road, the normal rules of life were suspended. Normal hours meant nothing. Laws that applied to regular citizens were stretched as far as they could be. Regular citizens were quick to help stretch them. They loved being in the aura of an entertainer. Policemen tore up speeding tickets and could steer a man to a willing woman and could get a gun for him. Hotel clerks could get women and liquor and just about anything a man wanted. And the women—it had once shocked Hank when he realized that otherwise decent women, men's wives and sisters and daughters, would rip their clothes off in abandon and do just about anything to get into that orbit and aura of a music star, even a minor one. Who was Hank to question such a fact of life? He had far more serious things to worry about, like how could you play Atlanta one night and drive straight through to St. Louis and be in decent enough shape to do a good show the next night? Or, where was the next song coming from? Which promoters were not out-and-out thieves? The questions were plenty.

Hank felt so good he decided to eat breakfast; his recollection of last night was hazy but what stood out was that he had finally gotten on that Opry stage and proved what ole Hank could do to an audience. He could do anything. He breakfasted on black coffee and scrambled eggs that were swimming in catsup—nobody recognized him in the coffee shop, but the place was nearly empty—and went back up to his room and put in a call to Shreveport.

"Ordrey, honey? It's ole Hank . . . aw, it went okay, how's my boy? . . . because I couldn't get to a phone till late and I didn't want to wake you up . . . I'm gonna drive back tonight . . . expect me when you see me."

He hung up the phone and tugged at his Adam's apple, which he always did when he was nervous. Audrey sounded all right, but you never knew with her. . . . He picked up the phone again.

"Hello, Pappy! . . . you betcha! . . . right! . . . I'll be in Shreveport. Talk at you soon." Well. Hank lit up a Camel. Pappy *thought* the Opry would offer him a regular slot. Hank *knew* they would. He thought. They would. He stood up abruptly and packed his Martin guitar and his overnight bag. He might as well be in Shreveport as here. He thought about calling his mamma but thought better of it. If she knew he was still in Nashville, she'd try to get him down to Montgomery. He could call her just as easy from Shreveport.

Audrey, in her housecoat, was standing at the door when he got there. She had the baby in her arms and she didn't look happy. He gave her a quick kiss on the cheek and took the baby from her.

"How's little Bocephus?" He was talking to the baby, not to her. He had nicknamed Randall Hank "Bocephus," after the name of Rod Brasfield's puppet on Rod's radio show. She preferred to refer to him as "Hank Junior."

"Your mamma's been callin' here ever' ten minutes," Audrey said. She moved around the room in vague motions, stopping to fiddle with her little doll collection on a knickknack shelf.

Hank was silent, still holding the baby.

"I *said,* your mamma has been callin'—"

"I *heard* you the first time. I guess you don't wanta hear about the Opry."

"I heard. Ain't you gonna call your mamma?"

Audrey had beaten him again, Hank knew. Without saying so, she had just told him he was neglecting her for his own career and ignoring her and even beyond that, had reminded him Lilly could intrude herself between Hank and Audrey anytime she wanted to and Hank would allow it. *Preferred* to allow it, for he was too weak to do otherwise. Personally, Audrey let him know that his big-shot career wasn't such a big deal—when she'd said "I heard" in her cold tones when he'd asked her about his Opry appearance, she had spoiled it, ruined it for him—and said that if other people knew the truth about him, he wouldn't be such a big deal.

Hank sat down on the sofa with Bocephus. "Where's Jughead at?" He called Audrey's daughter Lycrecia "Jughead" because of the size of her ears and because he would have invented some kind of name like that regardless of how she looked because all she reminded him of when he looked at her was Audrey being with another man. Hank had not offered to adopt Lycrecia and never would. "She's . . . next door," Audrey said. Lied.

Six-year-old Lycrecia was hiding in the closet. She knew a fight was coming on. She remembered seeing the last one: Hank had taken Audrey over his knee and beat her bottom. They were both out of control. Audrey had gotten away from him and thrown dishes at him, had connected to the face with a crystal glass, had broken a lamp over his head.

"Ordrey, put the baby to bed."

Audrey was surprised at the . . . *mature* tone in his voice. She knew he was sober, she wouldn't have let him in the door, much less let him hold the baby if he'd been drinking. She took Randall Hank "Bocephus" from him, avoiding Hank's eyes, and tucked the baby away in his crib in the bedroom.

She didn't want to but forced herself to walk back into the little living room. Hank was sitting there very still with his hands on his knees. His bald spots were getting bigger, she noticed. She sat down in her armchair and said nothing. Hank shook a Camel out of his pack, tapped it down on his thumbnail and made a ritual out of flicking back the top of his silver Zippo and striking the wheel—both motions made with his thumb in one easy movement. He inhaled deeply on the Camel and with his thumb flipped the lighter shut. The lid made a tiny clanking sound. Hank, as usual, was slumped on the sofa, practically lying down, and he blew a smoke ring at the ceiling, which had water rings of its own from rain that had soaked through from the last storm. Audrey was not used to seeing him acting with such confidence, with such authority. She suspected—rightly, she was sure—that now that he had finally got on the Opry, it had given him a little bit of a backbone. She would hear him out; she had certain terms of her own that would be eventually met, not necessarily tonight.

"Ordrey."

"Yes, Hank?" She was attentive and alert; schoolgirl-like.

He picked a fleck of tobacco from his lip, studied it lazily, and flicked it away with his thumbnail. He didn't look at her. "Ordrey, I'm goin' on the Opry." He anticipated her question and cut her off before she could ask it. "No, they *ain't* ast me yet. But they will. Pappy'll call tomorrow. We'll be movin' to Nashville."

Audrey couldn't help herself, had to blurt it out: "Well, what about me? I ain't gonna sit home and wash diapers all day. I ain't gonna do it. What about me singin'? You go off and be the star all the time, you ain't givin' me a chance to even try. You give me that chance, Hank, or I swear I will leave you, I will take the kids and *go*. Remember that divorce? All I got to do is pack up and leave and it'll all be legal. *I will do it, mister.* You better listen to me. I am a singer and you better let me sing. Or else you can just say goodbye to your kid!" Her eyes were flashing; she could barely contain the fury inside her.

Hank sighed. He had hoped it wouldn't come to this but had half-known it would. Audrey wasn't born no yesterday; she was always a step or two ahead of him. He had to settle for what he could get. He did love her, in spite of all the troubles they had and he loved his son perhaps more, loved being a father and having a son and looking forward to bringing him up and giving him things and giving him a life that he himself had never had. And, most important of all, giving him a full-time daddy. They would go hunting and fishing together, do all the things together that a father and son did. He would, though he wasn't ready to admit it to her, grant Audrey any concessions to keep little Bocephus. But there was one important thing he wanted.

He faced her: "I do not want my son to be no bastard. We ain't married. I want him to be legal. I want you to go to the judge and take back those divorce papers. You can do it. I know. I talked to a lawyer. *Will* you do it, honey?"

His urgency betrayed him. She knew she had him. It was her turn to ignore him while she leisurely lit a cigarette.

He finally broke the silence: "Well?"

"Well what? You heard what I said. Are you gonna try to give me some consideration, or not? I told you, I am a singer, I am not gonna be locked up at home."

"What to you want?"

The words tumbled out in a rush, she was on the verge of leaping across the room and clawing his face. "You know damn good and well what I want! Are you deaf? I

have told you *time and time* again! Do I have to hit you
over the head to get you to listen to me? You will not
even try to help my career, you try to ignore it, you just
want me to sit home and cook your dinner when you
want it and be your whore when you want it and take
care of the kids and clean house and never see nobody! I
don't have no decent clothes! I don't have no car! I have
to get Miz Jones across the street to carry me to the
grocery when you're gone! You've been sendin' your
mamma money! Don't you deny it!"

She knew she had really hit him in the balls with that
one. He flinched and started tugging at his Adam's apple
a mile a minute and tried to hide his confusion by getting
up and rummaging through his overnight bag for a fresh
pack of Camels.

Audrey had him on the run and she wanted to run him
to the limit before she let him rest. "Oh *yes* sir! Sendin'
money to your mamma, who has a boardin' house full of
young la-*dies,* when your own wife don't even have decent clothes. I heard you talkin' to her on the phone
when you thought I was a-sleepin'. 'Okay, Mamma, I'll
send you a money order. Don't tell Ordrey nothin' about
it,' *that's* what you said! Well, mister, it's time to think
about your wife! *What* about it?" She was almost spitting
sparks.

He was beaten. "Okay," he half whispered.

She was not gracious in victory. She had a vindictive,
lopsided smile that was not pretty and her voice grated.
"I want to be a singer! I want to sing with you again! I
want to make records! I took you to Fred Rose. It's the
least you can do to help your wife. When we get to Nashville, I want a decent house. And I want a housekeeper. I
have to be able to get out sometimes. I need some clothes.
I—"

Hank tuned out. He half-heard the list that she recited.
He sat back with his eyes closed tightly. "OKAY!" he
said.

She stopped.

"Will you take back the divorce, Ordrey? Will you do that?"

"Yes."

"Okay, then. I don't wanta argue no more."

She sat down beside him on the couch and rubbed his thigh. "Oh, Hank, I don't want to make you mad. But you *do* ignore me, you know that. Don't you love me?"

His eyes were still tightly closed. "You know I do, honey."

"Well, then," she whispered, her hand moving up his thigh, "we got to help each other. Right?"

"Yeah."

"Well, Hank, help me with this zipper, then."

He sighed. She sure knew how to fight.

Hank was sitting slumped as usual, as close as he could get to being horizontal in the back seat of his big Packard. He had his white felt hat tilted forward to shield his eyes from the bright July sunlight. The Packard and its box-like trailer—which held his band's instruments and was emblazoned with his name along with big letters reading "M-G-M Recording Artist" and "Direct from the Grand Ole Opry"—was bouncing along the highway north out of Nashville and heading for the county fair in Springfield, Ohio. It was the first date on his first tour as an Opry star.

He was frowning as he read *Billboard,* the music trade magazine. Hank had expanded his regular reading menu of comic books to include the music magazines. It was important to know what was going on. He thumbed through the magazine until he found what he was looking for. His lips moved slightly as he read the Best-Selling Retail Folk (Country & Western) Records popularity chart. Each entry listed the record and its position on the chart this week, its position last week, and how long it had been on the chart. Hank's eyes shot straight to the

number one slot. It was, as he knew, his own recording of
"Lovesick Blues" and that week of mid-July it was, after
nineteen weeks on the chart, still too strong to be toppled
from number one. What he wanted to see was how well
his follow-up to "Lovesick" was doing. "Wedding Bells,"
he saw with satisfaction, had moved up from number five
last week to number three this week. The only song sepa-
rating Hank's number one and number three songs was
Eddy Arnold's "The Echo of Your Footsteps." Hank
didn't know Arnold but he wished him no good will.
Hank frowned when he noticed that Arnold also had the
number four and number five records. *And* number seven
and number thirteen. George Morgan and his "Candy
Kisses"—more like "candy ass," Hank snorted—was
number six. Red Foley had four records on the chart.
Hank hadn't met Red but had heard he was all right.
Three of Red's four hits started with the word "Tennessee," Hank noticed. "Tennessee Polka," "Tennessee Saturday Night," "Tennessee Border." Now that was
something, Hank thought. It seemed to be that a state's
name made people like a song. He thought about that for
a while, the miles flashing by, his band members silent in
the Packard—steel guitarist Don Helms and guitarist
Bob McNett had been members of Hank's Drifting Cowboys before. Fiddler Jerry Rivers and bass player Hillous
Butrum didn't know him at all. The band had been assembled the day before, had backed Hank up on the Opry
that night, and in the early morning hours they had hit
the road. Hank's reception at the Opry had been tumul-
tuous, just as it had been in his debut appearance a
month before. He was now an Opry regular and the
WSM Talent Bureau was booking him out on the road as
often as he wanted to go. Like most Opry regulars, Hank
tried to be in Nashville every Saturday night to play the
Opry. Even though it paid only union scale, the Opry as a
power base was invaluable.

McNett and Helms had worked with Hank before but

they had no illusions of knowing him well and waited to test his current frame of mind before deciding how to react. He was moody and unpredictable. And remote. Not snobbish, just removed and uninterested in those around him. McNett had worked with Hank earlier that year in Shreveport and had seen Hank develop his *Billboard* habit when "Lovesick Blues" first hit the charts. Hank had fired him and the rest of his band in May. All he had said to McNett was, "If I call you tomorrow, you got a job. If I don't, you ain't." He didn't call and McNett had been rather bitter. He went back to the family farm in Rolling Branch, Pennsylvania. When Hank finally called in July, he came.

McNett was driving the Packard that day and asked Hank, "Where's that Ohio road map?"

"Shut up," Hank muttered, and didn't look up from the *Billboard*. State names . . . if Red Foley could put *three* records on the chart with "Tennessee" in the song title, that had to prove something. "Gimme a pencil," he said. He still didn't look up. The Drifting Cowboys traded uneasy glances. Nobody said anything. Hank got a pencil and started trying out song lines in his little spiral notebook. Red had already used "Tennessee." Alabama was the one Hank should use, anyway. He wrote line after line and crossed them out; no good. He kept a title, though: "Alabama Waltz." Just be a matter of time till he worked a song around that title and had a nice little hit with it. He sat up and smiled. "Who's got a smoke for ole Hank? I just wrote another hit. Are we there yet?"

There was a brief, almost forced camaraderie. "Hey, Hank, don't M-G-M give you enough dough for a packa butts?" "Yeah, Harm. If you want us to get there yesterday, get us some Cadillacs." "If you done wrote another hit, you can damn sure cover for some *hamburgers.*" "Piss call, piss call!"

"Okay boys," Hank laughed. "Hamburgers on ole Hank. Just gimme a smoke." His taut face creased when he smiled. He lit up and blew a smoke ring. "Stop at the next joint."

He went back to studying the *Billboard* chart. Down below Red Foley was Floyd Tillman's "Slipping Around." Good song. Below that was Ernest Tubb's "I'm Biting My Fingernails and Thinking of You." Hank liked Ernest Tubb, or appreciated him, rather; he hardly knew him. Tubb had been a country music legend for years and had encouraged Hank when Hank would go up to him at shows. Tubb had talked him up to the Opry management people when they had thought of Hank as a drunk and a problem. Ernest was raw east Texas and kind of saw a younger version of himself in Hank; saw the same kind of musical sincerity and drive and naivete. Tubb had come out of rural poverty and made himself what he was but didn't forget the kind of people he grew up with and wrote and played music for them. That's why he was successful, although he hadn't planned it that way. Ernest was so unassuming that people who met him were tremendously impressed with the way he did not act like a star. He certainly impressed Hank. Last Saturday night, Hank had gone out into the alleyway by the dressing rooms at the Ryman for a breath of air and a smoke. Even though this was Hank's third appearance on the Opry and he sure felt he belonged there, he still felt a kind of frost from some other performers and he just wanted to go outside for a minute and be alone before he went on stage. He was leaning back against the Ryman's red bricks and blowing smoke at the sky and thinking about nothing when a voice interrupted him.

"Howdy."

Hank looked around and gave Ernest a shaky, surprised smile. They shook hands; they had met before but Hank wasn't sure that Ernest remembered him. He did. "How are ya, Hank?"

"Fine. Good. How are you, Ernest?" He started to say "Mr. Tubb."

"I'm all right, Hank. I just wanted to tell you how much I like your songs."

Hank relaxed. He was being treated like an *equal* by one of the country stars. "Ernest," he said sincerely, "you and Jimmie Rodgers and Roy Acuff was the singers that inspired me. People used to tell me at first that I sounded just like Roy. Then, your records started comin' out, I started buyin' your records and learnin' your songs and then they'd tell me, 'Boy, you sound just like Ernest Tubb' and I got tired of that. So I got me a style right in between you and Roy and I just might stay there. Is that okay with you?"

Tubb laughed his big Texas laugh and slapped Hank on the back. "Hell, *yes,* son. You oughtta know by now you can do anything you want to."

"Aw." Hank was serious but liked what he was hearing.

"I *never* been more serious, Hank. You're as good as there is. Don't never forget it. But don't dwell on it all the time. You can't put it in the bank."

"Hell, Ernest, I can't put *nothin'* in the bank. Ordrey spends it before I make it."

They both laughed, but both knew it was true. Tubb, at thirty-five, was on his second marriage and he himself had once had occasional losing bouts with the bottle.

They had swapped small talk for a while: did Ernest still have Jimmie Rodgers' old guitar? Hank would sure like to see it some time. Had Hank looked for a house in Nashville yet? Ernest and Olene would be happy to help and looked forward to having Hank and Audrey over to supper sometime. Ernest looked at his watch: it was time for his Opry segment.

In the Packard, in Ohio, Hank half-dozed as he recalled talking to Tubb. He liked Tubb a hell of a lot. Tubb was one of the few stars who didn't seem to resent Hank's success and what they took to be his arrogance. It was too bad he and Tubb couldn't spend more time together.

But they were both on the road nonstop. They had to. The Opry was essential to keep their names out there before the public but it paid next to nothing. Record royalties didn't amount to all that much and were unpredictable, same as mechanical royalties from jukebox play and same as writer's royalties.

It struck Hank as he studied the *Billboard* chart that his two hits had been written by other people. They would get the writer's royalties; not him. That wasn't good. He was a hell of a writer; he ought to have hits with his *own* songs. He'd have to have a little talk with Pappy about that. At least his follow-up record to "Lovesick Blues" and "Wedding Bells" was a song he had written. He nodded with approval as he scanned the *Billboard* list of Advance Folk (Country & Western) Record Releases and, right there underneath "The Wine Blues" was his own "There'll Be No Teardrops Tonight." He had released one record right after "Wedding Bells" but it didn't surprise him when nobody bought it. To shut Audrey up, he had recorded two duets with her—"Dear Brother" and "Lost on the River"—and, brother, he thought, they should both be chucked into the river. Audrey's pig-headedness about her singing was going to cause one hell of a lot of trouble yet, he knew that to be a fact. It was one thing for her to get up on stage in Greenville or Andalusia; Nashville and the Opry were another world. Well, there was time enough yet to worry about that. Don't trouble trouble till it troubles you.

Hank put down his *Billboard*. "Are we there yet? Who's got a smoke? Is there a ballgame on the radio?"

"What about those burgers, Hank?" It was Don Helms asking. Helms was senior Drifting Cowboy; he had worked for Hank in Montgomery five years earlier. "Okay, Shag, you got 'em." Shag was Hank's nickname for Helms.

They pulled off the road into a diner's parking lot. Helms walked beside Hank toward the door.

"Hey, Shag, you remember when I hired you back in Montgomery?"

"I sure do, Hank. First thing you did was take us to a hock shop and buy us blackjacks."

"And I told you you'd need 'em. Was I right?"

Helms laughed. "You sure as hell wasn't wrong."

"Well, I hope you kept yours. You might need it yet." Hank said it seriously.

Helms noticed for the first time that Hank seemed to be walking with a slight hesitancy. He wasn't charging along like he used to in Montgomery, just a few years back. He seemed to be slightly favoring his right leg and his right shoulder was slumped lower than the left. Hank never mentioned it and nobody with any sense would ever ask Hank if there was anything wrong.

They ate quickly, with little talk. Hank doused his burger with ketchup and ate only half of it. "Let's go. We got to be there."

Jerry Rivers had noticed Hank's slumped right shoulder. He mentioned it to Helms. Helms said it was probably because Hank was used to carrying his hardware on that side: his .38 and his sapper and his brass knucks. They had a good laugh over it. Awe-tinged laughter that respected the myth forming around Hank, the myth that he was a strongman of country music, that he wrote songs all day while driving a big car across the South at eighty miles an hour and then sang half the night away for his fans at a honky-tonk and then drank and loved the rest of the night away.

Rivers was nineteen years old and, although Hank was still two months short of his twenty-sixth birthday, he regarded Hank as a revered leader of country music. Hank had changed country music's direction. He was not like the hierarchy of leading country singers; he was young and came across as a bit cynical and as a wise-ass; he obviously liked to have a good time and he appreci-

ated the ladies. And the bottle. Nobody thought of calling him a rebel, but he was clearly different. He was
cocky and defiant and challenging, not humble and hesi-
tant and ass-kissing like most of the country stars. His
attitude, when he took the stage, was that of an *elected
hero.* He didn't appoint himself. The crowd chose him, so
his regal attitude was accepted and applauded. People
didn't want heroes who apologized for existing. And
Hank was the first to make no secret of his personal problems; why try to hide them? It was nothing calculated on
his part. Everybody he knew had the same troubles, so
why not sing about them or talk about them? You can't
hide them, anyway.

Rivers was silent in the Packard. A few months before,
he had turned down an offer to join Hank's band in
Shreveport. He had preferred to stay in Nashville, the big
time, and wait for a slot in a band on the Opry. He had
refused Hank, but Hank, as soon as he was accepted by
the Opry and had to form a new band, had let it be
known that he needed band members. The supplicants
stood in line. Rivers had gotten the news after he finished
working a show at WLAC. The news that Hank needed a
band was a triple priority flash with Nashville's musicians: the new Opry star with the M-G-M recording contract and the number one country song was the most
desired and most courted man in town. Rivers felt like a
damn fool as he stood and shuffled his feet and waited,
fiddle case under his arm, to audition for the great man.
How could he have turned Hank down before? It had
been easy, he knew. Hank was just another picker who
was hoping for the big break. Now he had it. And that
made Hank regal and rendered people like Rivers foot-
servants. Rivers shifted his weight nervously from one
foot to the other while Hank sat comfortably on a stool
outside WSM's Studio A while Clifford, WSM's black
porter, shined his boots to a high gloss.

Clifford made his shinecloth pop like the crack of a whip. "There you go, Mr. Hank."

Hank put a sawbuck into Clifford's hand—"Thank *you,* Mr. Hank"—and motioned for Rivers to follow him into Studio C. Rivers was intimidated by Hank's confidence and his take-charge attitude, his air of complete authority. He picked up Rivers' fiddle and sawed out a recognizable version of "Sally Goodin' " and thrust the fiddle at Rivers. "Can you play that, boy?" Rivers could and did and Hank hired him on the spot. "We play the Opry tomorrow night and then hit the road.

Hank started out the door. Rivers stammered that he didn't have his musician's union card yet. Hank looked at him like he was feeble-minded: "Well, why don't we just *get* you one tomorrow?" Then he was out the door.

The next day, Hank got Rivers his union card, got matching black and white western shirts and pants for his band, got the Packard gassed up and serviced for the road trip, and played the Opry and drew ovation after ovation. It seemed like he couldn't move fast enough: he had a lot of things to do and wanted them all done right *now.*

They had stopped in Cincinnati to call on Nelson King, a country disc jockey who had a very influential radio show on station WCKY. Radio stations had to be courted like fickle suitors; airplay was like oxygen. Life for a country star did not exist without it. Disc jockeys were always happy to see a star and King had something to show off: he had just bought one of the first high-fidelity record players.

He played some of the new, small, thin 45 RPM records, that were replacing the old, large and thick 78s. Didn't that sound just amazing?

Hank looked at his watch. They should be going, they were behind schedule. Thank you, Nelson, good to see you. Good to have *seen* you. See you next time.

Hank could barely stand still. He was speeding: full of

bennies, the Benzedrine pills that many touring musicians lived on so they could stay awake. Speed was wonderful for them; they could go without sleep forever.
Until it was time to crash. Then they needed liquor or
downers to knock them out. Hank came to like the downers better.

"How you doin', Hank? Good to see you," the man
said, slapping Hank on the back. Hank flinched, then
looked around. People were sure starting to get friendly.
Hank looked the man over coldly; never saw him before
in his life. They were standing backstage at the Opry.

"How'm I doin'?" Hank asked in a tone that should
have warned the man that he was presuming a hell of a
lot. "I ain't doin' too bad for an ole Alabama boy that
was sellin' peanuts and shinin' shoes on the street. Ain't
that right, *friend?*" He pronounced "friend" the way it
was pronounced in a honky-tonk or a parking lot just
before a fight. There was no friendliness attached to the
word. It was a warning. The man got the warning and his
face reddened. His chance to look like a big deal by sucking up to Hank Williams, Opry star, was just killed by
one word. He backed away with a kind of shaky grin,
shamed in front of his big-deal friends who'd managed to
get backstage. Hank just shrugged (Who the hell was this
guy? They all wanted to be his friend now.) and turned
back to look at the audience.

Even though he hadn't been introduced yet, he could
see the people looking at him, eyes shining, waiting for
him. He smiled at a little blonde down there in front and
her face just melted. It was just downright amazing, the
way people reacted. A person could shine shoes and nobody would look at him sideways. But if that same person that shined shoes made a record and got on the radio,
people started getting excited and just lost control, got
out of breath and would do anything. But it was the *same*
person as before, same person that shined shoes. Didn't

people understand that? Hank couldn't figure it out. He did know that *everybody,* no exception, everybody that came up to him wanted something from him. They weren't offering, they weren't there out of the goodness of their hearts; they wanted some part of him.

At 7:30, broadcast time over WSM, the milling in the crowd subsided and everybody settled back on the hard wooden pews. Louie Buck stepped to the WSM microphone and announced, "It's Grand Ole Opry time! Another big show, starring Red *Foley!*" Red sang "Old Blue" and Hank paced backstage. The Opry was still not so routine to him that he could face it with the same stolid, almost cowlike indifference of the people around him backstage, who might as well be waiting to appear in traffic court for all the emotion they displayed. Didn't they know the public out there bought them their beans and bread?

Hank sure knew that; had known for years that it was the people out front who lined up and paid their quarters and dollars to see you that paid your living; it wasn't some big-shot in a fifty-dollar suit backstage slapping you on the back and acting like he and you were boyhood buddies, while his big-shot friends stood around to be impressed with being on the inside of the music stars' circle. Hell with that. Since he first hit the Opry back in June, Hank had been burning up that road, wearing out that Packard. He knew he had to get out there and sing for those people while they wanted to see him, while they would line up to get in and would call for encore after encore. And then he needed to be back in Nashville on Saturday to play the Opry, to reach out there into Radioland, where the magic millions were.

Hank had not stopped. He was on the road, he was on the Opry, he was recording in the studio, he was doing radio shows, trying to write songs. He didn't have time to drink; had no reason to drink; didn't want to drink. Even Audrey could see that he was in the grip of some bewildering and maybe incomprehensible but certainly undeniable wave of public adulation. They couldn't get enough Hank Williams.

He had made a quick trip to Lilly's in Montgomery; had hauled Audrey and Lycrecia and little Bocephus down to Mamma's, mainly to make sure that Audrey went back to court to cancel out her divorce from the year before. On August 9, 1949, Hank took a certain grim satisfaction in reading and then pocketing Judge Carter's legal paper stating that Audrey's divorce from Hank was now "amended nunc pro tunc"—which meant to Hank that it never happened. There was now no doubt that his son was legitimate.

He was in a hurry to move on. He needed to move his family to Nashville. He himself could live in the meanest garage apartment; he didn't care. Audrey could not and said so. There was also the matter of two children to house decently. Hank was impatient to get settled and then devote his time to music, where it belonged. Pappy had told him he'd have enough money coming in to buy a place. They decided on a three-bedroom brick house at 4916 Franklin Road. It looked like a big place to Hank. Audrey thought it had potential. "Ordrey! Do you know how much money forty thousand dollars is? That's more money than I ever made!"

"We . . . are . . . going . . . to . . . buy . . . this . . . house." Audrey was using her don't-tread-on-me voice. There was to be no arguing about it.

He was back on the road while she was furnishing the house. He was booked into Canada and then had an Opry tour of Germany coming up in September. He had no time to waste.

Hank leaned against the red brick back wall of the Opry stage, in the darkness behind the big canvas drops for Martha White Flour and Duckhead Overalls. Red Foley was finishing "Old Blue" and throwing in a few corny dog barks. Louie Buck was signaling the crowd to applaud. Hank stopped thinking about the stack of bills that Audrey seemed to generate every day at Franklin Road; stopped thinking about her demands to get a housekeeper to take care of the kids so she could get back to singing with him again, which was where she belonged.

Hank wanted to get out there before that audience, where he belonged. They were waiting for him.

Red Foley finished his song and said, "Oh, my, *my*. Thank you, thank you a lot, folks. And a great big hidy to all my friends and neighbors on the Grand Ole Opry!" The friends and neighbors fanned themselves in the pews and applauded.

Louie Buck took the microphone: "Boy, we're really rollin' tonight, Red, with one of the biggest crowds in the Opry's history, here to welcome Rod Brasfield, Minnie Pearl, Claude Sharpe's Old Hickory Singers, the Jordanaires, and the *entire gang!* And, for that extra special musical treat, our good friend, Hank Williams!" There was good applause for that and Hank straightened a bit with pride.

"Yessir!" Foley said. "That sounds like big doings for sure. Hey, who's first on the program?"

It was, as Hank knew, Rod Brasfield, a country cornball comedian. Baggy-pants, cross-eyed humor couldn't fail.

"Mr. Foley," said Brasfield, "since I seen you last, by Ned, I have got to be an inventor, buddy."

"An inventor?" Foley asked.

"Yessir," Brasfield said, "and my last invention is just sellin' like hotcakes, boy!"

"All right, Rodney," Foley sounded mock impatient. "You're pullin' my leg. What in the world did you invent that'd sell like hotcakes?"

Brasfield rolled his eyes: "I invented *hotcakes!*"

Hank didn't laugh—even he knew that joke—but the crowd did, warm and affectionate laughter rolling up toward the stage. Brasfield, who seemed to be rubber-faced, made his chin touch the top of his nose and crossed his eyes. More laughter. He continued: "That just *kills* me. But, Mr. Foley, not all of my inventions work so good. Naw. For instance, I tried to make shoes out of bananer skins and it didn't work."

Foley was impatient again: "Well, *of course* it wouldn't work. What in the world kind of shoes would you expect to make out of banana skins?"

Brasfield's eyes rolled. *"Slippers."*

Hank rolled his own eyes at that one and paced back-stage: *let me on that stage.* Brasfield's voice droned on and on. "People put ice in a glass to make it cold, they put gin in there to make it hot, they put sugar to make it sweet, they put lemon to make it sour. Then, they hold it up and say 'here's to you' and then they drink it *their-self!*" Finally, he was off. Hank tugged at his tie and nodded at his Drifting Cowboys to get ready.

Foley went back to the microphone: "Folks, now I want to bring out a friend of yours and a buddy of mine, too. He's written and recorded some of the best folk music of our day. I want you to give him one of your best welcomes. Here he is! The old Lovesick Blues boy, Hank Williams!" Wave after wave of applause washed over Hank as he walked to stage front. He looked down at the faces in the front rows. Puppylike devotion was what he saw in some faces, the younger ones, along with respect in the men's faces and affection bordering on lust in the women's faces. What he returned them was a remarkable mix of defiance, humility, lust and affection. Any time he met a person's eyes, that person felt that Hank was shar-ing a privileged and private feeling. That was a hell of a talent he had and it bordered on the hypnotic. He could give a crowd a fiercely personal intensity that he could never or would never manage with one individual. The first few rows at the Opry were already starting to weave and break ranks and charge forward. Hank *liked* it. They appreciated him and he liked that: they didn't ask too much of him. Just a few songs and they loved him totally, no strings attached, no conditions. They loved Hank.

Foley waited for the applause to recede and continued: *"Mighty* fine. You know, Hank," he read from a script, "I got a letter yesterday from some of my pals over there in Lancaster, way *up* there in Lan-kaster, Pennsylvania"— he was interrupted by a man whistling and cheering up in the balcony—"and they tell me you really bowled the folks over when you played up there last week."

Hank read the words mechanically—this was after all the part of the Opry that was staged just for the millions sitting at home in Radioland—and said, "Well, that's real neighborly of 'em to say that, Red. I always enjoy meetin' our friends out on the road person to person."

"Well," Foley read, "you know, Hank, we got about four thousand of our friends here tonight and we hope millions more out there listenin' in, so why don't you give the folks a treat with your latest hit, called 'Why Don't You Love Me.' "

"Be glad to," Hank said and then he really came alive when he nodded to Jerry Rivers to start the winding fiddle introduction to the song and he zeroed in his gaze on Don Helms and wordlessly told Helms to start his lovely chiming sound on his steel guitar. Unlike the cattle backstage, Hank played to the live audience and gave them all he had; he slipped in and out of yodels and sobs—he could now break a note, he knew with great satisfaction, as well as anyone who had ever stood on the wooden planks he occupied at the Opry—and he did what he always did best, which was to sound like the most lonesome man there ever was or is or ever would be. He sounded like no one could ever suffer the way he was suffering; he was inventing *new* ways of suffering and what a great suffering *that* was—he must be undergoing double and triple suffering pains compared to your usual hurting country music singer, who just had a pain or a

hurt or a heartbreak. He did mesmerize that crowd,
though, Jerry Rivers realized as he fiddled the mournful
equivalent to Hank's sobbing-but-strong vocals. Rivers
had seen a lot of country music singers but he'd never
seen one who could literally capture an audience. It was
something totally new. Country singers had been background music for a dance, or they had been received
lukewarmly as peers at a show; Rivers had never seen one
treated with hero worship. Hank was. People would do
anything to see him and just fell apart when they finally
did.

"Wonderful, Hank, wonderful," Foley said as Hank
finished "Why Don't You Love Me" to great applause.
"We gonna have Hank back here in a few minutes."

Hank looked at Vito's log on the wall backstage: next
came the Jordanaires and then Red Foley doing the
show's hymn and then Claude Sharpe and his Old Hickory Singers before Hank had to be back onstage for a skit
with comedienne Minnie Pearl before his next song. He
went out into the alleyway for a smoke. No one bothered
him.

He looked at his watch, flipped his cigarette away, and
walked back onto the stage just in time for Foley to start
Minnie Pearl's spot: "You know, Hank Williams, did you
notice all the pretty girls up there in Lancaster, Pennsylvania, boy?"

"Pretty girls, man?" Hank read, "I *sure* did, Red.
There was so many I got tired of lookin' at 'em and I got
to longin' to see that gal from Grinder's Switch and here
she is, Cousin Minnie Pearl!"

Minnie, who was a smart woman named Sarah Ophe-
lia Colley from Centerville, Tennessee, came out in the
country rube's costume of a bunch-sleeved gingham dress
and a straw hat with the price tag dangling off of it.

"How-*dee!*" she yelled. "How-dee," the audience
called back.

"I'm just so proud to be here," she said. "Hank, come *here,* Hank."

Hank searched for his lines: "Howdy, Minnie. I'm just so glad to see you."

Minnie chucked him under the chin and spoke coyly, "You're about the handsomest thing I ever saw."

Hank recoiled: "I am?"

Minnie laughed: "I want to be the first one to kiss you for your birthday."

"My birthday?" Hank asked. "Why, Minnie, my birthday ain't till September."

Minnie rolled her eyes as Hank started a mock-run offstage. "Well," she said, "I ain't the kind of girl that puts things off till the last minute. Whoo-eee—look at him go, runnin' off like a skeered rabbit!" Minnie liked Hank, the crowd could tell that.

When Red Foley came back out to introduce Hank's next song, Red was . . . *lacking* a little bit. "I want you folks to listen," he said hesitantly, "to this now-of-course it could be none other than tonight's guest, Hank Williams . . . Hank! Come out here, buddy, I'm a little bit stuck here. What was the name of that number you told me you were gonna do?"

Hank walked out: "It's a brand-new one, Red."

Foley persisted: "What's the name of it?"

Hank was getting a cut-the-throat motion, which he understood well enough. Cut it short so we can go to a commercial. "We got time for a little of it here," he said. "It's called 'They'll Never Take Her Love From Me.' " He had a remarkable facility to alter the pitch of his voice. When he mentioned a song title, he managed to put quotes around it just by injecting a certain worshipful tone and air to his voice. He was verbally taking off his hat. He also ran through the song fast; he didn't like having to chop a song down to fit arbitrary commercial slots. He and the Cowboys ran through half of "They'll Never Take Her Love From Me," and then he put down

his guitar and left. He still had to play the second Opry
show—he had to sing two songs on the second Opry
show between ten PM and midnight—but that didn't
mean he had to stand around like some store-window
dummy. He liked a little cul-de-sac in the alley where he
could sit unnoticed and have a smoke by himself. He
liked to do that. Sit alone. It was peaceful. No one walking by would have thought that the scissored-up guy in
the blind corner of the alley was Hank himself. Hank
could sit there and listen to the drunks as they lurched
by, could listen to young couples as they walked by. He
didn't have much of a chance anymore to just listen to
everyday conversation since he had become a star. It was
nice to sit in the dark and listen to people talk and hear
the rhythms of their talk. In Mobile, in the bars and in
the shipyard, it had been easy to be a listener. He missed
that now, missed being able to just fade into the wall and
be invisible when he wanted to. To write songs that people wanted to hear, you had to listen to what people
talked about. That got to be kind of hard when he got to
be a celebrity and people just wanted to sit around and
look at him and wait for *him* to say something. Hank
liked listening in on people when they didn't know anybody was paying attention. He could literally pluck song
titles out of idle conversation and arguments: "I've been
down that road before, you win again, I won't be home
no more, dear John, if you loved me half as much as I
love you, I can't help it, I'm sorry for you my friend, I
ain't got nothin' but time, someday you'll call my name,
no one will ever know, I wish I had a nickel, you're
gonna change or I'm gonna leave, no one will ever
know." They were everywhere.

He had talked once to Pappy about that. They were up
in Pappy's little attic studio in his house out on Rainbow
Trail. Fred, in his suspenders, was hunched over his piano, trying out tunes. Fred, although Hank didn't know
it yet, sometimes wrote country songs under the pseud-

onyms of "Floyd Jenkins" and "Bart Dawson." Fred thought those were tough-sounding hillbilly names, tougher than "Fred Rose." He plinked away at his piano. Hank was slumped on the little sofa, shuffling through his crumpled notes and scraps of songs.

"Pappy," Hank finally said, "seems like all I got here is a bunch of song titles. No songs."

Pappy swung around on his piano stool. "That's the best place to start. If you've got a good title, all you have to do is build a song around it. We can help each other."

"Well, I *know*," Hank said, worry in his voice, "but I got to wait for inspiration, seems like. I don't see how you can manage to just . . . *make* a song on the spot. I got to wait for the feeling, or it don't mean nothing to me. And if it don't, I just can't sing it."

"I know, Hank, but if you can tell *me* that feeling, we can both of us decide what that song should be. Give me one of those titles."

Hank looked through his scraps of paper. "I'm a long gone daddy."

"A long gone daddy," Fred said. "Now, if you're a long gone daddy, what does that mean? To *you?*"

"It means, Pappy," Hank said with some fever, "that I am telling that woman that I have had *enough* and she is treating me *wrong* and I am *leavin'*. I am *long gone.*"

To Fred, it was a hypothetical situation; to Hank, it was not.

"Well, then," Pappy said, pleased, "all we have to do is say *so* in the song. See what I mean?"

"I guess so," Hank was doubtful.

"I *know* so," Pappy said. "Now, 'I'm a long gone daddy' ought to be in the chorus, don't you think? That's a beautiful hook: I'm a long gone daddy. I like that. Now, all we have to do is start it out. If a man is going to tell his woman that he's had enough of the way she treats him, what's the first thing he's going to say?"

"Depends on who the woman is, Pappy." Hank was serious.

"No, now, come on. What would he say if he finally got worked up enough to actually leave? That's hard, to leave."

Hank knew that, for sure. Hard to leave; hard to stay. He thought for a minute. "Well. He would say something like, *first,* he would say something about the way she was actin' and then he would just flat out tell her, 'Looky here woman, I am steppin' out on *you.* I am *gone.* You done had your chance but you wouldn't treat me right.' "

Pappy was writing all this down. Rhymes were already dancing in his head.

"This woman," Hank continued, "would pass up supper every night if she got a chance to fight instead. The only time she closes her mouth is when she's asleep and that ain't a hundred percent sure. If she knew where to buy a ball and chain, she'd be the first one in line. If she gives you a kiss, you better check and make sure you still got all your teeth. If. . . ."

Hank was just getting warmed up and Pappy was writing furiously. The song was almost there. Pappy was just jubilant. These little attic sessions where he and Hank bounced ideas off each other had developed an electric, supercharged atmosphere. The way they complemented each other—the slick, world-wise tunesmith and the raw, rough, emotional, red-dirt hillbilly—was just amazing. Fred Rose, who had known Tin Pan Alley in New York, and Hank Williams, who could not be more rural. Neither one could really express an emotion except on a song sheet or in a recording studio. Fred had taken to playing piano on Hank's records, besides producing them and rewriting them and deciding how they should sound, and that was a strong and unspoken bond. They knew they shared a goal—turning out the best hillbilly music there had ever been and hitting millions of listeners right square between the eyeballs with it. With each other, the only subject they talked about was songwriting. Each, had he been forced at gunpoint to describe his partner, would have described him as a genius. When they were together—Fred discouraged his son Wesley from bothering them and Hank would never allow Audrey to accompany him to the attic—it was like the most exclusive club in the world. Only they were members. It was a comfortable feeling. Sometimes neither would speak for half an hour. Then Hank would read two lines of a song and Pappy would plink it out on the piano and they would argue good-naturedly about the words. Pappy would usually end up changing them a bit. He would throw in some imagery—purple skies and silent, still trees and the like— and would round out the melody. Hank really had no ear for creating melody. Once he found a good one, he hated to leave it alone. He might change the meter and tempo just a little bit, but he would ride a few simple melodies as long as they would hold him up. The melody for his "I Saw the Light" is identical to the melody of the Chuck Wagon Gang's "He Set Me Free," which came out in 1935. Once Hank heard a good melody, he wouldn't let go of it. He knew people liked familiar tunes; tunes they could hum. Words were what concerned him. Pappy, now, could write original melodies all day long and sometimes did. Fred was really held in awe in country music circles: he was the only outsider who had really come in and stuck, who was accepted. He seldom if ever went out around town, but that didn't matter—his presence was felt. Country music was just beginning to be a business in Nashville. There were no record companies, no recording studios, no management firms. In the beginning there was just WSM and the Opry. And then there was Acuff-Rose, which became a haven for hillbilly singers who knew nowhere else to go. An industry began to spring up around WSM, the Opry, and Acuff-Rose. Pappy was now recording Hank at Nashville's first full-fledged recording studio —the first outside WSM's Studio. D. Carl Jenkins and

Aaron Shelton, who had been sound engineers at Hank's
WSM recording sessions for Sterling, built Castle Studios
in the Tulane Hotel, at the corner of Eighth and Church
streets. Magnetic tape was just being introduced and they
still recorded directly onto black lacquer discs. There
could be no over-dubbing, no second chances. It had to
be right the first time. A lathe cut the sound into the disc
and the sound could not be recalled from the master disc.
It was like cutting granite; once it was done, it was done
and that was that.

Pappy was noodling at the piano in his attic studio,
fooling around with "I'm a Long Gone Daddy," which
was becoming a song real quick. An hour earlier, it had
been just a title in Hank's little notebook. Pappy and
Hank had sweated over it and had finally decided just
what a man would say to his no-account wife once he
finally decided to up and leave her. They were feeling
pretty good about it; it would be another of Hank's real
emotion-probing songs, which would hit the average guy
right in the gut. Every man had felt this emotion once or
twice; finally, here was a song that told him exactly what
he had been feeling or was feeling or *would* perhaps feel
one day when some woman he loved and trusted turned
on him. Hank had his hat off—his scalp was shining
through the few strands of hair he had left on top of his
head—and his jacket off and his sleeves rolled up and was
puffing away on Camels and downing black coffee. He
would never drink around Pappy and, anyway, he didn't
need to drink tonight. He didn't *like* to drink; it was just
that sometimes he *had* to. Lilly had told him—and he
had no reason not to believe her; they shared the same
distrust of doctors—that he had some kind of blood
sugar deficiency that required a certain amount or level
of alcohol to keep him on an even keel. He still had never
had a full physical examination by a doctor and didn't
want one.

Pappy, who didn't inquire into Hank's personal life any more than Hank would ask after his, cracked his knuckles and leaned back off his piano stool. "This is a *good* song, Hank."

Hank grunted an affirmative. He now knew it was; it had just needed Pappy to push it along a little. It was one hell of a good song. George Morgan, that candy ass, could never touch it with a damn blowtorch.

"Pappy, we got to cut this right away!" Hank was up and pacing. He found it hard to sit still for more than fifteen minutes. "This is *hot.*" They started recording it on Pappy's crude home recorder.

There was a knock at the door. Hank shot a hard glance at Pappy: their unspoken agreement was that nobody invaded their writing sessions up here in the attic. Pappy averted his eyes and shuffled over to the door in his slippers: "I wonder who this could be." He knew damn well who it was. He had called Roy Acuff earlier and pleaded with him to come by and meet Hank. "It'll mean so much to him, Roy." Acuff, who was the reigning king of country music until Hank came along, agreed. He had seen Hank perform once, in Montgomery, when Hank had been one of the opening acts for an Opry package show that Acuff headlined. Hank had sung a lot of Acuff's songs and had clearly *meant* them. Roy had appreciated that and remembered the boy in Montgomery. Roy was forty-five years old here in 1948 when he climbed the narrow stairs to Fred Rose's attic. He felt, though, that this Williams boy—in spite of all the talk about his drinking—was going to be a good one. Roy had risen from Maynardsville, Tennessee, to become a real whiz of a minor-league baseball player and was, in fact, drafted by the New York Yankees before a bad case of sunstroke—suffered during a fishing trip while at the Yankees' camp—shut off his baseball career. It took him over a year to recover. He was not real healthy to begin with—he weighed one hundred and twenty-plus pounds

and was nicknamed "Rabbit" because of his size. After
his recovery, he had worked for the L&N Railroad—the
same one that ran by Hank's house in Alabama when he
was a boy—and learned to saw fiddle and in 1932 hit the
road with a traveling medicine show. The next year he
formed his own band, the Tennessee Crackerjacks, with a
Dobro guitar—the acoustic forerunner of the electric
steel guitar, which Hank Williams favored as the lead
instrument of his group—as the band's trademark. Roy
became tremendously popular, first on radio in Knoxville, Tennessee. The Grand Ole Opry summoned him in
1938 and he was the Opry's first real star. Uncle Dave
Macon with his banjo back in the 1920s had been popular, but nothing like Roy.

Roy Acuff was so like his audience that he frequently
wept onstage when he sang a song that was about a trag-
edy that was familiar to his listeners. His eyes would
moisten up at the mention of trouble and he really felt it.
As such, he could not adapt to new audiences as times
changed. He didn't care and in the late 1930s and early
1940s Roy Acuff was better known to most Southerners
than was Franklin D. Roosevelt. His first record, "The
Great Speckled Bird" which was released in 1936, borrowed the melody of the Carter Family's "I'm Thinking
Tonight of My Blue Eyes," which itself had been pilfered
from Anglo-Saxon ballads that had traveled to the south.
Acuff was deeply religious and incredibly sincere; if he
sang it, you knew that he meant it. Many of Acuff's songs
were country music's last stand as purveyor of fundamentalist religion: "Speckled Bird" was a hymn in many
Pentecostal Holiness churches and in the Church of God
in the south. Hank himself had learned about conveying
emotion to a crowd from Acuff (with flourishes from Tee-
Tot; Hank still remembered him and his lessons). Nobody was better than Acuff. Hank, when asked about
southern singers, said, "It's Roy Acuff and then God!"
For years Hank had copied Acuff, until Pappy had gently

steered him toward his own style. Pappy, in dealing with authentic rustics like Roy and Hank, felt that he had become an authentic hillbilly, too. You couldn't go farther back in the woods and find better peckerwoods than Roy and Hank; you practically needed an interpreter to decipher what they were saying. It didn't matter: the U.S. Army's Armed Forces Network in Germany conducted a listeners' poll to see who was the audience's favorite singer in 1945. Acuff beat Frank Sinatra from today to Sunday. That's why Hank Williams went to Germany with an Opry troupe in 1949. They toured army bases: the army was basically blue-collar and hillbilly in its musical tastes. In the South, Sinatra was some kind of foreigner; Acuff and Hank were heroes. Roy tried three times—in 1944, 1946, and 1948—to run for governor of Tennessee. Jimmy Davis, who was governor of Louisiana, had written songs with Hank Williams and had been elected governor after a career as a hillbilly singer. Acuff wasn't so lucky. He was close in '48 but not so close as to decide to spend the rest of his life in politics. Roy was not the smartest man in the world, but he—with his wife Mildred's straight advice—decided that he ought to devote himself to what he knew best, and that meant country music. Roy was as nice a man as you could find and when Fred Rose had asked him to stop by to meet this young Hank Williams, Roy decided to do so.

It was his knocking that interrupted Hank's and Pappy's songwriting session up there in Pappy's attic. Pappy shuffled to the door, muttering under his breath as though he were irritated. "Who is it?" he called out.

"Oh, come in, Roy." Pappy swept the door open and acted like he'd never seen Roy Acuff before. He shut off the homemade record cutter he'd made. "Roy, have you met Hank? Hank, this's Roy." They shook hands awkwardly; they were both painfully aware of who each other was. Pappy shuffled off toward the kitchen; he wasn't going to be responsible for what happened. When he got

back, Hank and Roy were old friends. Hank was singing
Roy's "Wreck on the Highway." Then Roy sang Hank's
"When God Comes and Gathers His Jewels." Hank
jumped into Roy's "They Can Only Fill One Grave."
They were about to make each other weep. Pappy was
beaming.

Hank smiled at the memory as he sat in the alleyway
outside the Ryman. It seemed like a long time ago, but
things were moving so fast that everything seemed like a
long time ago. Well. He didn't have time to sit around on
his butt and daydream. He ground out his cigarette and
started back for the stage door. Time to knock them dead
in the second show. He would sing, he would sing—he
decided on "Moanin' the Blues" and "Nobody's Lonesome for Me." Some good sad songs that would really hit
the women.

5

"SO HOW was Germany, Hank?" Vic McAlpin asked. They were driving in Hank's Packard out Franklin Road. Vic was a songwriter Hank knew and he had run into him down at the Acuff-Rose office and asked him to come out and see the house and visit awhile and see Bocephus.

Hank laughed. "I'll tell you somethin', Vic. I wouldn't mind it a damn bit if I went back tomorrow. Those Fräuleins." He shook his head in amazement. "I never seen nothin' like it, the way they, uh, *appreciate* you, you know."

They both laughed. They knew about snuff queens.

"But the people, did they like the music?" Vic asked.

"*Like* it? Hell, they're more hillbilly'n I am. We oughtta move over there and open a damn record store."

"So they liked you?"

"A damn sight more than Nashville does. Do you

know—I had to put down a damn *five hundred* dollar deposit to get a damn phone put in my house when they found out I was a singer? Said I was a *risk*. Risk, hell. I oughtta show 'em what a risk *really* is."

They pulled into the driveway. Vic was mildly surprised at how modest the house was. Of course, he couldn't know about Audrey's plans for the house and Hank sure wasn't going to tell him, especially since he himself didn't know about all of her plans yet.

"Ordrey! I'm home. We got company." Hank and Vic stopped in the living room. It was only partially furnished, with what Vic guessed were oriental chairs, since they had shiny black lacquer legs and were covered with dragons and things.

Audrey walked into the living room. She was still in her housecoat, though it was late afternoon. "I was on the phone."

Hank kissed her on the cheek. "Honey, this's Vic. Vic have a seat. What can I get you? Cuppa coffee, coke, a beer?"

"A beer'd be fine, Hank."

Hank went into the kitchen and came stomping back out in a second, his face dark. "Ordrey. Where did that washer and dryer come from?"

"From the store, honey." Her voice was maddeningly calm.

"You know what I mean. You know damn good and well what I mean. We can't afford that."

"Of course we can, honey. You're a *star* now." The tone of her voice was infuriating. She was ready and eager for a big fight.

Hank was embarrassed in front of Vic. "Listen, honey," he said, "let's talk about it later."

"No. Let's talk about it *now.*" She turned to Vic: "Do you know what Hank did when he got his first check from M-G-M? It was five thousand dollars. He got it changed into one dollar bills and just threw it up in the air. He said we were nigger-rich. Now we can sure have a washer and dryer if we are nigger-rich, don't you think so?"

Her voice was icy.

Hank wanted out. "Uh, Vic, we oughtta run. Pappy said he wanted to talk." Vic was quite happy to get out of there.

They were silent during the drive back. Hank was chain-smoking and his knuckles were white from gripping the steering wheel so hard.

"You know," he said. He was almost speaking to himself but he obviously wanted someone to hear it. There was a tinge of despair in his voice. "When we lived in Shreveport and Ordrey would spend money and the bill collectors'd call me up, I'd tell 'em, '*Listen,* buddy, ever' month me and Ordrey put all our bills in a hat and the one that comes up first gets paid. Now, if you send me *one* more of them nasty notes you ain't gonna get put in the hat next month.' "

Vic laughed nervously. "That's tellin' 'em, Hank."

"Yeah. You know how women are. They got to have everything."

"That's right."

Hank dropped Vic off and stopped at a phone booth. He just didn't want to go home right then. He was tired. He deserved a rest, even if it was just for a day or two.

"Ordrey, it's me. Mamma left a message at Pappy's for me. She's down sick. I'm goin' down to visit." He hung up. Audrey or Lilly. It was a hell of a choice. At least Montgomery would be a change and maybe he could rest. He needed to think things out. Audrey was after him night and day to sing with him, on the Opry and on his radio shows on WSM and on the road. Audrey had clipped out and shown him the first magazine article that had been done about him, in *Country Song Roundup.* She had underlined one sentence: "Yes, girls, Hank is married to lovely and listenable Miss Audrey, featured on his program." That had burned Hank enough. What was just as bad was that Audrey had pointed out that a story on George Morgan filled up the page opposite his. He was gonna have to have it out with Morgan one of these days.

He had already busted his ass to get Audrey a recording contract. It couldn't be with M-G-M; they would've laughed him out of the country. Pappy had helped him—without a single question; what a friend—and had called Paul Cohen at Decca. Cohen—who had turned Fred down when he first came around with Hank—agreed to cut a couple of 78 sides by Audrey. They were just dreadful. She had recorded two songs she had written: "My Tight Wad Daddy" and "I Like That Kind." The second record was two of Hank's songs: "How Can You Refuse Him Now" and "Help Me Understand." There was no way they could have sounded worse. If Audrey were to swallow a canary, she would still manage to sound like crow. It sounded like she took a pickaxe to the melodies; it sounded like—Hank hated to think about it. She *liked* the records, though. She had them up on the wall in their den, along with Hank's 78s. Audrey was all geared up for her singing career. Life's highway had trouble signs posted every which way Hank looked. If he took Audrey on the Opry—the audience there was pretty tolerant but not that tolerant. If he took her out on the road—he just couldn't do it. It wasn't like the old days in south Alabama when they charged a quarter for people to get in and nobody listened anyway because all they wanted to do was dance and drink and fight and screw. Hank *was* a star now; Audrey's acerbic line was right on target. And people expected a star-quality show. You just couldn't get away with hauling a donkey up there on stage and introducing it as "Mrs. Star" and then having it bray and expect people to put up with it. They'd run you right out of town.

Maybe if he let her go on one of the morning or afternoon radio shows at WSM now and then, the Mother's

Best Flour show or the Duckhead Overalls show. The damage might be minor. But would she settle for that? Well, the hell with it for now. He was headed for Montgomery. Tomorrow could take care of itself; he just wanted to think about today.

He was sailing down Highway 31, slicing into the heart of Alabama. He felt better. He loved driving alone, with the windows rolled down and the fresh country air flowing over him, the radio turned up loud. He twisted the dial constantly, waiting to hear himself. These days he didn't have to wait too long to hear a Hank Williams song. He sang along; those *were* damn good records. His confidence slowly started coming back. Audrey could knock him down to nothing in a second. She shouldn't do that, he knew, as well as he knew that he shouldn't take that from her. Knowing it and doing something about it, though—well, that was just damn hard. You—he—had to take things one step at a time. He had Bocephus to think about; he had to provide the boy a good home and take care of his future. He had to watch his own career; he didn't have a hot record out at the moment and had not been writing much. There was so much else to do. The touring didn't stop and probably never would; there was always a crowd somewhere waiting to see him. He remembered the last date he had played. It was the Tri-State Fair in Amarillo, Texas, and he remembered it only because Ernest Tubb had also been on the bill and it was special to Hank to be Ernest's equal on the road and on stage. And he remembered Amarillo—he usually didn't remember towns, there were so many of them—because Ernest had given him a good-natured lecture. Hank had gone out and bought all this crap to take home to Bocephus. He bought huge stuffed dogs and panda bears and a giraffe—he had bought so much crap he couldn't carry it all—and was trying to stuff it all into the car. Ernest came up to him: "Hank, he's just a *little* baby. He's— what is he, six months old now?—not seven years old yet.

He can't play with these things. Let him grow up a little." Hank had gotten a little red in the face but finally
laughed. Ernest was all right, yessir. A good man. He
had known the bottle, too, knew what it could do and
couldn't do. Sometimes, when Hank and Audrey had had
it out and she left or he left and Hank had drunk a few
and was feeling that he was about to hit bottom, he
would call Ernest. Hank didn't feel that he could call
Pappy or anyone else. But he felt all right calling Ernest.
Ernest was stern with him, but fair.

"I told you, Hank. Don't call me when you're drinkin'.
I can't help you when you're drunk. You sober up and
call me back. I'll be here. I'll wait for you."

"Hello, Ernest?"

"Well, sounds like Hank to me. You drinkin'?"

"No. But I got a bottle and I might open it."

"Well, Hank, how about if I come over and we talk?"

Ernest would meet him, no matter what time of the
day or night, and talk to him man-to-man. Not that it
ever solved anything and besides he and Ernest were on
the road so much they seldom saw each other. Still, it
helped.

"Ernest, it's Ordrey."

"Well, son, tell me about it."

"I couldn't make enough money for her to spend if I
done struck oil out there in the back yard. As fast as I
can make it, she done spent it twice over."

"Well, Hank, that's easy, that one. Get you separate
checkin' accounts and put her on a budget."

"I'll try, Ernest. I just don't know what she'll do."

What she did was open charge accounts every place
that sold anything. The house on Franklin Road grew
like some expanding creature. Three bedrooms became
seven bedrooms; a two-story ballroom appeared; bathrooms were appointed with black marble floors and tubs
and gold fittings; the bar—he really needed a bar—was

dripping with music notes from his songs and with hearts; a wrought-iron fence with music notes from the song "Lovesick Blues" adorning it stretched across the front of the house; the windows were shaded by big awnings inscribed with the initial "W"; Audrey's fantasy room, which she called her "heart room," had white velvet walls and a white carpet and a white bed with a heart-shaped headboard.

The house grew like a fungus and eventually covered fourteen thousand square feet and was painted with gold-flecked paint and had six-and-a-half bathrooms with solid marble sinks. A person could get lost wandering around that house. The house had just gotten out of control and Hank knew it but he liked to keep Audrey happy; that way, he didn't have to worry about the lamp coming crashing over his head like it had in Shreveport or maybe —someday—the knife in his back.

He'd rather have her down in some furniture store all day than trying to climb on stage with him. The house bothered him, though. He never really felt comfortable in all that chintz and glitter and fancy stuff that he was afraid to sit on. He didn't know yet that Audrey—once she had overdone the house—was going to cultivate a taste for white furs and diamonds and shopping trips to New York City. The shops in Nashville, she would say, might as well be in . . . *Montgomery,* as out-of-date and . . . well, country as they were. Hank vaguely felt that all this money going out the window just so Audrey could feel stylish was a real betrayal of his background. When he was a kid, he and Lilly and Irene could have eaten for a month on what Audrey spent on one dress.

Still, he kept his mouth shut and went out there and earned the money and ran down to the Third National Bank and deposited it so that Audrey wouldn't overdraw the account. Hank had never made any kind of investment with his money and never would. All he understood was cash, greenbacks that he could see and feel. Some-

times, he wouldn't even count the cash from a show
when he deposited it: "That's your job," he would tell the
bank teller. He never knew how much money he carried
in his pocket and didn't care as long as he knew it was a
lot. As far as he had learned, money didn't do you all
that much good. It sure as hell didn't make life any better
or easier. The pressures got to be worse. He told Don
Helms when they were coming back to Nashville one
night after a tour and Helms was talking about getting
home to his little wife and so on: "Listen, Shag. When
you get home, Miss Hazel'll be there to meet you at the
door. When I get home, I'll have to give Ordrey half this
here fifteen hundred dollars and then she'll argue all
night about gettin' the other half of it." Helms and the
other Drifting Cowboys didn't say anything. They knew
that Audrey was trouble for Hank. "She won't let me
sleep. She's makin' life miserable for me," he mumbled.

Hank walked into Lilly's parlor in Montgomery.
"MAMMA! It's me." He sailed his hat ahead of him, the
way he always used to do. He was quite good at it and his
hat landed right on the settee where he'd aimed it. Sometimes, when a crowd was a little slow to call for an encore, he would stand backstage and sail his hat at the
microphone and usually hit it. The crowd loved that.

Lilly came bustling in from the dining room. "Son!"
She hugged him before she started her monologue: why
hadn't he called? She had no idea of how he was; he
could pick up the telephone and let her know. Where was
Audrey? Had she run off? How long would he stay? Were
they paying him enough money up there in Nashville?
(When Hank was on the Hayride in Shreveport, Lilly had
ridden the Greyhound there once to "visit," but in fact
the reason for her trip was to try to persuade Hank to
return to Montgomery.)

"I'm okay, Mamma. I'm sleepy, though. I want to
sleep."

"I'll make up your old room. We *will* talk in the mornin', though." Hank didn't doubt that a bit. At least she would let him sleep. Sometimes insomnia would keep him up for seventy-two hours, especially when he was upset. This night, in his old bed, he slept a blessed eight hours without nightmares.

He felt *so* good in the morning. The boarders had already breakfasted—the ones who got up before noon—and left, and he and Lilly were sitting in the dining room with their coffee.

"What's wrong, son?" Lilly would have had to be blind to not notice that something was bothering her boy.

"Oh." Hank avoided her armor-piercing gaze and lit a cigarette and fiddled with his lighter and the ashtray. "Just workin' too hard, I guess."

"It's that woman." Lilly made it a flat statement. "Is she talkin' divorce again?"

"No, Mamma."

"Well, what is it then?" Lilly was impatient. "I know she fritters away all your money." Lilly held up a hand in protest before Hank could reply. "You can't even try to help your mother with expenses no more."

Hank sipped his coffee and took a drag off his Camel. "It's just that she wants to sing, you know—"

Lilly was suddenly furious. "And she *can't* sing. She has the talent of this *table.*" Lilly rapped the oak table with her large knuckles for emphasis. "It's about time you told her what was what." Her eyes were burning.

"I know, Mamma." Hank didn't look up at her. "I will."

"You *better.*" He knew she was not kidding. "Don't bring that woman back here till you do." Her glance would blister paint from thirty feet away.

Hank just kind of drifted around Montgomery all day. He really had no friends to look up. Just acquaintances. He finally decided to call Braxton Schuffert, who had been the first singer he had known in Montgomery and who had been in his first band. Hank liked Schuffert. He had always done his best to try to help Hank and had never—unlike many people—tried to put the touch on Hank for money or favors after Hank became successful. He got him on the phone at the Hormel Packing Company, where Schuffert was a truck driver.

"Hello, Brack? It's Hank . . . I'm doin' all right . . . yeah, yeah, Mamma's fine . . . how's your wife and babies? . . . good, good. Listen, Brack, you still sing a song ever' now and then besides haulin' that meat around town? . . . Well, you oughtta come up to Nashville and get on the Opry, you're better'n some of them they got up there, you got your own style, you don't copy nobody else."

Hank wanted to do something for Schuffert; wanted to help in some way; wanted to show gratitude to him.

Help with music was the only way Hank could think of to help, to say thanks.

"Brack, I tell you. I'm gonna get you on records. I'll get you a recording contract and bring you up to Nashville . . . I *know* you got your family here and your job . . . I ain't listenin' no more. I'm gonna fix it up and call you and then you comin' up to Nashville."

Hank felt better after he hung up. He was ready to go home to Nashville, back to Audrey.

Hank woke up and didn't recognize the ceiling above him. There was a pain in his left arm; he looked and as his eyes finally focused he saw a . . . a damn *tube* stuck in his arm. It was attached to a bottle of clear liquid on a rack above what was obviously his hospital bed. He couldn't remember . . . the last thing he knew about was a drink or two he had had with . . . who was it with? He wasn't sure. But then he had decided to go back to Lilly's and get some sleep so he could get up early and head back to Nashville. He didn't know he had lost two days; didn't know Lilly had sent him to the hospital.

He was too weak to do anything but lie there. So his mamma had locked him away again. He felt like crying. He didn't remember phoning his daddy, calling up Lonnie whom he hadn't seen in years, and begging him to come to Montgomery and get him. Lonnie, who was as soft-hearted a man as there could be, drove up from McWilliams to Montgomery. At Lilly's house, he saw an ambulance pulling away. He followed it to St. Jude's Hospital. The doctors there wouldn't let him see Hank; they said Hank needed to be detoxed from drugs. Lonnie was shocked. He went back to McWilliams.

Lilly didn't visit Hank at the hospital. He lay there like a sick dog. A priest came through. He was visiting all the patients. Father Harold Purcell knew who Hank Williams was and was surprised to hear that Hank was there to bake drugs and alcohol out of his system. He stopped by Hank's bedside. He had expected Hank to be an arrogant star. Hank was humble and glad for company and knew enough about the Bible to ask Father Purcell some questions. They liked each other immediately. They seemed exotic to each other: a notorious music star meeting a holy man. Each was surprised to find that the other was just human. They vowed to keep in touch.

Braxton couldn't believe it. He had thought Hank was just talking the usual talk about that recording contract. But now Braxton had a recording session with M-G-M Records scheduled for Monday morning at 7; Hank had made him a reservation at the Hermitage Hotel in Nashville; Hank was wiring him money for the train tickets; Hank said he would meet him at the train depot in Nashville on Sunday. "Come on up, Brack. You're on the records. You're *on.* I *guarantee* it."

Braxton wasn't ready to give up his steady job driving a retail delivery route for Hormel and abandon his family. But he finally decided that it couldn't hurt to make a record in Nashville, especially when Hank was being so nice about setting up the whole thing. The foreman at Hormel told him he could have some time off; all he had to do first was find a relief driver and tell him the territory and the figures for each delivery. He did that Friday afternoon.

Hank met him at the train station Sunday and they drove out to Franklin Road, talking about old times when they played those skull orchards in south Alabama.

Audrey was nowhere to be seen. Fred Rose came over and he and Hank and Brack went back into the pine-paneled den to plan the recording session. Brack was impressed by Fred: he was strictly business. "Schuffert, Schuff-ert," he kept repeating and he turned to Hank and Brack. "That last name," he shook his head, "that last name just doesn't work. Not on a record label, not on a radio station. Let's make it—" He thought for a moment, mouthing the name: "Schuff-ert." "We'll spell it 'Shooford' on the record. People can pronounce that." He spoke with finality. Hank and Brack nodded; Brack was a bit nervous that his last name had just been changed arbitrarily but who was he to challenge the great Fred Rose?

"Now," Fred said, name change disposed of, "what songs are we going to do?"

Braxton froze. That hadn't occurred to him. Surely he was lost now. Fred would cancel the session.

Fred continued, ignoring Braxton: "Now, we're doing two records. The first one will be that Johnny Wright song, 'If Tears Would Bring You Back' and the other side will be that song you wrote, Hank, what is it, now?"

Brack was impressed by how self-assured Hank had become. Hank had his black-and-white boots up on the coffee table and was idly blowing smoke rings, just like he planned recording sessions with the great Fred Rose every day. "Oh, uh, Pappy," Hank finally said, "that'un's 'Why Should I Cry?' "

"Okay, we need two more songs, now don't we?" Pappy asked.

Without a word, Hank picked up his beautiful Martin D-28 Herringbone guitar from its velvet-lined case there beside the couch, ran his fingers across the steel strings, and started singing. His voice, Brack thought, was amazing. It was strong enough to cut through the din of a raucous honky-tonk; here in Hank's den with no driving band behind him, it sounded mournful and delicate, like a wild bird.

Neither Fred nor Brack said anything when he finished. Hank looked around for some kind of sign of approval: he was used to that. "Well," he said, "That'un's called 'A Teardrop on a Rose.' What do you think of it?"

"I never heard that one before, Hank," Pappy said. "You hid it from me, didn't you?"

Hank ignored him and looked at Brack, waiting for his reaction.

"Hank," Brack said, "that's one of the *most beautiful* songs I *ever* heard." Hank smiled. Of *course* it was. "Where'd you get it?" Brack asked.

"Why, I *wrote* it. You want it? I'll give it to you."

"Why, sure Hank, you *know* I want it."

"Well, Brack, you can record it in the mornin'."

He smiled, glad that he could give Brack something, glad that he could help someone who deserved it and appreciated it.

Such people were rare in Hank's life. And . . .

Pappy got up and headed for the living room. He stopped: "Hank, you need one more song. You and Brack sit here and write one."

They sat there, Hank on the couch that was upholstered with forest-green polished cotton adorned with horses; Brack on the tan vinyl settee. Hank found a pencil stub and a little spiral notebook. He seemed to be

absolutely confident that they could write the best song in
the world right then and there. "You got any ideas,
Brack?"

"I don't know, Hank . . . I . . . I'm not *lazy,* I'm
just *tired."*

"That's *good.* Now what oughtta come next?"

In about fifteen minutes, they went into the living
room and sang the just-written song "Rocking Chair
Daddy" for Pappy. He grunted his approval—"Just sing
it a little higher there at the end"—and the recording
session was all planned. The Drifting Cowboys would
play on the records; everything was set. Braxton couldn't
believe it.

"Hello, Brack? Brack? It's Hank. Why ain't you
called? M-G-M's lookin' for you. 'Teardrop' is sellin'
ever'where. Now, listen to *this."*

Hank paused. "Brack, you're on the *Opry!* I talked to
Mr. Denny about you and he heard your records, they're
goin' good ever'where. You're *on the Opry.* Quit your job
and get on back up here and we'll get you a buncha
musicians, anybody you want, Nashville is full of them
ready to go and then you're out on the road. What you
say, buddy? Ain't this *somethin'?* Brack, it took me *so*
long to get the Opry. Now it's *yours,* too." Hank was
excited and he seldom allowed himself to bubble over like
that for someone else to hear, even over long-distance
telephone. "Remember the first time I talked to you? I
was just shinin' shoes—"

"Hank, *please."* The tone of Brack's voice hushed
Hank's own. *"Hank.* I'm not gonna do it. I thought *hard*
about it. I just don't have what it takes for that life."

"Brack, Brack, you were in the band, we were on the
road—"

"I know, Hank. But since then I been in the army and
I promised the good Lord that if I ever got home from

there, if He got me home, I was gonna *stay* there. I got my family now."

"Brack, you *got* to come up here. We'll go on the road together. . . ."

"Hank. I can't do it. I'm gonna go over to station WJJJ here, do a radio show there. I'm gonna see how I can make it down here."

"Brack, you *can't* make it there. *No way.* When I left Montgomery, I couldn't even make a hundred dollars a week. *You can't make it.* M-G-M'll drop you. If you don't come up here and go out on the road and work and help 'em sell you, they'll *drop* you. You *can't* make it no other way. *Come on back.*" He was pleading.

"I'm sorry, Hank. I just can't do it."

They hung up. Braxton was uneasy. He had done what he felt was right but he was nagged by the prospect of what might have been ahead had he taken the highway that Hank was offering him: M-G-M Records and the Opry and whatever else all that could lead to. He would think about that for years and years to come. He admired Hank but he did know that it was not for him.

Hank sat and brooded and chain-smoked in the dark and envied Braxton: a man who believed so strongly in the solidity of his family and its happiness that he could without regret spurn what Hank valued so; could walk away from what seemed to be music stardom. Hank wished he had a family like that. What a joy that must be.

M-G-M Records declined any further association with Braxton "Shooford." Pappy never mentioned him again.

"If the good Lord's willing and the creeks don't rise, we'll be back for another visit. See you in a while, Bocephus!" Miss Ragland always turned on the radio for Hank's radio shows and if little Bocephus was awake, she told him to listen and he was always delighted and clapped his hands when he heard his daddy talking to him. Hank turned away from the WSM microphone after his usual sign-off after a radio show. Audrey had started forcing her way, and she did mean *force,* onto some of the broadcasts, but this morning she had overslept and Hank was never one to force *her* to get up at 4:30 in the morning to go down to the studio and sell Mother's Best Flour. "Let's go, Burrhead!"

Jerry Rivers heard Hank's order and picked up the pile of fishing poles and tackle boxes in the corner.

If they had to get up at dawn on the weekdays that they were in Nashville to do the live WSM morning broadcasts, they had decided they might as well use the early morning hours to their own advantage and go hunting or fishing. There was nothing else to do in Nashville at six-thirty or seven in the morning. They drove out to Rudy Ross's boat dock at Kentucky Lane, just past Waverly, and took Hank's outboard boat out and fished till the sun got high. The others were ready to leave; but not Hank. They called him a "nigger fisherman." He would put out a dozen fishing poles at once and fish from morning darkness till evening darkness. He was impatient; there was no reason why he couldn't catch ten fish at once, the way he saw it.

Hank anchored the boat, sank his minnow buckets (which held a couple hundred minnows), and put out his lines. Only Don Helms and Jerry Rivers were with him. Guitarist Bob McNett had quit the Cowboys to go back to Pennsylvania and bass player Hillous Butrum had jumped to Hank Snow's band. Hank needed to replace them . . . but not while he was fishing. Helms's steel guitar and Rivers's fiddle were the core of his band, anyway. Anybody who left didn't really belong. There were other guitar players, other bass players. Especially bass players. The bass player in country bands, in hillbilly bands, was traditionally the comic figure of the band. He blacked out his teeth, crossed his eyes, did the blackface routines—he was the "eed," which was short for "idiot."

Hank was still fussing with his lines and Helms and Rivers were dozing off when they heard the sound of a light plane approaching. It landed in the lake; obviously, it was an amphibian. There was no reason for it to be there.

In about two minutes, Rudy's powerboat pulled up alongside them. "Hank!" Rudy shouted, "Audrey's in the airplane. She chartered it! She said you got a big meeting this mornin'! She said you got to get back."

Hank silently swore. The son of a bitch whore would not even let him alone out here. What damn meetin'? He didn't remember any damn meetin'! Still, he got into Rudy's boat. "Oh, yeah, Rudy, I'm *late! Hit* it, hoss!" He really could not tell everybody that he and Audrey were dueling and that you had to wake up twice to try to get up before she did. *Bitch.*

The mist was rising off the lake and so was Hank's voice. Webb Pierce was fishing with Hank, and Webb thought it was just another fishing trip. Hank was hung over and some of his lines got tangled and he got tired of untangling them and pulled out his .38 from his beltline and fired off a couple of shots at the shore. Webb pretended he didn't notice. He was alone in a boat with a man who was shooting a gun. It was easier to get back home if he ignored the gun. Of course, he wasn't about to go fishing with Hank again, ever. The first thing he had to do was get home.

Everybody who went fishing with Hank learned a new rule. Vic McAlpin used to leave Nashville with Hank about three in the morning to get to the lake by sunrise. Rex's Cafe in Waverly would sell six-packs of beer all night. Vic quit stopping there with Hank, once he learned that. Vic started taking Hank by the bus station for

breakfast. The first morning they went in, Hank made a
swipe at their dirty table with a napkin, picked up the
forty-cent tip left there and said, "Hey, this might pay for
our breakfast!" The waitress heard that and Hank knew
that she had and he kept baiting her. She was furious. He
finally left her a five-dollar bill for a tip and never even
looked back to see what her reaction was. He was just
about past looking back at all.

"You know somethin', Vic?"

"What's that, Hank?" Vic and Hank were fishing
down at Kentucky Lake.

"Ordrey's just like this damn fishin' boat."

"How's that?"

"She got a flat bottom, she got no top, and she smells
like fish."

Vic laughed. "Yeah, but she still lets you get in her and
she don't leak."

Well, now, just what in the world was this? Audrey had
awakened at about seven AM; had *been* awakened, in fact,
well before she usually woke up, and the offender, the
disturbing sound, seemed to be a typewriter. It
sounded drunken, stuttering, stammering, erratic. Audrey wrapped her white velvet robe around her and went
forth to see what was disturbing her sleep. Her *husband*
obviously wasn't there to protect her, to shield her. Audrey had long ago quit depending on Hank and had, in
fact, started training her cannon on him. She had started
rethinking her first divorce action against Hank; had
started thinking that maybe she had been right.

Audrey padded barefoot into the den; the only light
came from the little lamp at her roll-top desk in the corner. She stopped; hands-on-hips posture. All she saw was
Hank and he was seated at her desk and was weaving
dangerously over her typewriter. Now and then he hit a
key. He didn't notice her. He reached out with a finger

and hit a key and then wavered upright; he looked like he might as easily fall over as not. He looked pathetic; looked like skin and bones. His eyes were vacant. Still, he pecked away at the typewriter.

"Hank." Her voice was tender, for a change.

"Yeah." His was empty, a hollow husk of a voice.

"Go to bed, honey."

"Why?" He was still suspicious, ready to fight.

Her tone of voice defused him. "Hank, *honey,* get into bed. I'll help you." He staggered off; his fight was gone.

Audrey helped him sprawl across the bed in his clothes; she was not often that generous in her treatment of him.

There was a reason, of course: she wanted to know what he'd been hunting-and-pecking away at on her typewriter. When he wrote songs, it was always with pencil and paper and he always kept the results on him. He never showed the song to anyone till he felt it was a hit. He teased everybody with his compositions: Owen Bradley, Chet Atkins. He would sing them a few bars of "Your Cheatin' Heart" and then stop and give them a shit-eating grin and ask, "Hey, is that good?" If they said "Yes," he would stop and say, "Well, then, that's too good for you. I oughtta keep that'un for ole Hank."

That infuriated other singers. That was just what Hank wanted. He couldn't be happier. Teasing other singers with his unrecorded songs was great fun. There was nothing he liked better than to pull some stained and scrawled lyrics out of his pocket and to read them to Opry stars backstage at the Opry and then to pronounce: "Well, that's just too good for you. Ole Hank'll have to record that 'un." People were furious. Hank sure liked that.

It took Audrey a while to get Hank off to bed; he was producing bravado up till the last waking second. Hank was a stubborn drunk and had to be coaxed and talked every step of the way even when he was already blind

drunk and had no idea of where he was or why he was
there or even who he was. Even when she got him onto
the bed and got his boots off and talked him down from
his drunk, he was more trouble than he was worth, as far
as most people who ran across him would think. Who
really needed a guy who wanted to punch out everybody
who swam across his field of vision? He finally nodded
off, and thank God for that.

Once Audrey was sure that Hank was down for the
count and would be out for a while, she went back to her
typewriter to see what Hank had been trying to write
before he'd fallen out.

He had written a letter and it was literate and should
be forwarded and should be published. It was just a letter
to a fan magazine. A letter to *Country Song Roundup*
Magazine. Audrey was trying to jump on him for writing
one letter to a fanzine. What he'd typed was this: "Dear
friends: a few months ago I was browsing through a issue
of Country Song Roundup and turning a page was surprised to see a picture of myself, gazing up at me. It was a
big thrill to see it in your fine magazine, a magazine that
I'm happy to say I've been reading since the first copy.
Matter of fact, I was so thrilled, I sat right down and
wrote you a letter of thanks.

"And now we come to the embarrassing part. I stuck
that letter in an envelope and put it in my pocket, meaning to mail it that night. My wife Audrey knows I'm
absent-minded but even she wouldn't believe I was as
forgetful as I was that day. You see, a little later I got an
idea for a song and I reached into my pocket for a piece
of paper to write it down and came up with that envelope. I didn't even notice the address as I hurriedly scribbled bits of lyrics on the back. It was about two months
before I wore that suit again. When I finally discovered
the envelope, I just knew I couldn't take the letter out
and send it in a fresh one. Too much time had gone by.
When I turned the envelope over, there was the lyric that

had done the mischief. If you can believe it, I had forgotten that, too. I read it over and I immediately had an idea for a tune. I finished it an hour later and recorded it for M-G-M Records the week after. It's called 'Moanin' the Blues' and if you'll accept it, it's dedicated to Country Song Roundup. Sincerely, Hank Williams."

Audrey was oddly touched. She had never seen him write a letter before; couldn't recall him *ever* writing any since he had been in Mobile, years ago, and had written her a couple of times. She sat down and retyped it for him, correcting the strike-overs and misspellings. She didn't even add her name to it.

There were no fishing poles stacked in the corner of the WSM studio. Audrey was there and she was smiling. Hank wasn't and neither were the Drifting Cowboys. They could all do without the presence of Audrey but she had insinuated herself into the "Health and Happiness Show" radio broadcasts, sponsored by Hadacol, the health "tonic."

There were two new Cowboys: Hank had replaced Bob McNett with Sammy Pruitt and hired Howard Watts—who called himself Cedric Rainwater in the comedy routines—in place of Hillous Butrum.

Announcer Grant Turner signaled Hank and he and the Cowboys started "Happy, Roving Cowboy" which was his theme song for the show. Turner came in with a voice-over: "Well, howdy, neighbor! It's Health and Happiness time with the Lovesick Blues boy, Hank Williams, and Miss Audrey and the Drifting Cowboys! Yes, the singing sensation of the nation, Hank Williams, is back again with some good news that'll make you mighty glad you tuned in."

Hank finished "Happy, Roving Cowboy." Oddly, it was the only cowboy song he ever sang.

Turner returned to the microphone. "Yes, friends, here's a fellow that's always welcome at your house and

mine, it's the old Lovesick Blues boy, Hank Williams!"
The Cowboys cheered and clapped and did their best to
sound like a huge studio audience.

"Thank ye, Grant," Hank said solemnly. "Thank ye a
lot and welcome friends and neighbors. Here we are
again. We hope everybody's just feelin' just as spry and
good today as you possibly can. All the boys and myself
and Miss Ordrey, we all feelin' good. We're gonna start
off here with a little advice in a song I wrote 'chere and
recorded a little while back, a tune called 'If you don't
change, honey, I'm gonna pack my suitcase and go home
and live with mamma.'" Audrey tapped her foot impatiently. That long introduction to "If You Don't Change,
I'm Gonna Leave" was not lost on her. She waited.

"Friends," Hank said. "Miss Ordrey's up with us today and she's got a mighty pretty little song all picked
out for ye that I know you folks are gonna enjoy. It's got
an awfully good title to it and, uh, a lotta good meanin'
to it. She says there's a bluebird on your windowsill."

"Right, Hank."

Even Grant Turner flinched as Audrey attacked "Bluebird on Your Windowsill." The melody emerged un-
scathed: she never came close to it.

After "hymn time"—Hank did a spectral-sounding
version of "Tramp on the Street"—Hank got the signal
from Turner to close out the fifteen-minute show.

"Well, friends," Hank said, "it looks like it's about
time we gonna have to get goin'. The clocks' gone all the
way around and that means we gonna have to go. But
this is Hank Williams speakin' for all the boys, sayin' if
the good Lord's willin' and the creeks don't rise we'll see
ye 'fore long."

Turner broke the silence that ensued. "Okay, Hank,
now we need to record one for next week."

Hank sighed. "All right. Lemme have a smoke first.
'Scuse me." Two long strides and he was out the door.

Audrey was trying to decide on what song to do for the next show. She didn't have a wide choice to pick from.

After "Happy, Roving Cowboy" Turner varied his introduction: "Yessir, when you invite this fellow into your home it just seems like the sun shines a little *brighter,* makes the day's work a little *lighter,* so let's give a great big old-fashioned welcome to Hank Williams!"

Even Hank had to smile at that. "Thank ye kindly, Mr. Turner, thank ye a whole heap. Welcome, friends and neighbors to the Health and Happiness Show. Hope everbody is happy and feelin' good today. Ordrey and all the boys and myself, we all feelin' just as spry as a two-year-old. We all ready. Start off here with a song I wrote 'chere a few years ago. This man got tired a his wife beatin' him on the head with a fryin' pan so he wrote a little song. The title of it is 'I'm a Long Gone Daddy.' " He sang it quickly.

"Now Miss Ordrey's up. She's got a little song here that looks to me like it sorta sounds like it was wrote as an answer to that first 'un, I'm leavin' now. What's the title of this 'un, honey?"

"I'm Tellin You."

"What are you tellin' me?"

"I'm only kiddin', Hank."

"You're only kiddin'. All right. Here we go."

He went back to the microphone when she finished: "Thank you, ma'am. I don't know whether you was kiddin' or not after listenin' to that."

They drove home in silence. Hank had finally traded in the Packard for his first Cadillac, an emerald-green jewel that he loved. Audrey soon demanded and got a yellow Cadillac convertible.

"What's wrong, Hank?"

"Nothin'."

When they got home, he stayed in the car. "I just remembered, Ordrey, I got to go see Pappy. I'll be back directly."

Audrey just shrugged and walked into the house. If he wanted to be moody, he could go right ahead without her. She didn't need that.

"Hey, Pappy."
"Ho, Hank. You all right? How about some coffee?"
"Okay."
Pappy waited till they were seated and had sipped their coffee and Hank was a third of the way through a cigarette before asking the reason for the visit.

Hank ran his hand through his thinning hair and tugged at his Adam's apple before answering. He really had no reason to visit other than to get away from Audrey and be with someone he felt comfortable with. He thought for a minute. He *did* have a couple of songs that were almost finished.

"Well, Pappy, I got a couple of new songs for ole Luke."

Pappy just grunted. He could take Hank's guise as "Luke the Drifter" and he could leave it. Mostly he could leave it. But if it kept Hank happy. . . .

Pappy knew that the records Hank made under the name of Luke the Drifter were cornball and not really commercial. Still, he didn't argue. He had fought with Hank once; had tried to keep him from recording "My Bucket's Got a Hole in It" because he thought it was a terrible song. Hank won the fight and the record did well. That was Hank, though, not Luke. Luke the Drifter recorded a lot of mournful recitations of heart-tugging music. Luke was pretty morbid and went to the funeral service of a poor Negro boy—"The Funeral"—and went to a courtroom where the judge's own poor little daughter was being tried for prostitution—"Too Many Parties and Too Many Pals"—and even lectured Joseph Stalin— "No, No, Joe"—and thought about mother and God a lot. He—Hank—actually broke down and wept while recording "I Dreamed About Mama Last Night" and left the sounds of his sobbing on the record. Luke could say a lot of things that Hank the Star couldn't. Hank said that the Luke records were "for the take-home trade. I don't like for these songs to make the jukeboxes. They are mostly sad songs about mother, funerals, death, and men with broken hearts." Hank had no illusions that people didn't know that he was Luke the Drifter, but he liked having Luke around to make the records that Hank really shouldn't. Luke was an upstanding man who went to church, didn't drink or whore around, defended his country, would instantly kill any man who said a word against his mother, was full of sage advice and extraordinary compassion and understanding and tolerance, and was generally a man to be greatly admired. He set an example for others to follow. Hank was proud of Luke the Drifter. One hell of a guy. If only there were more like him. . . .

Luke did, to be sure, kind of "borrow" one of his songs. "Pictures From Life's Other Side" had first been recorded in 1934 by the Smith Sacred Singers. Maybe it had come to Luke in a dream or something like that. Perhaps a divine visitation. Luke would certainly never appropriate someone else's work and call it his own. Everything he stood for would oppose that sort of thing. Hank had invented Luke as a combination of Sgt. Preston of the Mounties and Jimmie Rodgers. Rodgers was a wise drifter but some of his . . . more *relaxed* views in certain moral areas required Sgt. Preston's unyielding integrity.

Pappy finally took the bait. "Well, Hank, what have you got? Let's have a look." Pappy's mind was elsewhere. He and Wesley had been talking a lot lately about how to market Hank Williams the songwriter. Pappy knew in his guts that Hank's songs could be pop hits if the right people recorded them. All he and Wesley had to do first was knock down Tin Pan Alley's prejudice against hillbillies. Hillbilly hits themselves had been flukes, unexpected one-shots: in 1925, Vernon Dalhart's "The Prisoner's Song" had been the first hillbilly record to sell a million copies and Elton Britt did the same in 1942 with "There's a Star-Spangled Banner Waving Somewhere" but those were regarded as freaks. To hit the pop audience, the music industry reasoning said, you had to get a pop singer to sing a hillbilly or cowboy song, like with Bing Crosby doing "You Are My Sunshine" or "New San Antonio Rose."

Pappy and Wesley had spent a lot of time thinking and talking about what they needed to do or should do or might do or could do or should try to break that pop market wide open. They thought of everything. Red Foley's "Chattanoogie Shoe Shine Boy" was an entree. Close, but no cigar. Pappy went over every Acuff-Rose song again and again: maybe if he re-wrote that hook or wrote a new chorus. . . . Maybe if Wesley could get Hank's best songs to Nat "King" Cole or Rosemary Clooney or Tony Bennett or Vaughn Monroe or Frankie Laine or Tony Martin. That was a rough road, though. Admitting that you were from Nashville closed more doors than it opened in New York. Fred and Wesley themselves were so far removed from being hillbillies that singers in Nashville made up jokes about them (Why did Fred Rose kiss the cow? Because he had never seen one before and thought it was the Opry's new star) but they were still peddling hillbilly songs. That was a definite taint, like having an ounce or two of cowshit on their shoes. A problem, certainly. For all their hours and hours of strategy sessions, Fred and Wesley didn't know that they already owned the song that would forever shatter the wall between pop music and any other field of music —hillbilly, western, cowboy, race, folk, ethnic, sepia, and everything else that non-Tin Pan Alley songs were called.

Fred and Wesley had bet their careers that Hank's songs would be the ones to wipe out the barriers. They were right, ultimately, but the song that burst the dam and gave Hank his pop entry had nothing to do with Hank. It was a song that Pee Wee King and his singer Redd Stewart had written back in 1948. "The Tennessee Waltz," which Patti Page recorded in 1950, was the biggest song to ever come out of Nashville, made Acuff-Rose a lot of money, and taught record companies that they should pay attention to songs that came out of Nashville. It also made Fred and Wesley (and Roy Acuff) look pretty shrewd, but the song's success was an utter surprise to them. They recovered quickly from the shock and rallied to sell as many songs as they could to pop singers.

Pappy knew that he had to listen to every word Hank Williams said; if he missed something, it might amount to a hundred-thousand-dollar lapse. You never knew. It didn't matter what Hank was talking about: songs, comic books, a wino he knew, a flat tire, the weather. It *could* matter. So if Hank wanted to change into Luke the Drifter for a while, he should be offered all possible assistance with the transformation.

Pappy waited while Hank dumped the contents of his wallet to try to find the songs. He had old business cards, he had yellowing receipts, he had women's phone numbers scrawled on torn scraps of nightclub napkins, he had parts of songs written on matchbook covers, he had *pounds* of paper stuffed into that wallet. Pappy waited.

Hank sorted the pieces of paper into piles: receipts here, phone numbers here, songs here. Sometimes he wrote them on his shirt cuffs if he didn't have any paper handy and then he would just rip the cuff off and stuff it into his hip pocket. It was just a shirt, after all, he told a woman one night who was visibly shocked at the sight of a grown man writing on his shirt cuff and then tearing it off. He could always buy another shirt. Songs didn't come as easily.

"*Here* we go, Pappy!" Hank was smiling. "Now listen to this 'un. I'm gonna call it 'Ramblin' Man.' It's a hit, for sure."

Pappy listened. It *might* well be a hit. You just never knew.

6

H ANK OPENED the *Billboard* dated June 17, 1950
and turned straight to the Folk charts. He was
sitting in his green Cadillac parked outside the Nashville
bus station. He was waiting for someone coming in from
out of town.

The sales chart looked good. His "Why Don't You
Love Me?" had jumped from number four to number one
after just three weeks. Number *one*. That made him feel
better. But "Long Gone Lonesome Blues" had slipped
from number three to number five. And he frowned when
he looked down the jukebox chart: "Long Gone" was just
number three and "Why Don't You" was way down at
number eight. Moon Mullican was up there at number
one with "I'll Sail My Ship Alone" and Red Foley's "Birmingham Bounce" was number two. Moon and Red were
both good old boys but that didn't mean they belonged
above Hank. What the hell did he have to do, go out

personally and visit every damn jukebox in the country and make sure his songs were on it? He wished he could. He could use any little bit of help.

The pressures were coming at him from all sides. He was on the road all the time, it seemed like, but he had to do it. He had to get out there while he was hot and he had to make money. He and Audrey were buying a five-hundred-and-seven-acre farm out on Carter's Creek and Audrey was daily finding new ways to spend money. He had to hit the road and then hustle back to town to play the Opry and do the radio broadcasts. That was important. People expected that. He had to keep churning out songs and that got harder and harder when people didn't give him time to think. Audrey and his mamma were both after him all the time, both pulling at him. And they couldn't get along with each other; those two women were like polecats in a tow sack. And his back was acting up. Audrey was still after him night and day to let her sing with him on the Opry; she would just not let go of the notion that she was a singer. Now that his career was just busting wide open, she got more and more jealous of him. He was proud to show the *Billboard* charts to other people—when Vic McAlpin got sick and tired one day of Hank shoving *Billboard* in front of his face and had asked Hank why he kept doing that, Hank had told him proudly, "It's for all them dumbass folk who say ole Hank wouldn't be nothin' without that Lovesick shit!"— but he tried to keep it hidden from Audrey. It just made her mad to see him doing well. They had had the usual Opry argument last Saturday and then he stomped off to play the Opry. He *had* had a couple of beers but he wasn't drunk. Mr. Denny had smelled it on his breath backstage. "Hank, are you okay?"

"I'm all right. I got a reason for drinkin' and here she comes up them steps right now."

Denny turned: Audrey was advancing on them in her sequined white "A" dress, which was decorated with music notes and big "A" initials. Her three-thousand-dollar diamond ring was flashing. Denny walked away: those two didn't need any help to fight, he knew. Hank was embarrassed; he preferred not to fight in public and Audrey knew that and used it. He gave in but he was fuming. Later he ran into Steve Sholes backstage and came within an inch of decking him on the spot. Sholes produced Hank Snow's records for RCA. Snow had said he was going to record Hank's "You Better Keep It on Your Mind." Then, he didn't, after Sholes heard it. Hank had heard stories. He grabbed Sholes and spun him around and pushed his finger into Sholes's chest. "Listen, you fat Jew," Hank said through clenched teeth, "don't ever let me year you saying my songs are low-class again." He shoved him aside. Sholes was a large man but he said nothing, made no movement after Hank. He considered himself lucky, after all the stories he had heard about Hank's temper.

Hank looked at his watch and lit another cigarette. He was impatient. Where the hell was that bus? He had enough problems without a late bus. He pulled a sheet of paper out of the glove compartment and studied his tour schedule: Montgomery to Sioux City to Moline to Des Moines to Cedar Rapids. Shreveport, Tulsa, St. Louis. On and on.

Finally. The bus pulled in. Hank waited. The tall figure he was waiting for finally came out of the bus station and got into the Cadillac.

"Hello, Mr. Williams."

"How you doin', Paul? How about a cuppa coffee?" Without waiting for an answer, Hank started the Cadillac.

"Sure, Mr. Williams. How've you been?"

"Hank. Hank. Aw, I been all right. I ain't got a enemy in the world but all my friends hate me."

Paul started laughing but stopped abruptly when he saw that Hank seemed to be serious. Hank was moody and Paul didn't know how to react to him. Sometimes he was full of his cornball jokes—"Ask me what you oughtta do with your weekend, Paul?" "Okay. What should I do with my weekend, Hank?" "The best thing you can do with your weak end is to put a *hat on it!*"— and other times he was totally distant and cold. Paul hardly knew him. He had sold him parts of some songs he had written. Paul Gilley was a six-foot-nine-inch basketball player at Morehead State College in Morehead, Kentucky. He had been writing country songs for years —just the words, not the melody—but they didn't bear his name. Like many naive young songwriters, he fell for the convincing line in Nashville that his big break would come later if he worked hard now and let—"let"—some of the stars "work" with him and help him finish his songs and record them. Otherwise, he, as a total unknown, had no more chance than the average jackass of even getting the time of day in Nashville; it was a very common practice. Songs traded hands like playing cards in a poker game. Hank had sold songs when he was younger; it was all part of the apprenticeship, just something you did if you had to. Hank had cowritten "Long Gone Lonesome Blues" and "I've Been Down That Road Before" with Vic McAlpin and then bought out McAlpin for $500 per song so Hank could get full writing credit. That meant a lot more to him than money in his pocket.

"Whattya got, Paul?" Hank asked, once they'd sat down over coffee. Gilley handed him several sheets of paper. Gilley had once sold Hank the core of what ultimately became, after rewrites and additions first by Hank and then by Pappy, "I'm So Lonesome I Could Cry." That had been quite a good song.

Hank finished reading. "Not bad. Not bad. What's this 'un called?"

Gilley looked at the lyrics, which he had forgotten to title. "Oh—that's 'Cold, Cold Heart.' "

"I like it." Hank took out his poke and peeled off some bills.

The Drifting Cowboys got to the Adolphus Hotel in Dallas early on the afternoon of July 5, 1950 and were surprised to find that Hank was not registered. he had flown in while they drove—he had started doing that more often; he got impatient at the long drives and could never be comfortable sitting for long. They double-checked with the desk clerk. No Hank Williams registered here, he said. They finally decided to wait in the lobby to see if he would show up. Jerry Rivers finally saw a thin man wearing sunglasses getting on an elevator. He thought he looked familiar and pointed him out to the bell captain as the doors closed: wasn't *that* Hank Williams? No, it was Herman P. Willis. That was odd: that was Hank's usual epithet for one of the Cowboys whenever he screwed up. The Cowboys went up to Room 504 and found Hank. He was laughing. He handed Rivers a letter on Adolphus stationery. "This is to certify," Rivers read, "that Jerry M. Rivers is the general manager of Hank Williams and Band. Including Hank Williams. During my stay in state of Texas." Rivers raised his eyebrows; the letter had been notarized.

Hank didn't see anything unusual in it. He gave them an explanation in a few terse words: the promoter for their Dallas shows, Jack Ruby, had been pestering him to show up at his night club to shake hands with all of Ruby's friends. Hank didn't need any of that. It was easier to just disappear till showtime. Rivers, as his manager, could deal with Ruby. That made good sense, to *him* anyway.

Well . . . *okay.* What did the "P" in "Herman P. Willis" stand for, though?

"Pride, by gum!"

Rivers scratched his crew cut. When Hank had still traveled regularly with the band, he used to pluck

Rivers's hat off his head and give him a knuckle-burn on
the scalp: "That looks like a thousand daddy longlegs on
your head, Burrhead." Rivers knew that Hank was having the usual problems with Audrey and now and then
hit the bottle, but was he starting to get really squirrelly?
Rivers shrugged. He seemed okay.

Hank hardly said a word on the flight from Baltimore
to Nashville. He was too sick to. Jim Denny sat beside
him, like a virtual cop. Denny had had to come and fetch
him, like he was a sick kid at school, and take him home.
The Drifting Cowboys hadn't been able to handle him
and had been shaken up to find him in such bad shape
that he not only could not get on stage, he could not get
out of his hotel bed. And could barely talk. And made no
sense when he did. The Cowboys had noticed—and
closed a knowing eye to—little episodes of drinking and
buying pills and getting guns and getting young women
and things. But he was the boss and who were they to say
anything to him? Besides, as long as he got on stage and
did the show—that was what the crowds wanted. The
Cowboys had suddenly had it rubbed in their faces that
their boss was dealing with some demons that went beyond a mere hangover. He was out there in some kind of
thin atmosphere by himself, where the normal rules and
ordinary behavior did not seem to work. It was some
kind of frightening and vague territory that required
more than the experience of getting a road map and pilot-
ing a Cadillac to the next town in time for the show
there.

Denny, with Audrey's approval in a phone call, had
Hank committed to the hospital/sanitarium in Madison
to dry out. Audrey had learned about committing Hank
when they still lived at Lilly's and Lilly would lose her
temper at Hank when he was drunk and would pack him
off to St. Jude's Hospital to dry out. If he was still coher-
ent enough to fight, Lilly would call the police and let

him sober up in jail. Audrey was a quick learner. She was compassionate enough to never put him in jail, but she told Jim Denny and the Drifting Cowboys to take Hank to the hospital anytime he acted like he had gone over the line. She believed Hank when he told her his pills were to help him not drink. She thought a couple days in the hospital would help him.

When the Cowboys came by to visit him a couple of days later, things were a bit strained. They had, after all, watched him break down to almost nothing. The explanation of depression and a few drinks too many was a thin one but they accepted it. It used to be funny when he would say, "I ain't got a drinkin' problem. I get drunk, fall down. *No* problem." If he pissed on the sidewalk, that was the daring act of a man who had no use for conventionality. If he now and then shot off one of his pistols in a hotel room—well, he was a *gun collector* who was admiring his guns. He and Audrey had fights—*every* married couple had fights. So Hank took a drink now and then. He had a bad back, he had pressures. *Any* man would want a drink.

To think otherwise would be to step out onto uncharted ground.

Jim Denny and Fred and Wesley Rose thought that Hank just needed to sober up, get some rest, and eat some decent food and he'd be all right. Ready to hit the road again. Audrey agreed: if he was laid up in a hospital, he was not making money and certainly not letting her sing.

The Opry needed him, WSM needed him, the music business in general needed him. He was the biggest draw they had. If he needed a little pep pill or two now and then to face up to road fatigue or needed a couple of tranquilizers to smooth things out, there were people who would provide them. *Gladly,* no questions asked. It was a service to country music.

In his bed, out at Madison, Hank lay awake in the

darkness and waited to hear the footsteps that would come. That had better come *soon*. This business of being locked up in the hospital was wearing pretty thin and he'd be damned if . . . He heard the footsteps, *finally*. "Here you go, Mr. Hank." The Negro attendant pressed a bottle into Hank's hand and accepted a twenty-dollar bill in return. Hank learned pretty quick what a bribe would do even in a sanitarium. A few dollars would bring him whatever he wanted. He had quit buying speed—it was so common people were giving it to him—and started looking for chloral hydrate or Nembutal or the like. Morphine was best. If he had to, he would buy whiskey.

Hank twisted the cap off the pint of Old Crow and gasped after knocking back a mouthful and letting it burn into him. *Ah. That was good. Thank God for the niggers here. They knew what ole Hank was going through.* The doctors had been at him. He told them—and it was the truth—that he didn't remember Baltimore; couldn't remember locking himself in his room and howling about Audrey and refusing to set one damn foot on stage in Baltimore's Hippodrome or any other damn place else. There were getting to be too many damn stages. Too many parties, too many pals. Too many people telling him what to do and where to go.

He lay in the darkness and sipped at the Old Crow. Too much pain. Too much Audrey—she never let him forget about the career she should have and the sacrifices she had made for him. Not enough Audrey—where the hell was she when he called home night after night on the road?

"FUCK OFF!" He sat up and screamed it, screamed what he felt when people were closing in on him. The attendant padded softly down the hallway, toward the scream.

Hank had finished about a third of the bottle. He was half-mumbling, half-weeping when he dropped it. The attendant who caught the bottle before it hit the floor could hear Hank mumbling the name "Bocephus" as he passed out. There was no need to call the nurse: this patient had just sedated himself.

They looked like a real show-business couple. Hank and Audrey wore tailored western suits. Tastefully done, thought Nudie Cohen as he watched Hank and Audrey approach his Cadillac. Nudie should know: he had made both suits.

Hank had good taste, Nudie thought: mostly understated with just enough flash to let people know he was a real star and not just some stool jockey from Schwab's. Audrey, now, Nudie frowned slightly as Audrey approached, Audrey had to have too much of everything. If one row of sequins was enough for her dress, then she wanted *four.* She wanted longer fringe, shorter hems, more spangles, less *taste.*

Nudie had invented country flash. Before Nudie, hillbilly singers in the South and cowboy singers in Texas and the West had worn business suits or badly-done and homemade stage clothing. Nudie hadn't known that at first when he hit Los Angeles in the early Forties. He was Brooklyn-born and had shined shoes in Manhattan, been a small-time boxer, run a dry-cleaners and sewn G-strings and pasties for the burlesque houses in New York. In Hollywood he made friends with western singer Tex Williams and borrowed $150 from him to buy a sewing machine. He set up shop in his garage in the San Bernadino Valley and talked Tex into giving him free plugs on his radio show. Nudie's message was that country and western entertainers "owed it" to their audiences to dress up, to offer some fantasy. He was only echoing what all the singing cowboy movies had been showing. Nudie soon had to turn business away from his North Hollywood tailor shop. His mixture of costume jewelry and movie-star outfits and two-toned boots and fancy

hats was irresistible to white-working-class-entertainer
standards. Poor whites like to dress rich and high, is
what he knew. Hank had been one of his first customers,
and they had become friendly. Nudie had shined shoes
outside the Palace Theatre in Manhattan; Hank had done
the same outside the Empire Theater in Montgomery.
The experience was not so different, they had discovered.
Hank understood what Nudie meant about the importance of dressing "up in order to dress *down* to the audience" and he bought Nudie Suits (as they were quickly
nicknamed) as often as he could. Nudie himself would—
and did—make anything to the customer's design; bad
taste was not known at Nudie's. Cadillacs embedded with
silver dollars, with pistols for door handles? Nudie could
do it. Hank, though, dressed *down* to dress *up*. His staple
was Nudie's equivalent of the blue serge, the tan western
gabardine, with variations. Very versatile. Then he built
his wardrobe with the elegant white fringed suits with a
sequined horseshoe on each upper arm, a western yoke
front with a light row of sequins and fringe, and just a
green scarf loosely knotted for a touch of color. Other
suits became more elaborate and expanded the color and
design range available to him. White suits with red and
blue piping, brown-and-white buckskins, blue suits with
"Lovesick Blues" music notes splashed across them with
sequins, lavender, blue, brown, gray. On and on and on at
prices of $500. Nudie was proud of one: a black, double-
breasted suit with red, white and green piping. Not everybody would wear black that well. Hank and Nudie had
met when Hank was still on the Hayride in Shreveport.
When he hit LA for the first time he looked Nudie up,
even though Nudie was not well-known. Nudie later sent
him some boots as "a gift from Uncle Nudie." Nudie was
twenty years older than Hank and felt a bit paternal toward him, although Hank was a good six inches taller.
   Nudie jumped out of his tastefully-done white Cadillac
convertible, all white-on-white, which was pretty daring,

and embraced Hank. He gave Audrey a token Hollywood cheek-peck and hustled them into the Caddy.

"Well, folks, welcome to Holly-*wood,*" Nudie was smiling as he steered them down Sunset Boulevard. "Now, before we get you settled at the hotel, how about lunch. I got a table at Chasen's—" He was doubly interrupted.

"Hot dog's fine with me, I ain't hungry." That was Hank, who was idly looking around without apparent interest at his surroundings. He turned his attention to lighting a smoke.

"Mr. . . . *Nudie,* Nudie," Audrey was leaning over the seat. "Do you know James Stewart?"

Nudie could hardly believe what he was hearing. He started to answer Hank, but he had *no* answer for him till he dealt with Audrey. *She* wanted movie stars. *Okay.*

"Sure!" he yelled back at her over the seat. Nudie winked at Hank. That meant Audrey got dumped at the hotel with a token call placed to Jimmy Stewart—or somebody who knew his agent—and she could sit around and paint her nails all day and wait for the phone to ring. Nudie and Hank could hit the town. Nudie didn't mind hanging out with big recording stars.

He was all set to zoom off to Chasen's with Hank once they had dumped Audrey. Instead, Hank wanted three things and three things only: to go someplace where they could buy the latest *Billboard,* to grab a quick hot dog someplace where they could read the *Billboard,* and then to whiz by Nudie's shop so Hank could get fitted for some new threads. Well . . . *okay.* Nudie was used to weird things out-of-towners wanted to do in Hollywood. He just averted his head and closed his eyes in the hot-dog joint somewhere in San Berdoo when Hank was dumping ketchup over his hot dog while thumbing through *Billboard* and some guy, some . . . *tourist* at the counter was watching Hank and finally asked him, "Hey, buddy, why ya put so much ketchup on that?"

In a split second, Hank had broken the neck of that

bottle of Heinz ketchup over the edge of the formica counter and had the jagged edges of the broken bottle up and ready to rip Mr. Tourist's throat open. It took quite some talking on Nudie's part to get them out of there before the cops came. The Tourist and the counterman were pale and terrified: they didn't know what kind of skinny southern terror had just snarled at them to "Fuck off!"

They couldn't have known that just a few days earlier he had been released from a drying-out clinic and had gone home to a knock-down, drag-out fight-and-reconciliation with his wife and had, indeed, only two nights before, counseled with the venerable Roy Acuff. Roy had recorded, at Hank's suggestion, "Thy Burdens Are Greater Than Mine." When Hank had heard the record, he just shook his head. It was wrong.

When he finally ran into Roy, he asked him: "Roy, why didn't you sing that middle verse in there?"

"I didn't have time," Acuff said. "The record wouldn't permit that much time."

Hank just pursed his lips and finally answered the man who once had been his idol: "I *would* never have done that."

Acuff was not sure that he understood but he didn't press the issue.

Nor had the Tourist and the counterman witnessed the skinny terror's pleading with his wife before he went off to play five days at the Hippodrome in Baltimore, when she had wrung him through more hysterical arguments than a cheap southern lawyer would take to a washateria.

Acuff had been one living music idol: Ernest Tubb was the other. Hank had gone to Ernest, who was older and wiser, when Audrey had just gone beyond Hank's endurance. The issue of divorce and visitation rights for Bocephus versus Miss Audrey's rights to a singing career had just screamed to limits Hank didn't know existed, had careened into hours of haranguing and threats and mo-

Hank Williams, Sr. (courtesy Hank Williams Fan Club)

Hank and his mother. (Chet Flippo)

Hank's first band, circa 1937. From left: Hezzy Adair, Braxton Schuffert, Irene Williams, Hank, Freddie Beech. (Braxton Schuffert Collection)

Hank Williams and the Drifting Cowboys. (Chet Flippo)

Hank and Audrey examine her wedding ring. (Chet Flippo)

Hank and Billie Jean toast each other after their three weddings in the space of less than twenty-four hours. (Chet Flippo)

Hank on stage. (Chet Flippo)

Twenty thousand people jammed Montgomery's Municipal Auditorium and Perry Street outside during Hank's funeral. (Chet Flippo)

Hank's gravesite.
(Chet Flippo)

Hank Williams, Jr. with Waylon Jennings (Hank Williams, Jr. Collection/The Merrill's Home of Photography)

ments of dark tumult when she seemed to reach into some other dimension to pull out the vilest things he had ever heard.

Hank went to Ernest—he could not go to Pappy, who had made it clear by unspoken word that his advice was musical only; he would not go to Jim Denny for many reasons—because there was no one left to go to.

Ernest was greatly moved. He saw tears welling up in Hank's eyes as Hank walked up to him. "Ernest," Hank was pleading, "what am I going to do with her? She won't rest till she sings on ever' network show I'm on. I love her, but she can't sing. *What am I gonna do with her?*" Hank would never forget the helpless look and the sad face of his other music idol as Ernest Tubb had no answer for him.

Hank had his eyes closed as Nudie raced away in the Cadillac. "Nudie, I shoulda busted their heads *open. Wide* open."

Hank laughed at the first clipping he plucked from the piles of notes and song fragments and phone numbers he'd dumped from his wallet onto the coffee table. He unfolded it and read: "Williams grossed over $400,000 in the past eight months headlining Grand Ole Opry unit show coast to coast." That was torn from *Billboard's* April 8, 1950, issue. Hank laughed with little mirth. *He* sure as hell hadn't seen any $400,000.

He was sitting alone in his den and had just opened a bottle of Jax and decided to empty out the wallet, which was getting so thick he could barely sit on it anymore. He had just come home happy from Toledo—13,600 folks at *one* show there—and Audrey wasn't home. Miss Ragland, their housekeeper, didn't know where she was. Miss Ragland offered to make Hank some supper, but he just told her to put the kids to bed. He was still not totally at ease with Miss Ragland. Audrey had hired her and she was devoted to Audrey. The worst part was that she was also named "Audrey": Audrey Ragland. Hank did not really need an extra Audrey. After he kissed little Bocephus goodnight, he just didn't know what to do with himself so he got a beer and sat down and took off his "lightning bolt" boots—they were jet black with white bolts shooting back from the toes—and his white hat, which he wore all the time now. His hair on top of his head was just about gone. He had tried wearing a toupee for a while but had given it up after one morning when Vic McAlpin had come to pick him up to go fishing. Hank had slept in the den, right on that very couch, so he wouldn't wake Audrey when he got up early.

Vic thought Hank looked different somehow. He couldn't quite put his finger on it . . . then, he noticed. The part in Hank's hair ran from side to side, rather than from front to back. "Hank, Audrey done beat hell out of you last night. Your head's on crooked!" That was the last time Hank wore his toupee.

Hank unfolded an old telegram from the pile of papers. He knew its contents by heart but reread it anyway.

CONGRATULATIONS. MUSIC MACHINE OPERATORS OF AMERICA HAVE VOTED YOUR RECORDING OF "LOVESICK BLUES" BEST HILLBILLY RECORD OF 1949 IN FOURTH ANNUAL MUSIC POLL OF AUTOMATIC MUSIC INDUSTRY, SPONSORED AND CONDUCTED BY THE CASH BOX. SIGNED, JOEL M. FRIEDMAN, MUSIC EDITOR, THE CASH BOX.

Hank treasured that one.

He looked at another clipping: "Hank Williams, with white cowboy hat and formal cowboy suit, was a western Frank Sinatra. His warbles and voice tremors caused teen-age bobby soxers to squeal and swoon in delight." That was from the *Times-Picayune* in New Orleans, from

June 2, 1950. He remembered that well. There had been quite a bit of squealing in his hotel room that night, after the show. What was her name? He couldn't for the life of him remember. That had been a hell of a night, though. New Orleans was a good town for him. He lit up a Camel and closed his eyes for a minute. People in Louisiana had always treated him good, had always taken real good care of him. Those were good people over there.

He looked through some quotes from *Country Song Roundup.* "Hank Williams: Heart-Singer. He puts his heart into his singing!" "Hank Williams: Always Singing. He has been singing all his life." Next to the story was an ad for Dornol Pimple Treatment.

There were box-office figures: 10,500 paid admissions at Kansas City, January 29 to February 2, 1950; 16,750 at St. Louis, June 2–8, 1950; 18,500 in Amarillo, September 19–22, 1950. Nobody could beat those. Hank got another Jax.

There was a paragraph torn from his press release: "Hank Williams's records have sold in the millions of copies because of his down-to-earth style of singing. Here is a true country boy who makes no bones about it. Ticket-holders for ————'s performance(s) will be delighted with the variety of talent in the Hank Williams show. In addition to Hank, there's the rube comedian, Cedric Rainwater; the hot guitar specialist, Sammy Pruitt; steel guitar man par excellence, Don Helms; lightning-fingered fiddler, Jerry Rivers, and bass fiddler supreme, Howard Watts. There will be one (two) performance(s) of this outstanding Grand Ole Opry troupe ———— night, with ticket prices set at ———— (plus tax) for adults and ———— (plus tax) for children under 12. Advance tickets may be purchased at————."

Hank got up and walked over to the Victrola, slightly favoring his right leg, which was acting up a little, and decided that he would play some Hank Williams. The guy's press made him sound like Jesus Christ. What did he sound like, if he was so great? Hank put "Why Don't You Love Me" on the turntable and stood and listened and watched that mustard yellow [baby-shit yellow, he called it] label spin around and around. He sang along: that was one hell of a song. He ought to play it again. He stood there, beer bottle in hand, slightly hunched over, and listened to it a time or two again.

He read some more clips—". . . one of the country's most popular folk music stars. His fame as a songwriter is nearly equal to that of his singing reputation. . . ." ". . . one of the nation's top singers of folk music. Other than being a great showman, the Alabama musician has a voice that appeals to the wide following of his typically-American music. His fans kept yelling requests at both the early and late shows at City Auditorium."

He drank another beer. It was deathly quiet there in the house. Miss Ragland had gone to bed. Hank thought about calling up somebody and inviting them over but he finally decided there was nobody he really wanted to see right then. He hadn't talked to Lilly lately, but that could wait.

He finally decided to take a spin out to his farm and saddle up Hi-Life and ride him around for a while. Hi-Life liked that too; liked to get out at night and really open up. Hi-Life was a damned good horse and a damned good friend.

When he got home, he was drunk, as usual. Still, as usual, the first thing he did was to check the garage to see if Audrey's Cadillac was there, to see if she was home or out tomcattin' around town like he halfway knew she was doing every time he went out on the road. The Caddy was there. He felt the hood: the engine was cold. Well, sumbitch, he thought. Miss Audrey done stayed home for a spell. Still, he checked the speedometer to see just how much driving she had been doing.

He stumbled over a bottle in the living room and

kicked it. It shattered against the fireplace and he heard sudden sobs from the bedroom. He flung the door open. Audrey was crying, sitting up in bed, chain-smoking and drunk. Her hair, that lovely golden hair that he used to caress so tenderly was matted and wet with her tears. She threw him a glance that was half hate and half love. He ignored it and limped—his back and right leg were acting up again—to the ashtray, which was heaped over and smoldering. Not all the cigarette butts had lipstick on them. He turned to her: "Who was here, goddammit, who? You have some pretty boy here while ole Hank's out earnin' you money?"

Her only answer was a sob. Her underwear was on the floor, twined around the empty bottles. The giant Philco TV with the tiny screen droned a white sound.

He sat down, painfully, on the edge of the bed and, as usual, took off his left boot first. He threw it against the wall. It knocked down a picture of Jesus watching over an American soldier marching into battle. Jesus landed on a $2 pair of red panties. Jesus's expression didn't change, although his eyes continued to follow you around the room.

"No—no-*body* was here," Audrey finally managed in a choked voice. Hank bounced his right boot off the goddamn ridiculous bullfight picture that Audrey had paid good money for. *His* money.

"Motherfucker." He whipped his silver-buckled, hand-tooled belt off and threw it at the dresser. The motion sent waves of pain through his back.

He was spoiling for a fight. Usually, it was Audrey who started it but tonight she was acting so guilty that he wanted to just grab her and rub her face in the guilt, like you do with your dog when he shits indoors. Grab that sumbitch by the scruff of the neck and smear its goddamn face in that shit. He took out his pistol from his pocket—tonight he'd been carrying the snub-nose .38 he got from that cop in Shreveport—and set it down on the oak bed-

side table just heavily enough for Audrey to hear the
unmistakable clunk of steel against wood. That would
scare the bitch; she'd remember the last time he fired a
shot over her head.

She turned her back to him and continued to quietly
sob.

"Cocksickle," he said in a flat, matter-of-fact tone.
"Where's some fuckin' cigarettes?"

She didn't answer and he turned on the bedside lamp
—the goddamn silly lamp with a goddamn chintz shade
—and it was then that he saw all the new clothes. Boxes
and boxes spread all over the floor. "Bitch. BITCH! Why
you get all these new clothes? Where you got to wear
them to when ole Hank's gone? How much this shit cost,
huh?" He grabbed her hair and jerked her head up from
the pillow. She spat at him and he flung her away. In his
sudden fury, he ignored the terrible pain in his back and
gathered all those clothes up, the dresses and hats and
underwear and limped to the front door, threw it wide
open and heaved all the clothes into the darkness of the
front lawn.

"Hey, bitch, come lookit your new clothes." He was
shouting. He was surprised—and exultant—that for once
she wasn't fighting back.

"Hear me, bitch? HEAR ME? You ain't gonna run
around on Hank in these high-tone clothes." He went out
on the porch and kicked at a red chiffon evening gown.
He was starting to weave and went off to the kitchen. He
needed a shot of jack. He found a bottle and limped off to
the bathroom with it. He hadn't eaten in four days of
constant traveling. Hank slammed the bathroom door
shut behind him. He dropped his tailored $100 pants and
kicked them off, along with his BVDs. He sat down heavily on the toilet, dressed only in his blue cowboy shirt and
beige, rhinestone-studded $300 jacket. He fished in his
shirt for a cigarette, found a bent Camel, and lit up.
Three hours ago, thousands of people were calling his

name after he went offstage. Now, he threw back a swig from the bottle, "Sumbitch" came out as naturally as the first exhalation of cigarette smoke. His back hurt him, oh how it hurt so. He tried to cradle his head with his hands crossed over his bony knees. His body shook involuntarily with the first spasms of diarrhea and he felt a sudden chill. The cigarette dropped from his hand and landed beside the bottle on the tile floor.

He could still hear Audrey's sobs and he thought, for a fleeting instant, of saying "I'm sorry." But for him those words were as hard to say as it was for Audrey to even whisper "I love you." Words between Audrey and Hank had lost their meaning, become shorthand for unspoken insults and accusations. Jealousy and suspicion were now common nature for both of them. Women threw themselves at Hank on the road and Audrey threw herself at men at home.

He picked up the cigarette again and shakily took a drag. "Audrey. Mamma," the words came without him even shaping them. "Mamma, Audrey. Help me, oh please, please help me." Audrey couldn't hear him. She was too busy crying. He thought about calling Mamma, calling Lilly. But she was no better than Audrey, no help at all.

He sat there a long time, till the cigarette burned down to his knuckles and the pain startled him awake. He had been dreaming: he was back in Alabama at the old home and Lon and Lilly still got along and they were making him hand-cranked strawberry ice cream. Lilly let him lick the dasher and she hugged him. He was happy and safe and no one would ever hurt him.

When he awoke, it took him thirty seconds to realize where he was. He cleaned himself, forgot to flush the toilet and limped off to the living room with the bottle. After much difficulty, he managed to turn on the light and found a paper napkin and a stub of a pencil. He sat slumped, the way he always did, and stared at the picture above the mantel, the picture of him and little Bocephus, little Hank Jr., his only remaining pleasure. As he studied the picture, his face darkened, and he started scribbling on the napkin: "My son calls another man Daddy." He knew it would be another great song. He fell over, to sleep a few fitful hours.

The first time Hank took a shot at Audrey, he was too drunk to tell whether he hit or missed. He fled the house, flew to Los Angeles to his friend, Tex Williams, who ran the Riverside Rancho. "Well," Hank said after his first drink, "I done killed Audrey." Tex blanched, poured Hank another drink and slipped out to the kitchen and called Hank's house in Nashville. Audrey, obviously alive and fairly well, answered. He slowly lowered the phone. "Hank, Audrey seems all right."

Hank looked at his drink and then said matter-of-factly, "Well, then, I'll have to go back and kill her."

Hank flew back but Audrey was hiding out at Mother Maybelle Carter's house. He forgot about trying to shoot her. He went back to loving Audrey. Sometimes, she reciprocated. Sometimes, it was like the good old days when they couldn't keep their hands off each other, like when Audrey would sit on his lap in the '37 Chevy on their way to a show in Greenville. Before she wanted to sing and get equal billing. Before she tried to completely supplant Lilly as Hank's bosslady.

He lay awake in the dark. There had to be some way to slow things down for a while; slow them down enough for him to get his bearings. There was nobody he could talk to about it; he had known that for quite a while. Had come to almost accept the fact that everyone he met or saw wanted a piece of him. Now and then he managed to fight back; not often, though. It was usually in the form of rebuffing some rich asshole from Montgomery who wanted to talk about their "old days" together—there were none. He had felt some sweet vengeance when he'd played Mobile and stopped by the studios of station WALA. When they saw him walk in, they were falling all over themselves with star-worship and they got all ready for an interview with the "STAR." All he'd said was, "I wasn't good enough for this radio station when I lived here and tried to get on this station; I reckon I still ain't good enough for it." He'd walked out. That had been sweet.

They didn't come around every day, though, that kind of chance. Most days were just grinds of demand after demand.

Something nagged at his memory; there was somebody he'd told himself to remember, some guy who'd been decent and really offered to help. Who was he? The name wouldn't come.

Maybe, maybe he could just disappear for a while, just drop completely out of sight. He'd done that once for four days when he was a kid, had hidden out here and there. When he went home, though, Lilly hadn't really cared.

Disappearing still appealed to him a great deal. Hank Williams might vanish today and Herman P. Willis might appear in his place somewhere where they would never think of looking for Hank. Hiding out at Lilly's to get away from Audrey was not the same thing; nor was holing up for a day or two at the lake cabin down at Camp Kowaliga in Alabama. The people that ran the place knew who he was.

Purcell! That was the name he'd been trying to think of. Father Purcell. Father Harold Purcell. The priest who had visited him in St. Jude's Hospital when Lilly sent him there to dry out had really talked to him like he was just another man; not like he was the big income-generating star. Maybe he'd go and see Father Purcell. He had just about run out of other places to go. He'd go talk to the priest. First, though, he had to go and play Indianapolis on New Year's.

7

SHE STALKED to the breakfast table in a palpable fury; steam was almost rising off her. Audrey was pissed off, Hank could sense through his morning fog. She was pasty-faced and her blonde hair was dirty and rumpled and there were puffy bags under her eyes but those eyes were flashing and sending out death-ray danger signals. She was puffing away on a cigarette like that damn little steam engine in Lycrecia's coloring book. Audrey's white satin robe was dirty and she was barefoot —hadn't taken the time to locate her white feather-trimmed mules. She bore down on Hank like a kamikaze plane.

He was sitting there at the breakfast table, where Miss Ragland had put some cheery marigolds from the garden in a cut-glass vase in the center of the white lace table-cloth. Cheering early morning Nashville sunlight danced through the white valences over the windows. If things had been a little different, Hank might've told Audrey this new joke he had heard: "Why does the sun rise in the east?" "So the folks in east Nashville can get up first and cook breakfast for us."

There was a mockingbird singing merrily outside. Hank sat, as always, slumped on the base of his spine, chin on chest, eyes half closed, his bony legs thrust directly out in front of him. He silently cursed the sunlight and the damn mockingbird—he'd almost thought "goddamn" instead of "damn" before catching himself. He might swear, now and again, but he had once made a silent promise to God never to take His name in vain. He had even kept a cigar box in the car when he traveled with the Drifting Cowboys and made everybody who said "goddamn" put a quarter in it; as penance.

That damn mockingbird. If Hank could just see well enough to get his gun, that damn mockingbird would change his damn tune right quick, yessir, you could bet your sweet ass and two of your Uncle Herman's prize Herefords on that one, Bo. Hank reached out a trembling hand for a cup of Miss Ragland's chicory coffee, that lovely chestnutty coffee that he'd brought back home from his friends in south Louisiana. *Fine* coffee. He burned his tongue as Audrey sailed up to the table and fixed him in her death-ray gaze.

Miss Ragland retreated in double time to the kitchen and hauled Lycrecia with her: "Come on, honey, it's time to get you off to school."

Hank had not spoken to Lycrecia, as usual; he said as little to her as possible. The sight of her was a constant invocation of the sight of Audrey in the arms of another man, a sight he definitely did not need to be told about or reminded of.

"Hank." She wasn't yelling. That was a bad sign. The word came at him again, hissed through clenched teeth, the sound slapping at him like the tail end of a bullwhip snapping across his face. "Hank!" She knocked his coffee

cup out of his hand. White bone china didn't make much of a sound when it broke.

The hot coffee on his hand didn't hurt too badly; in fact, it almost took his mind off his headache and his raw stomach and his back, of course. Everything hurt today, but his back—that sumbitch was always there, simmering like a fire.

As the torrent of her words washed over him, he didn't even flinch. His only motion was the usual little tug with his right hand at his Adam's apple, which he always did when he was nervous. Then he raked the fingernails of his left hand up the side of his neck up to his chin, the only sound being a rasping of the nails against the stubble on his unshaven neck and chin.

"Clothes." He finally heard that word popping out of Audrey's lecture. Something about clothes. He thought detachedly that he was finally getting what he deserved for marrying the first gash he fucked more than once. He should've waited, he thought wearily. There were plenty of them now, gash was lined up from here to Little Rock and points west just aching and waiting to fuck Hank Williams. Things might be different now, if he'd just waited. . . .

Audrey's voice rose to window-rattling level. Hank couldn't even hear the mockingbird anymore. He tuned into what Audrey was saying: ". . . ought to goddamn kill you. You have shamed me in front of the neighbors. Thank God Miz Ragland got up early and cleaned up the mess before Lycrecia, my poor darling daughter, saw it, saw what was happening to her mother. My new clothes all over the front yard . . . just *ruint.* Hank, how could you do *such* a thing? I ought to call the po-lice. You belong in jail or in the nuthouse. Don't you care a *thing* about me, honey?"

He didn't know what the hell she was talking about. "Ordrey, what do you mean, honey? Looky here, I just got up and my head is splittin' open. Just lemme have some coffee—"

She stopped crying and the fury intensified. She grabbed up a knife off the plate of bacon and tried to stab him. Hank reacted without even thinking. He grabbed her wrist and twisted it until she screamed and dropped the knife.

She slapped him, hard, with her left hand, before he could do anything else.

She screamed: "What do you mean, what do *I* mean, you goddamn drunk. What I mean is all my clothes you ruint last night. My clothes that you threw in the front yard. You'll pay for this, oh *how* you'll pay." Her voice was shaking and she ran out of the room.

Clothes? Hank rubbed his eyes, dug his thumbs into his eyes till it hurt. He couldn't *remember.*

Audrey reappeared with an armload of dresses covered with mud and grass stains. She dumped them on the table, right in the middle of the bacon and biscuits and eggs and grits. *"There,* you drunk!"

Hank trembled a bit. This could be *serious.* He was beginning to get a few mental flashes, scattered scenes, of clothes getting stomped underfoot.

He got up slowly—look out for that knife. "Aw, Ordrey, honey, *baby,* did I do that? I'm *sorry.* Ole Hank didn't *mean* to do that."

She wept: "Didn't *mean* nothin'? Didn't mean *nothin'*? Look at this. Now I ain't got no clothes to wear. You won't never let me have nothin' or do nothin' or go nowhere or sing with you; you don't trust me, you don't love me!"

He took her in his arms: "Sugar, baby, ole Hank loves his Miss Ordrey. He'll buy her anything she wants, whatever her little heart desires. Ole Hank'll buy her all the clothes in the world."

"Really?" She asked it in a tiny voice and looked up at him through fluttering eyelids and tears.

"Whatever you want, darlin', you got it. Just name it."

"Oh, Hank, I *do* love you." She took his hands and led him into the bedroom. "Come on, baby, I'll make it right for you." She grabbed his crotch and giggled as he thrust his hand inside her robe.

"Got to buy you some underwear first thing, Ordrey. You ain't got nothin' on, have you."

She shed the robe and pressed up against him and he started to forget the back pain. She undressed him slowly and deliberately and he lay back and sighed as her head bobbed up and down at his crotch. That road pussy was okay, but Audrey was the only one who knew how to love him up right. For some reason, he had started having trouble getting an erection. Audrey knew how to get it up for him.

When she had snuggled up into the crook of his left arm and he had lit cigarettes for both of them, she stroked his thin body. "Hank, do you remember that first time we done it?"

He sure did. He didn't say anything.

She was almost purring. "I 'member you were *so* excited." She giggled. "You came in about *two* seconds and got it all over me and the back seat of the car. It's a wonder your mamma didn't notice it on the seat."

Hank winced. Lilly *had* noticed it, had found the tell-tale stains in her car and deduced where they'd come from. She'd cuffed him around awhile and made him take a bucket of hot water and some Dutch Cleanser and a rag and clean it up. The only time she ever referred to the incident again was the next night when Hank was getting ready to go out.

"If you got any ideas, boy, about seein' that blonde tramp again, make sure you use one a those things you been carryin' in your billfold so you don't catch nothin'." Hank had colored. The Trojan rubbers in his billfold were supposed to be his secret.

Audrey stirred and rubbed him and got him hard

again. She straddled him and pumped away until the pain in his back receded. He was suspended in a kind of billowy half-sleep and lightly rubbed her back while she nuzzled his face. Maybe, Hank thought, maybe things would get better. Maybe it would be like the good old days. He dropped off to sleep.

After Audrey had showered and dressed—where she had found a white mink, he didn't know, since she had sworn to him half an hour before that she had no clothes to wear—she walked with quick, impatient steps back into the bedroom, where Hank lay smoking another cigarette.

"Get up!" she snapped, pulling on a white glove. "Don't you try to forget what you promised me. We're goin' shoppin' to buy me some new clothes."

Hank felt his back pain return, in a rush.

They were riding along in the Cadillac back to Nashville. Hank was stretched out as close to horizontal as he could get in the back seat, and the Drifting Cowboys arranged themselves as best they could. Hank didn't often ride with them anymore; he usually flew. Hank finally put away his copy of *Billboard* and his copy of *The Cash Box* without reading the charts out loud so that everybody would know where he was on the charts that week and could share his joy. He had folded away his press clips: Hank Williams draws 16,500 paid admissions in Indianapolis, New Years, 1951. There was a longer one, that was now a pain in the ass to the Cowboys, they had heard it so many times: "[Alabama]Governor James E. Folsom has paid an official tribute to one of Alabama's hillbilly songwriters, Hank Williams. Folsom issued a formal citation proclaiming that 'Alabama is proud of Hank Williams and wishes for him many more years of eventful singing, playing, and composing. . . . The folk music field of America has been greatly enriched by his works.'"

His works, his works, his works, his works. Hank nodded off to the rhythm. His cigarette burned down to his lips before one of the Cowboys noticed it and plucked it away. That was starting to happen often. He would nod off and his cigarette would burn down to his lips or his fingers and he wouldn't even feel the pain from the burn: he was totally unconscious. Hank didn't even wake up. He had a bottle of pills in his left breast pocket, a loaded .38 in the right breast pocket, and his boots were full of tiny airline bottles of whiskey. He was armed against anything.

The Cowboys stopped outside Nashville and Don Helms called Audrey from a phone booth—by prearranged order. She had ordered the band to call her every time they were coming back into town and to give her a reading of Hank's condition. If they had time to give her a graphic description over the phone, then he was obviously in no condition to come home and bother her. She told Helms to drop Hank off at the Madison sanitarium. On *her* orders. That was all the authorization that was needed. Put him in the deep freeze until he was needed again. Off Hank went. As long as they kept him sedated and let him have his comic books and as long as he was able to bribe the attendants to bring him whiskey, he didn't mind too much. Until his brain started to clear and he thought about his little son and then he started to howl.

They shot him up with Nembutal and he finally slept.

White-up, red-down, white-up, red-down, whiteup reddown. Hank was reciting the words over and over to himself as he threaded his way through the crowd at Tootsie's on his way to go take a leak. He hadn't slept in two days and there was an unnatural heightened paleness about his gaunt face. His skeletal cheeks had an unhealthy flush. His eyes were glittering and his mouth was dry and he kept grinding his teeth and cracking his knuckles and talking too fast and laughing too loud. He was on speed. Speed was the fuel on which musicians ran. Everybody knew you couldn't play Georgia tonight and drive to Arkansas in time to play there tomorrow night without a little speed. The truck drivers had it first but once the musicians discovered it they adopted speed like it was Jesus and whiskey and pussy all wrapped up in one little pill. It was magic: you could play one-nighters all week and then get back to Nashville in time to play the Opry, thus meeting your contract demands. (The Opry was a stern mistress—she booked you on the road for good money but she demanded that you come home Saturday nights to play for scale.) It was just that at some point you had to come down and sleep; you could just not stay awake forever. Musicians had tried and failed. When it was time to come down, you could try alcohol, which was risky, or you could try downers. Equally risky, but more dependable than alcohol.

White-up: Hank had to remember that the white pills in his ornate silver pillbox were uppers. *Red-down:* he had to know that the reds were downers, tranks, tranquilizers, usually "cold pills" that were mostly codeine. Whites were ahead. Once he got to roaring, he didn't want to ever stop. Keep the drinks flowing and keep the juke-box going, he said. With speed, Saturday night could now and then be stretched to last all week. You could howl and roar for days.

Hank had been going at it ever since Tony Bennett's recording of his "Cold, Cold Heart" had hit number one on the pop charts. He had the *Billboard* chart ready in his pocket, if you didn't believe him. Being number one on the folk chart was one thing—hell, any fool could do that and *had*—but the pop chart was the *outside* world.

Hank, popping his whites with a Jax beer chaser, didn't know that Tony Bennett hadn't just one day decided to record a song by that genius, Hank Williams. Tony Bennett had never heard of Hank Williams. Mitch

Miller at Columbia Records finally decided he liked
"Cold, Cold Heart" and he persuaded Bennett to record
it. Bennett's version was as smooth as Hank's was raw.
But it didn't matter; the outside world was beginning to
notice Hank's genius.

Hank was yelling for Vic McAlpin, as he weaved
through the packed bodies and smoke and noise. "Vic!
Girl here knows where they's a party. We got to move it
on out of here, hoss." Hank was lurching a bit and hanging on to an overstuffed young lady.

When Vic finally got Hank out to Franklin Road to
put him to bed, Audrey wouldn't open the door. So Hank
spent the night at the Tulane Hotel, which was becoming
a frequent home-away-from-home for him. Vic helped
him to bed. He was shocked at how light Hank was: he
seemed to weigh next to nothing. People at the Opry
called Hank "gimly-ass" and joked that he could change
clothes in the barrel of a shotgun, he was that skinny. Vic
felt a profound pity for his friend; undressed and in bed
he looked like a stove-up wino. But there was nothing he
could do about it.

"Cold, Cold Heart" was a runaway hit, both for Hank
and for Tony Bennett. Hank even put an extra check in
the mail for Paul Gilley.

When he did "Cold, Cold Heart" at the Opry in late
January of 1951, he got a tidal wave of applause. He was
rubbed a little bit raw, though, by the way Red Foley
introduced him. He had referred to Hank as "tonight's
guest"—which was fine as far as it went, for Hank sure
felt he *ought* to get star billing—and then Red had said,
"He's welcome here every week if he can make it." So
what if he missed an Opry show now and then? Didn't
everybody? There was no need to talk about it on the
radio. And not too long ago, Red had after Hank finished
a song, said, over the *air,* "Now, Hank, don't stray off too

far; we want you to come back later in the program and
do another number." As if he was in the habit of wandering off like some drunk. Hank was a little hot and he'd
told Red so; Red apologized. He didn't mention that Jim
Denny had started, after the Baltimore Hippodrome incident, to hire personal bodyguards for Hank when he was
on the road. Their only job was to protect him from himself: to keep him from drinking. They didn't know he
actually wasn't drinking all that much—and it didn't
take much for him anyway. It was more the drugs and
the combination of those drugs with alcohol. Drugs became easier for Hank to get than alcohol. He could get
uppers and downers—everybody took them—in a *parking lot* if he had to. The stronger stuff he had discovered
in his drying-out spells in hospitals. The doctors used
massive amounts of tranquilizers on him.

He liked those drugs, especially as his back pain got
worse and his wife problems and his mother problems
plagued him more and more. On the road, he would bribe
anybody to get him anything in the way of sedation,
whether it be alcohol or chemicals. He never even
thought about the next day anymore; he just wanted today to black itself out, and as soon as possible, please, if
you don't fucking mind.

It was a bad one, he knew that when he woke up. He
was bad sick. His brain was numb and he could only
think in slow motion but everything else hurt, oh how it
hurt. His back was just a hornet's nest. His stomach felt
like it had collapsed. Everything else ached; his liver was
throbbing, it hurt to take a breath, his heartbeat felt ir-
regular and weak. He knew if he tried to get out of bed he
would die. He looked around as much as he could without moving his head. He was in a hotel room. Patches of
memory started coming back. With great difficulty and
pain, he reached the phone and told the front desk that
he needed a doctor. He lay back, exhausted by the exer-

tion. He remembered: the awful fight with Audrey when he'd told her what he'd been dreading having to tell her for years. It wasn't *his* idea, he'd told her, but the Opry people and the people at WSM had asked him—very nicely—not to have Audrey on as part of a duet anymore, because it just wasn't working out. *Not* that she couldn't sing; it just wasn't working and could Hank please tell her that. It worried him sick for days. He knew he had to tell her and he didn't know how. Finally, he just flat-out told her. She was silent at first and he thought maybe she had guessed the truth all along and was going to take it with no problem. Then, she seemed to start . . . *swelling up*. It frightened him. Then she seemed to just explode and come apart at the seams and called him everything there was to call him and accused him of everything she hadn't yet accused him of. She started raining dishes on him and he knew he had to get out of there. He had fled to . . . Montgomery, to Mamma's. He got an icy reception there: "What're you doin' here, son? Why ain't you workin'? It's that woman again, ain't it? I done told you, if you can't handle her, don't come runnin' to me with your tail tucked between your legs." Lilly was jealous, of course. She had gotten no checks lately from Hank; he had been busy covering Audrey's overdrafts. It was as if Lilly and Audrey ran separate armed camps—neither would venture into the other's territory —and Hank shuttled back and forth like some poor double-prisoner-of-war. If Audrey felt neglected, then Lilly would feel twice as neglected and even betrayed. There was no solution, no answer for Hank. He finally had to flee from Lilly. He couldn't go back to Audrey. Where could he go? *Louisiana,* he finally decided. They liked him there. Shreveport was his town, anyway.

Hank heard his hotel room door being unlocked. Two ambulance attendants wheeled a stretcher in. The desk clerk at the hotel in Shreveport, after seeing and hearing about some of Hank Williams's parties the last couple of days, had called an ambulance instead of a doctor.

Since all they had on their hands seemed to be a drunk and not a medical emergency, the Wellman's Ambulance attendants took Hank out to the North Louisiana Sanitarium. He told them he'd been there before. They dropped him there at one PM, May 21, 1951.

Once he was admitted and put to bed in Room 215, Dr. G. H. Cassity went up to examine Hank. They talked quietly; Hank did not seem to be in too bad a shape. He was clearly disturbed, though. Dr. Cassity gave him one-hundred milligrams of Demerol first thing, to calm him down. He gave orders for the nurses to start an intravenous solution of Vitadex and Vitamin B flowing into Hank's thin arm: the man looked malnourished.

Dr. Cassity went back to his office and wrote his preliminary report. For "working diagnosis," he wrote "acute alcoholism." Hank's temperature, he noted, was 99.2 degrees. Hank's "facies and general appearance" was "dull." In the section for "physical findings," Dr. Cassity wrote, "No lesions or physical abnormalities found except in lower spine. He complains of severe pain from five lumbar vertebra to end of sacrum. His symptoms are something like those of a displaced disc, however, he recalls no injury to this region."

Dr. Cassity started a new page for his "Personal History." He wrote that the patient seemed to be suffering from "acute alcoholism" as well as a "herniated intervertebral disc." He wrote that his patient "has been drinking about four days and otherwise seems in good physical condition. Seems to think he has a lot of mental worries."

"Correction," Dr. Cassity amended to that, "he has some kind of a very painful low back condition not yet diagnosed."

Hank was already asleep. When he woke up, they X-rayed him and another doctor looked him over. The Demerol came around again at four PM and he nodded

off. He got another hundred milligrams of Demerol at ten
PM and another at one AM and another at four AM and
another at eight AM. He threw up his breakfast, so they
hooked up the liquid vitamins again. They stopped the
Demerol and tried sodium luminal and Nembutal sup-
positories. Then they added the Demerol for his back
pain. Plus the Nicotinamide in two-hundred-milligram
doses.

His "Personal History" now included the comment
that for the past several months he had "noticed pain in
his low back and right leg. He thinks that he has gradually gotten worse so that he can hardly get about at times
. . . possible rupture of the fourth or fifth lumbar
disc. . . . Patient was measured for a lumbrosacral brace
which will be fitted within the next few days."

His X-ray report said that Hank had a spina bifida
occulta of the first sacral segment of the lower spine, a
birth defect that had never been treated or diagnosed before. No attention was paid to that. Dr. Cassity wrote
that the back pain was "probably a dislocated disc. . . .
The patient does not distinctly recall any serious injury to
his back."

The birth defect was not bothered with; only treatment
in early childhood could have eliminated its effects. Now
it was too late.

After three days in bed, Hank was—as Dr. Cassity
wrote down—"completely cleaned up [but] complaining
of back." At 2:30 the afternoon of May 24, he was discharged. They had given him a back brace but it didn't
help. There was nothing anybody could do to help him.
He recalled a saying he used to repeat to himself in south
Alabama: "Ain't no country boy seen a city doctor and
lived to tell about it." Hank had never had a physical
examination until he tried to enlist and that had been
such a cursory exam it was laughable. Once, even when
he was nurturing the secret belief that he had "spinal

TB," he had held the outside hope that big-city doctors might be able to help him. Didn't seem to be so.

He went back to Nashville, to Franklin Road, to see what was waiting for him there. "Cold, Cold Heart," he noticed when he finally located a copy of *Billboard*, was holding up nicely on the charts. He had to go see how his "family" was holding up. After three days of being tranked out, he was a little fuzzy, was feeling a little vague. He needed a little help to get his confidence back. He thought about holing up at Camp Kowaliga or somewhere else for a couple of days: no. He just remembered that he had come to Shreveport to do just that before things got so . . . out of hand. He had no idea what he'd been doing right before he'd gone into the sanitarium, who had helped him spend his money, helped him drink and dope himself into a corner. All he had to do was to show his face and "friends" would pop out of the walls.

Sometimes he kind of enjoyed having a carnival swirling around him and he would peel the bills off his poke to keep it going. People knew that, he guessed. He could never remember their names or faces, even if they showed up at party after party.

Well, the hell with that. He wanted to go home and see his little baby boy again.

Audrey was surprisingly . . . *cordial.* Not friendly, certainly not romantic, and yet not overtly hostile, either. She was fairly decent, she was . . . What the hell she was *polite,* Hank finally decided. At first that made him madder than if she'd been hissing and throwing daggers at him. He was used to that. He could dodge knives easier than he could live with a woman who just seemed to pleasantly treat him like another piece of her precious Chinese furniture. He didn't know and she wasn't ready yet to tell him that what he took for a sudden change in Audrey was fairly drastic. What he saw on the surface was easy to explain but he couldn't see it: she had discovered vodka. No one could smell it, it mixed well with everything from morning's orange juice to afternoon's Coca-Cola to . . . anything. When she had drunk before it had always been rather savage and out in the open, to compete with him. No more. Now it was done behind the kitchen door, in the pantry, after he went to sleep. He and Audrey had trouble talking—they always had, but now it was worse. It made Hank real uneasy. He couldn't figure her from one minute to the next. She had quit harping on her singing career. Hank noticed that she still put up his latest records on the wall in the den: "Cold, Cold Heart" and "Howlin' at the Moon" were up there. "Oh yeah," she said distantly, her voice seeming to float in from about a half mile away, "Pappy—I mean Fred Rose—wants you to call him sometime, when you get a chance."

When he got a chance! The damn cunt! He held himself back. The reason he went to a hospital was so he could get well so he could be with his family and continue his career, wasn't it? Well, then, he had to do just that.

Things became very strange at Franklin Road. Bocephus was too young to notice it. Lycrecia lived in a constant tension: Hank was the man of the house but he wasn't her father and he really didn't like her. Things between Hank and Audrey were very strained. Miss Ragland tried to just do her job and work around the emotional time bomb that the house was seeming to become. Hank worked away at his large gun collection on the rare night that he wasn't touring, and Audrey, while she seemed to be placid, was carving and sharpening her emotional knives on that whetstone of jealousy that she would never let go of. Hank and Audrey, when they did talk, might scare Miss Ragland or Lycrecia, not so much with what they said as with the way they said it. Hank had a no-nonsense, this-is-the-way-it-will-be tone about his talk usually and Audrey mostly was shrill and demanding. It got to be scary when they changed attitudes. He got hysterical; she was grim and matter-of-fact.

Hank never dared mention his personal life to all the people besides Audrey and Lilly who were making money off him: Fred, Wesley, promoter Oscar Davis, WSM, the Opry, Jim Denny, M-G-M, Frank Walker, and many more. He was personally afraid that if he didn't keep the money pouring in, they might drop him. *Hey, motherfucker,* he himself would say, I know you're good, but what can you do for me *tomorrow?* He knew, Hank knew, that he was good—but he had no guarantees, he had no way of knowing whether or not he might be shit-canned tomorrow morning. He knew that he *wouldn't* be but he also knew that he *could* be, and he started to think about the very slight difference in meaning between the two words: *wouldn't* and *could.*

Hank knew that he had good records following "Cold, Cold Heart." He had "I Can't Help It" and "Howlin' at the Moon" and "Hey Good Lookin'." He wasn't sure about what came after that but he didn't think that far ahead. Anytime he started to feel his back acting up bad or when he started to get bad danger signals from Franklin Road or from Montgomery, all he thought about was: Where is there some drugs, and is there enough alkie around?

Hank still had no manager, no lawyer, no friend he could trust. He had no idea whether or not he was getting stolen blind on all the money he was supposed to be making. He heard about certain sums of money, he read about certain sums of money in the music trades; he didn't know if that was true or wasn't true. And he didn't know who to ask, or who to trust to ask, which was actually more important. He was afraid to talk to Pappy about it; he *knew* that Pappy was honest. He didn't know Wesley well at all, but he figured that if Pappy had turned the business over to Wesley, then Wesley must be all right. The other people—he just didn't know, but what

the hell could he do? It was all he could do to make all
the road dates (and he missed some of those), and to try
to keep the terms of the Grand Ole Opry Contract, which
called for him to play the Opry 26 weeks of the year,
which was half the year, and to play it for scale, for
peanuts, for *no-thing.* It was enough to make him depressed; it was just about enough to encourage anybody
to have a drink. He had one. Audrey had two. He had
one. She had two more. He started getting a bit uneasy.
He was supposed to be the drunk in this family. Audrey's
shrill voice pinned him from the darkness of her chair:
"Go ahead, Mr. Big Star, drink your drinks and think
your thoughts and forget about us you leave behind."

He jumped up. He didn't have to hear that kind of
crap. He went out in the backyard. His dog Skip, a mon-
grel who was a damn smart squirrel dog; and Jimmy,
who was Audrey's ignorant collie dog, both came up to
lick his hands. He patted them both on their heads. He
remembered his old song about being in the doghouse,
"Move It on Over." All of a sudden, a dog's life wasn't
looking too bad, compared with what some human be-
ings had to go through.

There were some good times, too, he knew. Lycrecia's
eighth birthday party: he had really tried to warm up to
her. Hank bought her Trigger, a beautiful pony, and
Lycrecia rode in the Robertson Academy Horse Show.
Pappy had come over to Franklin Road for the birthday
party and had played the piano while he and Hank sang
duets. Fred took home movies with his new Bell and
Howell movie camera. Hank had asked Audrey, "Do you
think she'll ever call me Daddy?" Audrey had to rush off
to the kitchen to take off some thing or other before she
had a chance to answer, and the subject just wasn't
brought up again.

They used to—he and Audrey used to act just like high
school kids who couldn't keep their hands off each other.
He ought to have known, back there in Montgomery

years ago, when he and Audrey were on rival radio stations and he kept talking around town about her as "that cunt that's buttin' heads with me" because he and she were the two young hot acts in town, he ought to have seen that she couldn't control the ambition inside her. She had joined his band and he knew that she was just a mediocre singer at best. Still, he didn't care.

He'd almost fought his Cowboys one day when they thought he was asleep and were talking about how they hated to try to play behind Audrey's singing, it was like chasing down a damn butterfly: "She sounds like a bastard cat in heat. But Hank lets her sing because he just wants to protect that pussy." Hank started to jump up and tear their heads off, but he realized they were right. He laughed to himself; hell, it *did* show that he cared about his pussy.

Nashville was changing her into something he disliked and distrusted: a woman who thought that jewelry and fine clothes and a big house were the most important things you could have and *should* have. They'd had a bitter argument one day over a couple that Audrey wanted to invite over. Hank knew them; he thought they were ass-kissers who would have snubbed him as an ignorant hillbilly if it wasn't for his fame, and he told Audrey so. Audrey got her back up: she had informed him that this couple was the sort of people *"we ought to be associating with in our present position."* That's just what she had said: in our present position. He couldn't believe it. He said there were pigs and goats he knew and *their* present position was that they wouldn't allow that particular couple to share their damn pigsties with them. Audrey looked around for something to throw and he was out the door, gone. In our present *position*. In a horse's ass.

Her jealousy of his success—Hank automatically, unconsciously felt his back pocket to make sure that the latest *Billboard* chart was there ("Howlin' at the Moon" was moving up nicely)—and her sudden desire for social climbing were things he just could not understand.

Hank sat outside and chain-smoked and thought about things till he was sure she was asleep. Then, and only then, did he go inside and pour himself two fingers of sour mash. He had to go to Montgomery soon and he knew that would stir up more trouble. Well, there was no helping it.

July 15 had been a big day. Mayor James Worthington had officially designated it as "Hank Williams Day" in Montgomery. They'd had a big show at the coliseum with Mother Maybelle Carter and her daughters and Hank.

Hank's old friend Braxton Shuffert had gotten up on stage and sung with him for the first time in a dozen years. They were sitting around backstage before the show, talking over old times, when a teen-aged boy with a guitar sneaked in past the backstage guards. "Hey, Hank," he said, "I gotta sing on your show today."

Hank looked the boy over without sitting up from his slump and without changing expression. The boy was pleading, he could see that. Hank decided not to throw him to the police.

"Well, son, I wouldn't mind it myself but the program's already made up. There ain't no more room on the program."

"Please, Hank, I just wanta sing *one* song on your show. I don't sing nothin' but your songs."

"Weeellll. I'll let you sing *one,* then. Which one do you wanta sing?"

"I wanta sing 'Hey, Good Lookin'.' "

"Wait a minute, *I* was gonna sing that."

"Please, Hank, oh please, let me sing it."

"Well, okay. I'll just havta sing somethin' else, I guess."

* * *

Braxton couldn't believe that, and that evening as they all sat around the big dining room table at Lilly's, he told the story to everybody who would listen. Hank's Montgomery friends—many of them friends he didn't know he had—were crowded in. Hank and Braxton had driven Audrey and Bocephus straight out to the airport after the show: she needed to get back to Nashville right away, she said. She and Lilly didn't get a chance to say hello. Lilly was smiling, for a change, that evening. Her son, the one that *she* had started out in the music business, had come home driving a golden chariot and the townspeople turned out to honor him. It was quite a tribute to her and to all she had done for her only boy. It was quite touching, when you thought about it.

Lilly's purse was thicker, thanks to a wad of greenbacks added to it that afternoon. She smiled and squeezed her baby boy's shoulder.

Before he left Montgomery, Hank slipped out to visit awhile with Father Purcell. They had a long, sober talk. Hank wouldn't listen to the doctors at St. Jude's, so the doctors had gone to Father Purcell. The priest spelled out to Hank the exact nature of his birth defect and the rate at which it was going to gradually cripple him. Ironically, Father Purcell's obsession was working with and trying to help spastic children. Hank broke down and wept with the priest and prayed with him. When his tears dried and they had finally talked it all out, Hank pledged to send four hundred dollars a month to help Father Purcell's work. Maybe it was too late for him, but he could help the children. He did not tell anyone that he was contributing four hundred dollars a month to a Catholic orphanage.

Hank and Dudley liked each other on sight. Dudley saw before him a genuine, no-bullshit superstar whose massive appeal was his authentic simplicity. He didn't smile unless he meant it, which wasn't often, and he told Dudley right up-front just what Dudley could expect for his money: "I like it plain and simple, no hot licks and no extrys. I like my music *vanilla.*" Dudley knew he had a rare specimen in this Williams fellow, whom he invariably called "Mr. Hanks." This fellow *commanded* respect, he didn't have to demand it or ask for it. He was a *centurion* or whatever it was those Roman leaders were called in *King of Kings,* which Dudley had just seem. It spelled *box office,* and that always made Dudley happy.

Hank. for his part, was amused by Dudley: a fast-talking banty-rooster-sized southern politician. Hank knew a lot of politicians; knew Governor "Big Jim" Folsom of Alabama, knew Jimmie Davis, who had been governor of Louisiana, knew a banty-rooster state legislator in Alabama named George Wallace. Dudley, though, didn't seem to take it seriously.

Dudley liked to have his fun and he understood what entertainment was—it was not far from politics and vice versa. Dudley himself fussed over his "official" biographical press release until he was satisfied that it presented an accurate portrayal of him. It began: "The fabulous story of Senator Dudley J. LeBlanc reads as if it might have been written by a most imaginative spinner of tales." That it did. Dudley claimed that he was descended from Rene LeBlanc, "the notary public of [the poem] "Evangeline." He came out of rural Louisiana, enduring a self-professed struggle that included not only putting himself but also four brothers and two cousins through college. Dudley went on to earn a field commission in World War I, organize an insurance fortune, sell tobacco and much more—the man was a dynamo.

"After several years devoted to the study of nutrition," his biography notes with complete seriousness, "he developed the wonderful medical compound—HADACOL. Although recognized as a marvelous boon to humanity, the miraculous growth of the Hadacol enterprise in four short years is a phenomenon of never-ending amazement. But Senator LeBlanc has not been content merely to minister to the physical needs of his fellow men: their political well-being has also been close to his heart. He decided to take time from the manifold demands of his extensive business to do something concrete for the betterment of the people of Louisiana. Always an effective speaker, he campaigned for and was elected to that august law-making body, the Senate of the Sovereign State of Louisiana." It went on and on. Hank, when he read it, laughed and laughed. He loved Louisianians and Dudley was one of the best. Dudley had sponsored Hank's "Health and Happiness" radio show and now was mounting his greatest campaign ever. Medicine shows had been profitable throughout rural America, but always on a modest scale. Dudley had a grand vision of a mammoth Hadacol Caravan traversing the length and breadth of America, introducing one and all to the glories of Hadacol and—while he was at it—to the political worth of Senator LeBlanc. Hadacol itself, said Bob Hope, who was part of the Hadacol Caravan, was "Seven-Up with a dash of alcohol, but they say there was more alcohol in there than there was supposed to be. I think they slipped a little extra vial of something funny in there . . ." Dudley had mixed motives for what he did to promote his twenty-four-proof medicine and himself: he wanted to try again for the governorship of Louisiana, he wanted to make Hadacol respectable enough to slither past the increasingly stern gaze of health authorities, and . . . well, he just couldn't help himself: he wanted to throw a hell of a bash. That's mainly why Hank liked Dudley.

He decided to stage the biggest tour the country had seen. Before he started booking entertainment and venues, he secured twenty-one railroad cars for the Hadacol Caravan, plus five long-haul trucks to carry equipment. Everything would be first class. He started booking entertainment: Dick Haymes, Carmen Miranda, Jack Demp-

sey, Tony Martin and his Orchestra, Sharkey and his
Dixieland Band, Cesar Romero, acrobats, circus clowns,
midgets, giants, jugglers, and—to satisfy the hillbillies,
since the Caravan would venture no farther north than
Indiana—Minnie Pearl and Hank Williams. Bob Hope,
Milton Berle, Jack Benny and Jimmy Durante were
scheduled for some of the bigger cities. Dudley had
booked the tour straight through from August 15, 1951,
to October 2 without a single day off: one nighters all the
way, by Pullman car. From New Iberia, Louisiana, on
August 15 all the way through Mississippi and Alabama
and Georgia and South Carolina and Virginia and West
Virginia and Kentucky and Ohio and Indiana and . . .
It just didn't stop. Hank tucked the itinerary into his coat
pocket that first day in New Iberia and went to find Dudley, trudging across the high school's football field. Hank
wanted to tell Dudley that he approved of this forty-nine-
stop whistle tour; it was just the sort of thing somebody
should be doing for audiences. The price of admission
was a Hadacol box-top and fifty cents.

"Dudley." Dudley flinched a bit.

"Yes, Mr. Hanks?"

"Dudley, you just as full of shit as a Christmas turkey,
but I'm gonna be easy on you, because I *like* you."

"Well, Mr. Hanks, we all just one big happy family
here."

For a while, Hank thought that was true. The entertainment was so varied that there was little jealousy, even
though Hank was soon picked to close the shows because
no one could follow him on stage: the crowds wouldn't
allow it. They wanted Hank.

The Drifting Cowboys saw a new Hank: he had never
been so cocky and self-confident. He strutted his stuff
backstage while Tony Martin kicked off the show with
"Wagon Wheels" and Hank drew his own little entou-
rage. The chorus girls had never seen anything like this
hillbilly ramrod, so cool and authoritative and so sure of

himself and so able to handle a crowd. Hank didn't need
the bottle: he was getting laid every time he turned over
in bed. He was the undisputed number one country
singer and songwriter alive, he was slaying audiences
nightly on the Hadacol trail, he had to beat the pussy off
with a stick, he was just flying high.

Bob Hope was flown in to make one of his two
Hadacol appearances in Louisville. Hank, who closed all
the Hadacol shows, was moved to next to last: next to
Hope. After he did "Lovesick Blues," though, the crowd
wouldn't let him leave. He begged off after three encores
but the roar wouldn't subside. Bob Hope tried to go on.
The crowd ignored him. Hank passed Hope backstage:
"Good luck, hoss, I wouldn't go on neither, if I was
you." Hope finally put on a cowboy hat and went out and
introduced himself as "Hank Hope."

Hank was watching and liked what he saw.

In Kansas City, Milton Berle flew in to close the show
and to be the M.C. Berle got on Hank's fighting side as
soon as he got there. Hank heard that Berle was trying to
eject a photographer friend of his. Hank charged Berle:
"This boy is just tryin' to make a livin' like the rest of us.
Don't you be tellin' him what all he should be takin'
pitchers of. Don't tell him nothin' and don't be touchin'
him." Berle backed off: what had he descended into? Still,
Berle couldn't stop being the ham. While Dick Haymes
was doing "Old Man River," Berle put on an Aunt Je-
mima kerchief and started miming "Mammy" on the
stage apron. Hank said he would break his damn guitar
over Berle's head unless Berle cut that shit out. The message was received and acknowledged. Berle didn't even
try to close the show. Hank did.

Bob Hope had already gone to Dudley and told him he
was not going to follow Hank on anymore shows. He
didn't need the ridicule. He knew when he was out of
place. He still had, as even he called it, the last laugh. He
was the only entertainer on the Hadacol Caravan to get

paid. Only thirty-four shows (thus thirty-four straight days worked) were played before Dudley's Caravan stuttered to a halt in Dallas. Bob Hope had demanded and received a check for $30,000 for his two shows. Nobody else got anything but expenses and memories.

Hank had not even been angry when the great medicine show fraud folded around him. He had known Dudley to be nothing but a big-talking empty tent. He had been fun, though.

Hank was quiet in Henry Cannon's Beechcraft Bonanza on September 18 as he and Minnie—who was married to Henry—and Henry flew back to Nashville. Several times during the Caravan's run, Hank and Minnie had flown back to Nashville to play the Opry on Saturday night before rejoining the Hadacol tour. The past few weeks, Hank had started calling home four and five times a night. Audrey was never there. That's when he started wanting to fly back more often to play the Opry. Something was bothering him.

When the Hadacol Caravan began, people around Hank thought he was getting healthy again. By the time it was over, they were worrying. He would race his Cadillac out Franklin Road, search the house, and then start hitting all the night spots, looking for Audrey. A lot of Nashville women tried to dissuade him: he was quite the catch, even if he was known to take a drink. He still chased after Audrey, but his glance grew darker and darker every time he came home to find her "out." Miss Ragland didn't know where she was.

Hank wrote—or pretended to write, you could never tell with him; he would "write" the same song two or three times for different people to impress them—some of his sadder songs in Henry Cannon's airplane. Still, people around him always knew that he was writing. He and Moon Mullican, the great piano stomper out of Texas, put their heads together on Henry's plane to write

"Jambalaya (On the Bayou)" but only Hank's name was listed as author.

Hank's Hollywood offer came through. The moving pictures finally appreciated what Pappy and Wesley were trying to sell every day. Producer Joe Pasternak had first flung out a small redneck role as bait for Hank. Nothing. He wasn't biting.

Then, M-G-M gave Hank a blank check. He signed a movie deal before he went to Hollywood. Frank Walker of M-G-M Records signed it with him. Then, Hank went to Hollywood to meet with Dore Schary at M-G-M. They did not get along and the M-G-M movie deal was killed, very quietly. Wesley said it was because Hank was discourteous to Mr. Schary and had neglected to take his hat off and had put his feet up on Mr. Schary's desk and had otherwise acted disrespectful. M-G-M denied that there had ever been a movie deal.

Hank shrugged it off. If it was real, he'd see it again, he figured. It was all he could do to keep up with what was happening every day. He didn't seem to have the time to write songs as much as he used to and he wasn't recording and hadn't seen Pappy in a while. And anyway, Pappy never called him. Wesley seemed to be running things and *he* never called unless he thought it was urgent business.

Hank had his *Billboard* charts—they had three charts now for the hillbillies: jukebox play, retail sales, and radio play. Hank was not doing as well as he ought to. He was scattered across all three charts at lower positions with "Hey, Good Lookin'," "Crazy Heart," and "Lonesome Whistle." That did not make him feel good. He should be doing better than that. He called Pappy. Pappy was not reassuring. He sounded a little bit vague, as a matter of fact. It was like he was hinting that Hank ought to call back later when he had some hot material to record. Hank knew that wasn't what Pappy said, but that was the message he felt. And he felt really kind of cut loose and abandoned. He knew it wasn't so, but Hank suddenly felt that his Nashville support was eroding. He knew that everyone had traded stories about his Vegas mess: he was drunk at the show at the Last Frontier Casino; the audience was full of rubes too poor and too stupid to gamble. Las Vegas had decided that hillbillies were a poor bet, at best.

Hank had tried to convince them otherwise: he had told them about the time that he was three or four hours late getting on stage at the Sportatorium in Dallas and how all the crowd had waited and cheered him when he'd finally walked out on stage and said "Good mornin'." And there was that other time, where the hell was it, an outdoor show somewhere or other and when he'd been held up by the weather or something, just the sight of his airplane buzzing the stadium before landing had produced a standing ovation.

Hell, Hank figured, things would be bad if he wanted them to be bad and wouldn't be if he didn't want them to be. He still had everything going his way: everybody told him that he was the number one country singer around. Nobody was writing country songs that were getting covered in New York but him. He *was* the hoss, wasn't he?

He had published, with the aid of a ghost-writer, Jimmy Rule, a slim volume titled "Hank Williams Tells How to Write Folk and Western Music to Sell." It was not much of a book, but it was entirely practical and Hank's voice could not be found anywhere in the writing. The little book warned about the "song sharks" that lived in Nashville and were just lying in wait to steal songs from writers. Everybody in Nashville hooted about it, but Hank was rather proud of it. Nobody else had bothered to turn out a book like that, one that might actually help the civilians. Hank felt quite proud.

He also felt more and more alone. He had never been one to go out and drag people in to visit him, he knew that, but all of a sudden nobody would ever come to

Franklin Road but Audrey's friends. And those were people that—he hated to badmouth anybody, but those were people in danger of dying from their own bad breath. Those were not people he would personally drag out of burning buildings and give mouth-to-mouth resuscitation to. He might give them—and he would start to tell them what he would give them when he felt damn good and ready—the sweat off his balls if they were dying of thirst. Maybe. Of if they were on fire, he might piss on them. Maybe.

Hank finally agreed to Audrey's demands to open a store. He thought it might give her something to do and might calm her down a little. Audrey pointed out to him that Ernest Tubb was doing well with his record store, so why couldn't they cash in too? She finally decided on a western clothing store: Hank and Audrey's Corral. She rented a shop down on Commerce, near Tubb's record store, and had it decorated in true Audrey style. The outside was fake-log cabin, there was a big wagon-wheel lamp hanging over the entrance, and there was a big neon sign with pictures of Hank and Audrey on it. The interior was equally rustic. Hank was a little surprised to see the little Hank and Audrey dolls that were on sale. Hank really didn't think the public would tear down the store's walls to buy crap like that, but you never could tell. He talked WSM into broadcasting the grand opening of the Corral. He and the Drifting Cowboys sang and then Audrey had to sing and Big Bill Lister, whom Hank had open his shows for him, sang. Not a bad little show.

If he had actually thought that it would mollify Audrey, she had let him know right quick that it hadn't.

He came in off the road and she wasn't home. Miss Ragland didn't know where she was. No, Hank told her, he wasn't hungry. He poured whiskey into a water glass and sipped from it while he just kind of wandered around the den.

He thought about taking a gun and going out and looking for her, but he was just too damned tired to. He had started wearing his back brace and sometimes walked with a cane when his leg was acting up. He wandered in to check on Bocephus and his eyes misted up a little bit at the sight of the boy, his boy, now almost three, sleeping peacefully with just the soft glow of the nightlight on him.

Hank went to his desk, shoved aside the fan mail and the unopened letters from the bank, and poured out his heart in an awkward little poem to his son. "Little Bocephus" told Hank's son that he was his daddy's best pal and warned him about all the pitfalls of life, the sorrow and heartbreak that he himself knew so well. Hank was weeping by the time he finished it. [Although he never intended it to be anything but a father's note to his child, the poem later found its way into that great copyright catalog known as "Fred Rose Music" and, many years later, M-G-M would persuade Hank Jr.—Bocephus—to record it, with an appropriate tear-jerking instrumental background.]

Hank was back out on the road in a fury: if nothing else, he still had his audience. He was performing with an intensity that the Cowboys hadn't known was there, a reservoir of energy above his usual effort. Offstage, he spoke little. He was moody, his band decided.

He was also having to pay off a few people to hush certain things up in the area of offstage behavior. In Chattanooga, a hotel maid went into his room to clean and found him putting a needle into his arm. When he saw her, he reached for a pistol, aimed at her and pulled the trigger. The gun misfired and she knocked him out with a lamp over the head. In Birmingham, he gathered framed portraits from the hotel's hallway, lined them up, and used them for target practice. Police caught him in his hotel room with a fifteen-year-old girl, who was stripping for him while he played guitar. The police everywhere were usually pretty tolerant of him, but his cases of entertaining minor girls cost him a little bit. He started telling police he was actually Herman P. Willis, which didn't always work, or that he was George Morgan, which did work several times. He would sing Morgan's hit "Candy Kisses" to prove that was who he was. Morgan was furious when he found out that he was acquiring a police record, but he was afraid of Hank.

Hank's board of directors—WSM, Acuff-Rose, the Opry, Audrey, and Lilly—saw that Hank was meeting his touring obligations and that looked fine to them. He didn't seem to be writing songs and was not recording at all. He and Pappy didn't talk often. Sometimes when they did, the talk was distant and abrupt, like the time Hank threatened to leave both M-G-M and Acuff-Rose.

"Go ahead, Hank, if you're so goddamn independent," Pappy snapped.

"Now, Pappy, I was just kiddin'."

"Well, I *wasn't.*"

That scared Hank a little. He used to stand up to Pappy. When he first brought his Drifting Cowboys in to recording sessions with him instead of using studio musicians the way they had done before, Pappy objected. Hank had stood up for his Cowboys.

"Pappy, if these boys are good enough to play on stage with me, they're good enough to be on record with me. Besides, I got to sleep with these boys on the road."

He had won that argument, just like he had won some earlier ones about song selection and even about very minor things. Hank pronounced the word "picture" as "pitcher" and couldn't change that and insisted on recording it that way, over Pappy's objections.

But now Pappy sounded . . . *indifferent.* Was it just Hank's imagination, or were things kind of conspiring against him? Bad luck seemed to be always a step ahead of him. It had scared him in New York when he'd finally

sobered up and heard what he'd done. He and Don
Helms had flown up to do "Hey, Good Lookin' " on The
Kate Smith Show. At first they wouldn't let him bring
any of his musicians up but he had told them he had to
have Shag and his steel guitar or it wouldn't sound like
Hank Williams. Hank didn't like New York City a damn
bit, to start with. He had almost gotten into fights with a
couple of waiters in restaurants who tried to make him
take off his hat. Then he'd gotten drunk. M-G-M's Frank
Walker came over to Hank's suite at the Savoy Hotel and
Hank got to fooling around and shoved Walker, who fell
against the radiator and hit his head and knocked himself
out. Hank was too drunk to notice. The hotel maid came
in to turn down the bed and found two figures laid out on
the floor—one with a bloodied head—and called for help.
Hank was bitterly ashamed when he came around and
learned what had happened. He had let himself down,
had let his weaknesses betray him. He quit drinking for a
while. But now and again he had to have the drugs, when
his back was aching so and he would call home five times
a day and Audrey was never there. Morphine could dull
the ache pretty quickly.

Hank snored on. The woman got out of the bed and
threw up in the direction of the wastebasket, thin ropy
strings of whiskey and brown foam streaking the rug.
When the convulsions from her dry heaves finally
stopped, she rolled over in a ball and cursed Hank Williams. Some fuckin' king of country music . . . can't
even get it up . . . fuckin' drunk . . . just wants a blow
job . . . fucker will by Gawd pay for this. She knee-
crawled into the bathroom and threw up a cupful of
foam, hauled herself to her knees by the sink and threw
cold water over her face. When she could walk, she located her step-ins and dress. On her way out of the room,
she rifled Hank's pockets and came up with $437.
Shoulda been more. Cocksucker.

* * *

If he moved, the pain moved and got worse. So he tried to will his aching body to lie still. Mercifully, the light was off and the curtain was drawn over the window. Still, what little light there was hurt his eyes when he opened them. he had no idea where he was, not even what city he was in, or what time it was or even what day. The last thing he remembered was staggering onstage in Oklahoma City. Or was it San Antonio? All the goddamn cities looked the same to him these days. He barely remembered that the doctor had given him a shot of something in his left arm and he could still feel a slight sting there where he had had to dig around with the syringe before finding a vein that would accept the needle. He remembered holding onto the microphone stand to keep from falling off the stage and looking down off the low wooden stage into the first few rows of people and seeing the mockery and derision in some of those eyes. He remembered singing "Jambalaya." Or was it "Lovesick"? And forgetting the words; the goddamn words were there in his mind but they slid around somehow and just wouldn't make it down to his voice, goddamn it. He had tried to explain to the people how he felt. But they could never know.

He squeezed his eyes tight, so tight that he saw stars flashing under his swollen eyelids and tried to forget that. He tried to pretend that he was invisible, like he would sometimes do at parties, when he would hide under a coffee table or squeeze into a corner and then no one could see him and if someone did talk to him he would just say, "This ain't ole Hank. Ole Hank done left. I'm George Morgan." Or sometimes he would be Herman P. Willis, which was his favorite. The other person would be named Herman, too. That way, they could never get to him.

He thought maybe if he became invisible, the pain would have no body to inhabit and would go away. He gripped the chenille bedspread and willed himself invisible. It wasn't working. The pain spread and seemed like a white ball of heat broiling throughout his right side. It was swollen and throbbing. His lower back was a huge needle of pain. He could feel his swollen liver pressing against his ribs. He felt around on the floor with his right hand. Thank God. There was some beer left that was still fairly cold. He sat up long enough—goddamn, the pain! —to find the church key and popped a bottle of Jax and drank half in one long swallow and praised God that it stayed down. He grabbed another bottle and lay back and pressed the cold bottle against his aching liver. That helped some. Oh God. What now? He couldn't take a deep breath without it hurting, he couldn't goddamn move. He prayed to sweet Jesus that he didn't have to play a show somewhere that night; it would kill him, he knew it would, if he had to do that. Please God, let me rest, he prayed. Involuntarily he began weeping, silently, the tears coursing down his gaunt, unshaven cheeks. Dear God, sweet Jesus, just let me *live,* let me live to see my sweet baby boy, my little Bocephus. God, I'll do anything for you, I'll quit drinking, I'll go to church but please dear God drive out this pain and let me *live.*

Where did things go wrong? He and Audrey had been happy once, they were a real family and he had his horses and dogs and could go fishing. And the crowds loved him, goddammit! They loved ole Hank. Nobody but nobody could follow him on stage, not even that goddamn Bob Hope on the Hadacol Caravan. Nobody could close a show like ole Hank.

It was just that constant pain in his back, that fucking stabbing pain that would sometimes drive him to his knees with tears of pain. It wouldn't leave him alone. And Audrey—that motherfucking whore of a bitch Audrey who wouldn't leave him alone and spent twice what he made and was running around with everything in pants in Nashville, he was sure of that. He ought to kill her and just be done with it. The worst mistake he ever made—no, the second worst, the fucking worst one was marrying the bitch—was letting her get up on stage and sing with him. The cunt couldn't carry a tune in a wheelbarrow but she thought she was singing like a goddamn bird. A fucking buzzard. Yeah, like a fucking ugly turkey buzzard. Jesus. If he killed Audrey, Lilly would come after him with the wrath of God and he was more scared of Lilly than of Audrey. You can't kill your mother. You could get away with killing your wife—people would understand that—but not your sweet old mother. If only he could disappear, just become invisible like The Shadow, it would all be so easy. Maybe just vanish into the bayous down in south Louisiana with the cajuns. Now *there* were some goddamn people who appreciate ole Hank. Gumbo and beer on Saturday night. Maybe they would hide ole Hank while he just kinda rested up and got his strength back. But then he wouldn't be able to see little Bocephus. What the fuck was he gonna do?

He heard the door open and could hear a soft footfall on the wooden floor. He opened one eye and flinched and cursed. Goddamn. All he could see swimming into his blurred field of vision was the doctor. And he was opening his goddamn black bag and taking out a needle.

"Hank. How ya feel, son? You gotta be onstage in an hour."

Hank wept.

Hank knew the time had come. He had to see a real doctor about his back. He could barely walk. Like a damn fool, he had gone out hunting with Jerry Rivers. Skip had run on ahead of them—he was the best squirrel dog around and Hank had traded his diamond-studded watch to a farmer to get Skip—and all of a sudden Hank and Jerry heard Skip send up a distress yelp. He was in trouble. Rivers outran Hank and killed the groundhog that had cut Skip half to pieces. Jerry looked around and couldn't find Hank. He went back and found him lying flat on his back in a gully he had tried to leap over. He couldn't walk at all.

"Howdy, friends, this is Hank Williams." The frail voice, over an instrumental version of "Cold, Cold Heart," wafted out to the crowd in the armory in Washington, D.C. "I hope y'all havin' a great big time here at the show." There was no one on stage; it was a transcription.

"I'd like to say thanks to my good friend Jimmy Davis for comin' up here to Washington and pinch-hittin' for me. Also my wife and my boys. I had been lookin' forward to visitin' you folks here in Washington today but on the thirteenth of December I had to have an operation I'd been puttin' off a long time. It got to where I finally couldn't even walk. When I had the operation I was told that I'd be down about ten days if ever'thing went fine. At the time of the operation I knew about the date here and I was thinkin' all the time I'd get to make it. But after the doctor started the operation, it's called a spine fusion, he got into my back and he found a lot of stuff wrong that he hadn't anticipated before. So after he did this he went ahead and had to fix it all. I had two ruptured discs and the first and second joint in my back was bad. So he had to do quite an operation. I stayed on the operatin' table over three hours. So I was brought home Christmas Eve mornin' from the hospital in an ambulance and I'm in bed at home here now. I haven't been able to get up yet. Me and Mr. Denny at the station, we tried to talk the doctor into lettin' me take an airplane to Washington, an ambulance airplane and then have an ambulance meet me at the airport and carry me to the armory and roll me out on stage and let me sing or say hello or somethin'. But we couldn't talk him into it. He said it might tear down all that he'd accomplished. So I hope you folks, I know you will, in fact, have a good show with Jimmy Davis and all my boys. Ordrey's gonna say hello to you for me. I'd like to say thanks to you for buyin' my records and listenin' to 'em and I'd like to promise you that just as soon as I get up out of this bed I'm gonna try to get up to Washington and make an appearance. Till I see ye, thanks a lot. I know you gonna have a great big time at the show. Thank ye a lot."

He sounded like an invalid. A few people in the crowd wept.

Jim Denny forced him to record that and it had pissed Hank off. He could not get out of his fucking bed and the damn Opry Artists Bureau engineers swarmed through his bedroom with their microphones and wires just so the fucking Opry package show in Washington would have a dramatic sickbed moment. They were fucking afraid that the Hank Williams fans might demand their money back. They *fucking* should! He was the fucking star. And Hank was doubly pissed off that Audrey, who some weeks ago had left his bed but continued to spend his money, had jumped on the bandwagon to appear in his place while he was sick. She was practically wearing widow's weeds, she might as well have been wearing a black veil. She took very well to the role of being the long-suffering wife of the unpredictable star Hank Williams.

Hank had forced his way out of bed Christmas Eve to try be part of the family Christmas. He had been hurting and was short-tempered. Lycrecia was jumping about and yelling. She got on his nerves. He turned to Audrey: "She ain't got no business in here. Make her go to bed." Well, that started a fight and he was too sick to keep up his end of the argument, so Hank crawled back into bed.

He overheard Audrey telling Lycrecia, "If it wasn't for you kids, I'd divorce him right now." He cried after hearing that.

He and Audrey had quit speaking to each other, altogether. He was too sick to get out of bed, anyway, so they didn't even see each other. She drank her whiskey and

received callers and went out alone. Their last evening
together had ended in a brawl; punches were thrown,
clothes and furs were thrown out into the front yard.

He had just about had enough of her whoring around.
He had shot at her and a friend when he had come across
them entwined on the couch. Then, on New Year's Eve,
when Hank was barely able to hobble around after his
operation, Audrey was in the living room with two Nashville women whom Hank knew to be nothing more than
snuff queens. They were taking about all the men they
had fucked. Hank got his .38 and fired above their heads.
You would have thought he killed the president. Audrey
called the cops and then refused to file charges but let
everyone in Nashville know that Hank was getting so
weird that he had tried to shoot two elderly women who
had visited Audrey.

Even while she was gladly filling in for him on the road
while he was flat on his back, Audrey had filed for separate maintenance.

She was off in New York City, trying to get a record
contract and buying clothes, when Hank decided to just
call her bluff and call her down by moving out. He
thought that would shake her up. He packed a few things
—he never needed much—and told Miss Ragland, "This
has been the happiest time of my life. I've been so happy
I couldn't even write a song. You know, sometimes I feel
my body bein' torn apart. Mamma's pullin' one way,
Audrey's pullin' the other way. Even on the road I'm
bein' pulled apart."

He called up Ray Price, a young singer from Dallas
he'd worked with many a time. They had cowritten
"Weary Blues From Waiting," and Hank knew Price was
living alone in a two-bedroom apartment. Price said sure,
come ahead. So Hank moved out to Price's duplex on
Natchez Trace. Price didn't yet know about the suitcases
full of pistols and the eighteen-year-old girls and the

"doctors" who would deliver packages in the early morning hours. All Ray knew was that Hank was the reigning king of country music and if he was having a little trouble with the little lady and needed an apartment for a while, that was by God okay with Ray.

8

"**B**OYS, THEY ain't expectin' any shit at customs and we sure ain't gonna give 'em any," Hank said to his Drifting Cowboys as their Cadillac neared the Canadian-U.S. border. None of the Cowboys said anything. Hank had sobered up fast after the unpleasantness at that night's show in Peterborough, Ontario, but the aftershock remained. The show had been a total disaster. Hank had discovered that if he got drunk, the promoters couldn't make him go on stage. And he was getting tired of going on stage. He had gotten so drunk in Peterborough that he couldn't walk, but promoter Oscar Davis forced him to go on. He had literally crawled out on stage, hoisted himself to his feet by grasping the microphone stand, and had sung the same line from "Lovesick Blues" twelve or thirteen times. He introduced the band members five or six times and got them all mixed up. He forgot which one was which. He lost his grip on the mike stand and toppled off stage, tearing the hell out of his back. His boys dragged him out while the crowd booed. Helms asked for and got a police escort to the border. Hank had fast worn out his welcome in Canada. They had had a close call when another car forced them off the road and four guys jumped out, ready to tear them to pieces. The Cowboys didn't know that Hank, drunk again, had been giving the finger to that other car.

The strangers surrounded the Cadillac: "Let the sumbitch out here."

Jerry Rivers, who was driving, tried to calm them down: "C'mon, let him alone, he's just drunk."

"Let him out here so I can beat the shit outta him."

"C'mon, that wouldn't be fair, the man's just drunk."

"Drunk, hell. If he's that drunk, let him out here so my dog can get at him."

They had barely gotten away, and the Drifting Cowboys started to reevaluate their positions. Things had long since ceased to be fun—like when they would put loads in Hank's cigarettes and that time that the buzzard flew through the windshield of the car—and were now getting to be downright grim.

Hank had been on a fearsome tear, he wouldn't listen to anybody and he would take or drink anything put in front of him. He just didn't care.

He tried to tell himself that he and Audrey would get back together, but every time he read her suit for separate maintenance, filed January 10, 1952, it just ripped his guts apart. She was obviously not hitting on all cylinders. First of all, she claimed that she and Hank had gotten married in 1941; he had never heard of her in 1941. Then she said that she had made Hank move to Shreveport in 1947 because she was ashamed to show her face anymore in Montgomery after the way he mistreated her, even though she had returned to him after filing for divorce, which she forgot had actually been in 1948.

Audrey had claimed that Hank made $92,000 in 1950

—he didn't know what the hell he had made—and had made more in 1951, although she didn't know how much.

She listed their assets: the Franklin Road house was valued at $55,000, $10,000 of that still owed; "rather expensive" furnishings for that house, and "the defendant has indicated to the complainant that he considered the furniture as belonging to the complainant ["Ordrey, this fuckin' furniture looks like shit!"]; three Cadillacs; the farm, on which they still owed $45,000 after putting $15,000 down; a herd of white-faced cattle, value unknown; Hank and Audrey's Corral, with an inventory of about $8,000; joint bank accounts that amounted to only $725 since Hank had allegedly been withdrawing large sums of money; mystery bank accounts that Audrey alleged Hank had opened under pseudonyms to hide his money; Hank's music earnings, yet to be toted up.

Audrey charged, Hank read with mounting anger, that he had suddenly turned into a rich asshole, a raging bull: "During the very early years of their married life, before the defendant had become a successful artist, the parties were comparatively happy, having the differences of opinion normally to be expected early in the marriage of young people. The defendant's conduct just prior to the year 1947, however, and his mistreatment of the complainant became such that complainant was forced to separate from him."

What bullshit! he thought. He read on about how Audrey had taken him back and then persuaded him to move to Shreveport to start a new life together, where he suddenly started to become successful. Then, she charged, he became an animal.

"Finally, in 1949, the parties removed to Nashville, Tennessee, since which time the defendant's attitude toward complainant and toward his home has become progressively more unsatisfactory and more unreasonable, without any occasion for such change in attitude. About nine months ago, the defendant's conduct and attitude toward and mistreatment of the complainant became intolerable. While he had been inconsiderate, and even cruel at times before, he then became most abusive, cursing the complainant without provocation, and striking her on numerous occasions. On the afternoon of Saturday, December 29, 1951, the defendant, after berating, cursing and abusing her, in extreme anger struck her with such force and violence as that she would have been knocked to the floor had she not caught on a desk to prevent herself from falling. This cruel attack occurred in the presence of the complainant's two young children. In order to avoid a repetition of this scene before the children, complainant left the home, taking the children with her, and did not return until the . . . next day. Defendant was at home on this Sunday, December 30th. Petitioner returned in the company of several of her friends, who are elderly ladies. She asked these people to go with her, since she feared that the defendant might inflict even greater violence upon her than had been done on the preceding day if she returned alone. When she did enter the home the defendant again became most abusive, cursing and threatening her, and was prevented from inflicting more violence upon her only by the hurried departure of complainant. . . . Upon her return to the home . . . on January 3, 1952, the complainant learned that the defendant had departed. He left no funds whatsoever for the complainant.

"The foregoing specific instances are but samples of the cruel and inhuman treatment which has been inflicted upon the complainant by defendant. . . . Defendant is a man of violent disposition when aroused and this violence is particularly aggravated when the complainant herself is the object thereof. . . . Defendant does not hesitate to make a physical attack upon the complainant. She is desperately afraid that when this bill is served upon him, he, if not prevented by the process of this court, will inflict more grievous and serious bodily injury and harm upon her than ever heretofore. The defendant, particularly in the past few months, has been engaging in the wildest extravagances and wasting the funds which come into his hands. At the same time defendant left her no funds with which to pay even living expenses."

Hank couldn't believe what he was reading. He was ready to punch a hole in the wall with his fist. Who the hell was she talking about? It couldn't be him.

He read on: she was taking him to the cleaners, no doubt about it. Handcuffs were to be snapped onto his income and any hidden assets he might have, she wanted half of all future royalties and income, she wanted a peace bond slapped on him to forbid him from ever "coming about, interfering with, or molesting the complainant, Audrey Mae Williams, at any place, either in public or in private, at her home, on the streets, at the store known as 'Hank and Audrey's Corral,' or elsewhere. . . ." She wanted him enjoined from trying to sell or otherwise dispose of anything he owned, she wanted custody of Bocephus, and she wanted Hank to pay all lawyers' fees. It was a staggering suit. He wanted to answer back: hey, what about *her?* What about all the shit she had pulled? She had once called a tow service to come out and take all the tires off his Cadillac while he was drunk, so he couldn't go anywhere. What about her whoring around? What about. . . .

Without even talking to a lawyer, he knew that Audrey could win any kind of lawsuit against him. Any rube shyster lawyer could trot out Hank's medical records—not to mention his arrest record—and persuade any judge or jury in the world that Hank Williams ought to be shot for the good of mankind. They could even sell tickets to the execution.

Hank still kept calling Audrey; he couldn't help it. He knew what she was, but he couldn't get her out of his mind. She refused to talk to him.

He tried to keep his career together but he was moving

in slow motion, like a man walking underwater. He wasn't writing or recording. He had quit looking at the *Billboard* charts. He had quit strutting into the Opry's backstage area and announcing that his latest song had just sold 60,000 copies right out of the chute. He had quit showing lyrics to other singers and bragging that he had just written that song and what did they think about it? *Good?* Bet your ass it was good, so good that ole Hank should keep that song for himself. He didn't do that anymore. His self-confidence seemed to have been shaken. The Opry regulars gave him a wide berth: they had been jealous of him to start with and his sudden misfortunes seemed to be just what his arrogance deserved.

Jim Denny had Hank searched before allowing him backstage at the Opry. Hank bribed people to sneak him some liquor backstage. He tried to get a disc jockey to buy a fifth and suspend it at the small of his back (by a length of twine around his neck) so that it would not be noticed in the backstage frisking. People started claiming that Hank was drinking Sterno and antifreeze. No one offered any help. He might as well have lived in a vacuum. People started treating him like he was invisible. His "friends" looked the other way when they saw him coming. He became more bitter; everybody thought he was just a south Alabama dirt-eating redneck and they had only sucked up to him because of his money and his success. Now that he was regarded as a drunk, the same people who had drunk his liquor and eaten his food and called him friend suddenly acted as if he were just a bad smell in their presence. They were lucky, especially the hypocrites at the Opry, that he didn't use them for target practice with his .44 or his .38 or his other guns.

Richmond, Virginia, was all a-twitter. Hank read the newspaper stories as he and the Cowboys drove into town. Hank's shows that night and the next, on the 29th and 30th of January, 1952, were comparable to General

Lee's last visit. B. C. Gates, who was booking shows at
Richmond's Mosque, had passed out ballots to concert-
goers weeks earlier to vote for their favorite hillbilly star.
Hank had won by a large margin, so B.C. booked him
into Richmond, for the first "Hillbilly of the Month"
event. Hank's back was a mess; he was drugging and
drinking constantly to block the pain. But he didn't have
any money; Audrey had frozen his income and his assets,
whatever the hell they were. He had to tour and grab the
cash and run.

By stage time January 29th, he was a wreck, but he
tried to go on stage to collect the money; he had to.

Of course, someone should have been merciful enough
to put him to bed instead of on stage. But, everyone there
stood to make a percentage from his show, so no one said
a word.

It was pathetic, his show. It was so pitiful that a few
sensitive souls in the audience were crying at the spectacle of the king of country music sprawling in the gutter.

Ray Price opened the show, backed by a pickup band
of Don Helms and Cedric Rainwater from the Cowboys
and a local guitarist and fiddler. Price was tolerated; the
crowd wanted the star, wanted Hank Williams. There
was a half-hour intermission. Price apologized for Hank,
saying that he had had a back operation. Hank stumbled
out and had a lot of trouble remembering the words to
"Cold, Cold Heart" and he fractured "Lovesick Blues."
People got up and left. "Lonesome Whistle" was no better. People started lining up at the box office, demanding
refunds. They started getting pretty hot when the man at
the box office said he didn't have the authority to refund
tickets. Pretty soon, ten policemen showed up to try to
quiet the crowd down.

Price went back on stage and sang for a while. He
heard a lot of people shouting about Hank and just where
the hell was he anyway? Price went offstage and returned

to tell the crowd that "The situation seems a lot improved, here's Hank Williams!"

Hank was at least standing up. He acknowledged the boos he got: "I wish I was in as good shape as you are. Hank Williams is a lot of things but he ain't a liar. If they's a doctor in the house, I'll show him I've been in the hospital for eight weeks. And if you ain't nice to me, I'll turn around and walk right off." He drew jeers and he started to take off his jacket and shirt and exposed his back so the audience could see the scar on his back.

Price tried to preserve some of Hank's dignity. He went out on stage and pleaded with the crowd, "We all love you, Hank, don't we, folks?" The crowd laughed and clapped.

Hank lurched through "Move It on Over," "I Can't Help It," and "Cold, Cold Heart" again, before wandering off backstage. The crowd was angry and confused.

He still had a second show to do that night. Charlie Sanders, whom Jim Denny had traveling with Hank to keep him from drinking, knew that he had better get Hank into some kind of shape to do that second show. Sanders had not done too well that day at keeping Hank sober. He took him out and forced him to eat a sandwich and drink coffee. Then, he made him walk, coatless, in the frigid cold until he started to come around. The second show was adequate.

The Cowboys were humiliated. Howard Watts left for Nashville; he had had enough.

The next day, the Richmond *Times-Dispatch* printed the most damning review of a Hank Williams show that was ever published. It was surprising: most newspapers did not even review hillbilly acts, to begin with. This was one of a handful of reviews Hank received during his career. When they did review one of the top acts, they were invariably kind. This review trashed Hank twelve different ways. Hank started drinking when he read it. He was furious. Edith Lindeman, who wrote the review,

had actually done him a favor, although Hank didn't
realize it until Charlie Sanders showed up at Hank's
room. Sanders threw out Hank's whiskey and beer and
called a doctor, who shot him up with Demerol. It wore
off in time for that night's shows. Hank was pacing backstage that night. He could hardly wait to get out on that
stage and teach Edith Lindeman a lesson.

After Price introduced him, he loped out to the microphone and dedicated his first song, "Mind Your Own
Business," to "a gracious lady writer who you all know."
He got an ovation; he had recaptured his ability to hold
an audience.

Hank was stinking drunk when he showed up at Car-
mack Cochran's law office on May 29 to sign the final
divorce decree. He didn't say a word. Cochran, Audrey's
lawyer, had done a good job. She was getting quite a
settlement. To start with, Hank had to pay Cochran himself $4,000 in legal fees. Audrey got Bocephus, the Frank-
lin Road house, her Cadillac, and—most importantly—
she got one-half of all royalties ever due him for songs
and records written and recorded in the past, present, or
future. That would stop only if she remarried. She had no
plans to remarry.

The terms were meaningless to Hank. Money didn't
matter. He hadn't challenged Audrey on any of her demands; she could have anything she wanted. (He knew
she'd come back eventually.) She had given him the farm,
the Corral, visitation rights to see Bocephus, and his
other cars. It didn't matter. Hank had already signed
over power of attorney to his banker, San Hunt at the
Third National Bank, so that Sam could take care of all
his bills for him. He just wasn't interested. It looked like
his little songwriting "partnership" on "Cold, Cold
Heart" as going to cost him about $10,523.78, which was
what the writing royalties so far were worth. He didn't
care.

He had been in a daze ever since it had sunk in that his family was no more. He had disappeared for a while and later told Price, off-handedly, that he'd been in the hospital in Lexington, Kentucky, to dry out. Lexington seemed an odd choice of a location to dry out. He had never been to Lexington before and had no reason to go there, unless it was to check into the federal narcotics hospital there to get off the needle. Lexington and Fort Worth had the two big federal narcotics hospitals in the country. Hank was in better shape when he got back from Lexington. Now he just had to shake off the bottle and try to put his career back together. He hadn't been in the recording studio since the previous August. The only thing he had on the charts was "Half as Much," and it was not lighting any bonfires. It was just so damn hard for him to write, anymore. It was all he could do sometimes to round up enough liquor and drugs to get through the day. He had come dangerously close to overdosing several times, and on the road, the Cowboys had to routinely check on him to make sure that he hadn't passed out again with a lighted cigarette and set fire to the mattress.

He had gotten really knee-crawling, commode-hugging screwed up after his final trip to Franklin Road. Audrey wouldn't let him see Bocephus, wouldn't talk to him.

He stopped on his way out: "Miz Ragland, I guess this is goodbye. I want you to take care of the kids and if you ever need anything, call me." He had just given her a .38 pistol so that she could "take care of herself." He had allowed her to pick any gun she wanted from the collection in the trunk of his Cadillac. She had settled on a .22, but he made her take the .38. The .22, he said, wouldn't "take care of anybody."

Hank was bouncing off the walls backstage. Nudie was trying to talk to him. Hank was trying to put himself back together with a brief California tour. They always

liked him in California. Tonight in Long Beach, he was
drunk and he had deliberately gotten drunk because he
was just plain tired and didn't want to go on stage. Nudie
spoke to him earnestly: "Hank, I understand why you
don't want to go on. God bless you. They're all leeches.
But, just get up and sing for your *friends.* Come out on
stage with me." He went on stage; he figured he needed
every friend he could get. He refused to sign autographs
after the show: "Can't let these good people smell my
breath."

Hank was too drunk to go on stage in San Diego, but
they made him. They were helping him up the steps and
Hank stopped to look at Minnie Pearl. He was pleading:
"I can't work, Minnie. Tell 'em I can't work." There was
nothing she could do. He was able to do only two songs
in the first show before he was on the verge of collapsing.
Between shows, Minnie and Maxine Bamford, promoter
A. V. Bamford's wife, took Hank out for a drive around
town to try to sober him up and to keep him away from
liquor. The women were singing: they didn't know what
else to do. Hank finally sang a verse of "I Saw the Light,"
then he stopped. "Minnie," he said, "I don't see no light.
There ain't no light."

In Oakland, in the Leamington Hotel, Hank got a glass
of water from the bathroom and startled the reporter
sitting in his room by popping a huge handful of multi-
colored pills. Hank seldom gave interviews. He just
didn't see any point in it and he didn't think that newspaper stories were worth a shit, anyway. But the local promoter, Wally Elliott, who called himself "Longhorn Joe,"
had persuaded Hank to talk to Ralph Gleason of the San
Francisco *Chronicle.* Hank swallowed the last of his pills
and he and Gleason went to get breakfast.

Hank gave him a perfunctory personal history while
they had coffee and waited for their eggs in the Leamington's coffee shop. He said he was doing about two-
hundred one-nighters a year and earning . . . oh, about

$400,000 a year. And he had written about a thousand songs.

Gleason knew nothing about country music and was surprised when Hank called his music "folk music. Folk music is sincere. There ain't nothin' phony about it. When a folk singer sings a sad song, he's sad. He means it. The tunes are simple and easy to remember and the singers, they're sincere about them. I don't say I ever write for popularity. I check a song by its lyrics. A song ain't nothin' in the world but a story just wrote with music to it. I can't sing 'Rag Mop' or 'Mairzy Doats.' But the best way for me to get a hit is to do something I don't like. I've been offered some of the biggest songs to sing and turned them down. There ain't *nobody* can pick songs. Because I say it's good, don't mean it'll sell. I like Johnny Ray. He's sincere and shows he's sincere. That's the reason he's popular. He sounds to me like he means it. What I mean by sincerity, Roy Acuff is the best example. He's the biggest singer this music ever knew. You booked him and you didn't worry about crowds. For drawing power in the south, it was Roy Acuff and then God! He done it with 'Wabash Cannonball' and with 'Great Speckled Bird.' He'd stand up there singing, tears running down his cheeks. Fred Rose, it was my good fortune to be associated with him. He came to Nashville to laugh and he heard Acuff and said, 'By God, he means it!' "

That night, at the San Pablo Hall in Oakland, Gleason was converted by Hank's power and sincerity and tried to tell him so. But Hank was too high to recognize him and the backstage "friends" Hank was surrounded with seemed pretty rough and unfriendly. Gleason left. Hank no longer seemed to be the same person who had talked to him wistfully a few hours ago about how much he loved his farm and wanted to settle down there and watch "them cattle work while I write songs and fish."

* * *

Ray Price was starting to wonder a little bit about just
what he had signed up for when he had agreed to share a
place with Hank Williams. Granted, Hank *had* helped
his career along and had gladly lent him his band and
had helped him get onto the Opry. But . . . how many
mornings could Ray take of strangers passed out in the
house, of broken bottles everywhere? How many nights
of hard-eyed guys and heavily-made-up women reeling
around the place while the record player was practically
blasting down the walls?

Ray Price was a serious young man and moral, too. He
had tried to tell Hank, tried to *counsel* him that there
were a lot of people living off him, that these party-goers
were not real friends. And that, while Ray really liked
Hank, things at the house here were starting to get out of
hand, and Ray might have to move out unless things
quieted down a bit.

Hank listened to him, nodded, and promptly forgot
what he had said. Hank had finally gone back into the
Castle Studio on June 13 and recorded "Jambalaya."
"Window Shopping" was the flip side of "Jambalaya"
and Hank also recorded "You Win Again" and its flip
side "Settin' the Woods on Fire," as well as two Luke the
Drifter sides, "Be Careful of Stones That You Throw"
and "Why Don't You Make Up Your Mind." Pappy had
helped him a great deal in polishing the lyrics; Pappy, in
fact, had written "Settin' the Woods on Fire" with a
friend named Ed Nelson, and had done a hell of a lot of
work on the other songs.

Still, Hank was starting to feel a little cocky again. He
had some good songs in the can; he wasn't done for yet.

That feeling didn't last long. He wasn't touring; local
promoters were wary of the Hank Williams drunk reputation. He felt a distinct deep freeze whenever he went to
the Opry. It was like he was a leper; people averted their
eyes and just kind of let him know he was scum.

Ray Price moved out on him. Ray just couldn't take the mental strain that living with Hank was producing. Hank walked in while Ray was packing his bags. "Don't leave me," Hank said. "I'll be all right."

"I got to," Price said, and he was gone.

The house on Natchez Trace came to resemble a permanent party; a tawdry one. The place was a mess; ashtrays were always overflowing, empty bottles were everywhere, underwear remained wherever it was dropped. Broken windows stayed that way. The word seemed to have gotten out that Hank Williams was a free lunch and that faction of country music fans which included a parasitic element stopped in to sample the buffet. Hank ate only when he remembered to; he lost weight rapidly. He kept his cane handy; sometimes he couldn't walk without it. Yet despite everything else, he managed to keep a few women on the string.

Billie Jean already knew all about him, although Hank had never noticed her before. Billie Jean Jones had been what you might call highly visible around the Shreveport area for years. They called her "Seabiscuit" after the sleek red thoroughbred race horse of the same name that was tearing up the race tracks. She was what they called an early bloomer.

When Hank first got on the Louisiana Hayride in 1948 and he and Miss Audrey moved to Shreveport and settled down in their little house on Modica Street, Billie Jean's house was just down the street. When she would come home from school, she would sometimes see Hank going out for the evening and would just stand there and watch him walk out to his Packard, this lanky stud in his tailored western suit and shiny boots and white hat, just kind of unfolding himself with that rolling gait. And he never smiled. That impressed Billie Jean. He seemed to belong to another world. She told her mother one day:

"Mamma, one of these days I'm gonna grow up and marry that cowboy."

Meanwhile, while she was still in high school in 1949, she married some Air Force uniform named Harrison Holland Eshlimar and had a kid by him and got tired of *that* right quick and went back home to Mamma.

Billie Jean went to work for the phone company. Even though she was always saying to anybody who would listen that she "never listened to any of them damned hillbilly singers," she started going out with Faron Young, also known as "The Singing Sheriff," and went with him to Nashville. Faron was on the Grand Ole Opry along with Hank by then. One Saturday night at the Opry, she was in the front row when Hank came on. He spotted her and called out, "Hey, girl? You married?"

"No, sir," she said.

"Who you here with?"

"FARON YOUNG."

"You gonna marry him?"

"No, sir."

Hank turned to Minnie Pearl: "Isn't this the purtiest girl you ever seen? Bring that kid out known as Faron Young."

Hank was drunk, as he was nearly all the time by then: Audrey had thrown him out and though he didn't know it he would soon be fired from the Opry. Billie Jean had caught his eye, though, and he wanted some of that gash. He talked Faron into "double dating" after the Opry that night. Hank picked up a girl and the four of them got into Faron's car and headed for the Nocturne Club.

Hank and Billie Jean talked about the "old days" on Modica Street in Shreveport. Faron and Hank's date were silent. Hank kept trying to lurch over the back seat and kiss Billie Jean.

"You gonna be ole Hank's girl, you know that, girl?"

"Well, you gonna have to have a session with black coffee first."

After coffee at the Nocturne they stopped off at the Natchez Trace house. Billie Jean began to feel that Hank needed someone to take care of him. She didn't know, as he struggled up the stairs with a heavy suitcase that he had painfully heaved out of the trunk of Faron's car, that he was lugging a suitcase full of guns. Nor was she aware that Hank took Faron aside in the bedroom. Hank was still about half drunk and he had a pistol in his hand: "Looky here, Farn, I don't want to cause no trouble but I *love* this gal."

Faron backed off quickly: "All *right,* hoss." They all went out happily to sing at Ernest Tubb's Midnight Jamboree, his radio telecast from the Ernest Tubb Record Store down on Broadway.

In July of 1952, Billie Jean left her daughter home with Mamma, moved to Nashville, got a little apartment on Shelby Street for $10 a week, and went to work for the phone company there. And continued to see Hank.

One day in August she said she was homesick and wanted to go see her folks in Bossier City. "Please, Old Bone, come and meet my mamma 'n' daddy."

Hank hired a driver and off they went in his Cadillac convertible. They put the top down and had a merry time. They stopped at a Dairy Queen outside Memphis and Hank bought her some vanilla ice cream. He smiled as he watched her licking the ice cream and winking at him. The wind blew ice cream into her hair as they rode along, and all over her lovely skin and her tight blouse that was knotted at her navel, leaving a creamy strip of flesh above her short shorts. She was barefoot and Hank thought he had never seen anything so beautiful.

"Bone," she said, all wide-eyed, "they's ice cream all *over* my clothes." She stuck her feet up in the air and wiggled her toes.

They stopped and bought her more clothes; shorts and blouses, each one size too small. Hank was wearing his

usual off-duty sloppy white shirt, black slacks and baseball cap.

He started talking about Audrey. "She's a whore,
Baby. One a these days her cheatin' heart's gonna pay."
He handed her a pencil and told her to write down the
words as he on the spot wrote perhaps his greatest song,
"Your Cheatin' Heart."

"One thing about you, babe," Hank said as he kissed
her. "Ole Hank could never be ashamed of you."

They pulled up to the Jones house just after dark. Billie
Jean's mamma was out emptying the garbage. Billie Jean
skipped up to her, barefoot, dragging Hank by the hand
and said, "Mamma, I want you to meet *Hank Williams.*"

Mamma Jones looked this oaf up and down and curled
her lip: "Son of a bitch, you ain't no Hank Williams."

He didn't say a word. He unlocked the trunk, got out
his guitar, planted one foot up on the Caddy's bumper
and started singing "Lovesick Blues."

"See," he smiled, "it's ole Hank."

They stayed a couple of days, Billie Jean sleeping at
her folks' house and Hank bedding down at her brother
Sonny's house across the street. Hank wet the bed that
night, and all were greatly upset, especially because
Sonny had just gotten married and had all new furniture,
courtesy of his father-in-law who was a contractor. They
sure didn't like to see a grown man pissing on new furniture. That was the first time Billie Jean knew that Hank
was having that kind of problem and just wrote is off as
something that alcoholics did.

They left for Nashville on Friday—he was due on the
Opry on Saturday night—stopping along the way to buy
five pounds of fish for a big fish fry when they got back to
the house on Natchez Trace. When they got there, it was
after dark and they could see lights upstairs and hear
music. The glass in the front door was broken out and
there was a pair of women's high-heeled shoes on a chair
in the living room. They started upstairs and, even

though he hadn't been drinking, Hank began staggering. Billie Jean bumped into him and he fell backwards down the wooden stairs. He lay there at the bottom in a heap and laughed: "What the hell did you want to knock ole Hank down for?"

Billie Jean retreated to the living room where she found that one of Hank's lady friends had moved in while they'd been gone. She and Hank got into a fight upstairs and Hank threw her downstairs.

Billie Jean yelled at Hank, "I ain't never gonna be second to nobody, so have the chauffeur carry me home. There ain't gonna be no fish fry."

Hank begged Billie Jean to stay; he said he was throwing the girlfriend out. Meanwhile, he had the other woman in a headlock, and they wrestled their way out the front door until he threw her off the stoop into the yard. She got up and threw Hank off the stoop. Billie Jean got into the back seat of the Caddy and said she was leaving. The girlfriend declared that she too had had enough and was leaving and got into the front seat. Hank lurched into the back seat with Billie Jean and off they went.

Hank followed Billie Jean into her little apartment. "Bone, I'm gonna have the phone company transfer me back to Shreveport. I am done finished with this town. You promised to *marry* me when my divorce came through."

She was crying and running aimlessly around the room while she tried to pack. Hank just stood there, swaying, arms hanging limply. Billie Jean's only luggage was a couple of large Kotex cardboard boxes.

"If you want me, Hank," she wept, "you got to straighten yourself out."

Hank went home and passed out. His driver called Billie Jean and said Hank would like to talk to her. She said, coldly, "Tell him it's marriage or nothin'." She said she would never settle for second place. She went back to Louisiana, when she didn't hear from Hank right away.

He went on a nonstop binge. His absences from the Opry had become so frequent that Jim Denny drove out to Hank's house to talk to him about it. He said that "management" was forcing the issue, that the rumors and Hank's no-shows were hurting the image of WSM and the Opry. Denny said that if Hank didn't show up for the Opry's "Friday Night Frolics" program on Friday night, he would be suspended from WSM and the Opry. Hank listened to what Denny had to say and then shrugged his shoulders. What could he say? He was who he was and he planned to do whatever he planned to do and if somebody else applied pressure on him he couldn't guarantee what he would do.

The days went by in a blur. The parties went on. Drug contacts showed up, uninvited. Hank didn't mind; he wanted to be either asleep or sedated.

On August 11, Jim Denny called him. He said in as few words as possible that Hank was off the Opry and off WSM. That he had been fired for being a chronic no-show. Sorry, there was no chance to talk it over; it was a corporate decision. If Hank would straighten up and conduct himself right for a year, then he could call back. Hank was sullen, but resigned to it.

Ernest Tubb had been in Denny's office and saw Denny wipe away a tear after the phone call. Tubb reminded Denny that he—Tubb—had noticed a few months earlier that Hank was getting on the edge and had told Denny that he should take Hank off the road for a while. Denny had ignored him. The executives still regarded the singers as semibright slaves. Denny himself had started at WSM as a broom-jockey but he had developed the proper executive arrogance as he rose up through the ranks. Executives had to be tough, he was taught. Everybody involved in the firing of Hank Williams—all the top executives—said it wasn't their decision; that it was a "corporate" decision. Denny, Fred Rose, WSM program manager Jack Stapp, WSM president Jack Dewitt, WSM advertising director Irving Waugh, WSM chief engineer George Reynolds, and National Life and Accident Insurance Company president Edwin Craig; they had all heard the rumors and decided that Hank Williams was a bad risk and a negative factor and a poor representative when it came to projecting an advertising image. Not at all what they needed.

Johnny Wright was with Hank when he got the gold-watch phone call from Denny. Denny had paid no attention when Hank had told him to check the "fucking *Billboard* charts and then call back." Hank was *right;* "Jambalaya" was becoming a hit very fast and "Settin' the Woods On Fire" was a pick hit in *Billboard*. "Jambalaya" would soon be number one. WSM insisted, though, that it could not employ a person like Hank Williams. And it didn't.

Ernest Tubb left Denny's office and as he was getting into his car in the parking lot, encountered Edwin Craig, the chairman of the board of National Life and Accident Insurance Company, which owned WSM and sponsored the Opry. Craig, who always acted like a big country music fan whenever anyone from the newspapers approached him, seemed to be serious as he stopped Tubb. "Ernest, I hear that Jim just fired Hank Williams."

Ernest was serious, he had never been otherwise in his life: "Yes sir, Mr. Craig, he did. He told him he did it to straighten him up." Ernest was amazed to have an executive address him directly.

Craig said, "Well, I hope Jim knows what he's doing, because it could help Hank and it could kill him."

"That's right, sir."

There was some rejoicing backstage at the Opry, some talk of the "chickens coming home to roost." They talked about the time he walked into the Last Frontier Casino in

Las Vegas and automatically checked the jukebox to see how many of his records were on it. There were none! In-fuckin-credible! He went out and bought a jukebox, had it stocked with only Hank Williams records, and had it delivered to the Last Frontier with his compliments. "This one's got some good records on it," he said. What incredible arrogance, some Opry regulars said, as they dissected him. And remember that time he had told someone that he'd sure like to get into her pants and she said, "You can't. I already got one asshole in there!" That was telling him, for sure! Nobody was exactly breaking his back to rush to Hank's aid or defense.

He packed up and went home to Montgomery, home to Lilly. Nashville wasn't Hank's town anymore. He hadn't even seen little Bocephus since Mother's Day, when Miss Ragland took Bocephus and Lycrecia over to the Natchez Trace house to visit Hank. She had been surprised to find Lilly there. At last Hank seemed to be sober.

He went back to Lilly's two-story boarding house at 318 North McDonough and Lilly pulled down the shades. He didn't emerge for days. Lilly said that he had fallen down, hit his head, and developed blood poisoning. That explained the doctors' visits and the deliveries from the pharmacies. The neighbors were accustomed to Hank's "problems": they had seen ambulances come and get him and take him to St. Jude's Hospital and they had seen police cars come and get him when Lilly got furious with him and decided to let him dry out in jail instead of in a hospital bed.

On August 17, he slipped out of the house and met a girl at the Russell Hotel in Alexander City, up by Martin Lake. The police station got a call later that night about trouble at the hotel. Police chief Winfred Patterson drove over to take care of it. He found Hank, shirtless but with his white hat on, running up and down the hall, scream-ing that somebody was whipping old ladies and he wanted to find them and make them stop it. The girl was nowhere to see seen. Patterson got Hank calmed down and hauled him off to jail and locked him up. All he said to Patterson was, "I been in better jails than this, I been in worse jails than this." The girl paid his fine the next morning, peeling bills off a wad that "would choke a horse, it was so big," onlookers said. The story around town was that Hank had thrown all his furniture out the window of the hotel and that when he was locked up, he said, "How much is this damned town worth anyway? I'll buy it and tear it down, and turn it into a damned pea patch."

9

"**P**APPY!"

"How are you, Hank?"

Hank was happy to see him. Fred Rose had come all the way from Nashville to see him. They sat down in the parlor. They both felt a little awkward.

"How you been, Pappy?"

"I'm fine, Hank. You been taking care of yourself?"

"Oh, yeah. I get a little ache sometime."

"Well." That was enough polite conversation. "Let's have a look at those new songs of yours."

That's what Hank had been waiting to hear.

He went to get his guitar and his notes. Pappy was surprised to see how painful walking seemed to be for Hank.

"Now, Pappy, this is a good'n. It's a wooden Indian that falls in love. Kowaliga." Hank was surprised to see that Pappy's close-in vision seemed to have gotten so bad that he had to hold the sheet of paper almost against his nose. Hank didn't remember anything like that before. Maybe he just hadn't noticed it. Pappy was nodding as he read the words. It was good, but it was too serious. Pappy could see the makings of a great novelty song: what if the wooden Indian fell in love with another wooden Indian there in the store and somebody came and bought the Indian maiden he loved?

"Um hum, good. What else have you got?"

They worked over the songs for hours: "Your Cheatin' Heart," "I Could Never Be Ashamed of You," "I'll Never Get Out of This World Alive." Pappy thought that last one was a bit too serious too and decided to give it a major overhaul.

"All right. How soon do you want to record these?"

"Tomorrow!" They both laughed.

"I'll call you when the session's scheduled." Almost as an afterthought, Pappy said, "Oh, Hank. Jim Denny and I were talking and wondered if you might like to go back on the Hayride. Henry Clay would be proud to have you over there."

Pappy averted his gaze. He knew Hank was too proud to take charity and knew that the Hayride was still second to the Opry.

Hank thought for a moment. "Well sir, I guess so." There was no emotion in his voice but he was thinking a mile a minute: the last time the Opry had shunned him, he'd made them hire him after he just got too big for the Hayride. There was no reason he couldn't do it again.

"Good," Pappy said. "I'll call Henry. They can get you back out on the road, too, whenever you get ready."

"I got no band, Pappy. My boys are with Price now."

Pappy just laughed: "Well now, I imagine you've hired bands before."

Hank laughed with him: "I damn *shore* have."

* * *

Hank felt pretty good on the drive to Shreveport.
Things were falling back into place for him. He had some
good new songs, he was going to be the Hayride's star
attraction—no doubt about that, and just a couple of
weeks back the town of Greenville had turned out in a
Hank Williams Homecoming Celebration. Police said the
crowd was about 8,500. And he'd been getting thousands
of fan letters—the post office was starting to complain—
at Lilly's, once word got out that he was sick and had left
the Opry. And waiting for him in Shreveport was his
ultimate weapon against Audrey; a lush, red-headed fian-
cée. He'd called her after Pappy had left. "Baby, this is
ole Hank. I'm comin' up to Shreveport and we've got a
[wedding] date for October nineteenth." He told her to
find him an apartment and to get ready for the return of
Hank.

When Audrey heard about the wedding plans, she
would, he hoped, bust a gut in anger. Billie Jean was
younger than Audrey and better-looking too. He was determined to get even with her. The last incident had
made him want to kill her. She had let him take Bocephus out on the road with him—a ploy, he now thought,
to try to get Hank back—and then she had appeared in
Oklahoma City just as he was introducing his little son
on stage. She had grabbed Bocephus and taken him
home. Well, Hank thought, let's see how she takes to a
wedding.

Before leaving Montgomery, Hank had gone by to visit
Father Purcell. Hank had given him the first donation, a
thousand dollars, for the construction of a fifty-bed hospital building at St. Jude for the treatment of spastic children. And he had agreed to do a benefit tour with all the
proceeds going to treatment of spastic children. As
Hank's leg and back worsened, he started to give some
thought to birth defects.

* * *

Hank ran a quick tour through Texas before starting on the Hayride on September 20. He had signed a year's contract for $250 a week, to appear every Saturday night. Things went well, but Shreveport was just not the same as the first time, when he had really cut a wide path through town while on his way to the Opry. He liked challenges and the Hayride audience the second time around was not one.

There were other things. Lilly had persuaded him to take on one of her friends, Clyde Perdue, as his manager, although Clyde wasn't experienced. The little apartment Billie Jean had gotten for him, in a building on Shamrock, turned out to be part of a family affair pattern. The building was owned by Billie Jean's brother's father-in-law. That brother, Sonny, also became the lead guitarist in Hank's new band. Any time Hank even acted like he was on his way to getting drunk, Billie Jean offered to let him either go to the hospital or to jail and she volunteered to call up her brothers Sonny and Al to make sure he went.

Three days after he was back on the Hayride, he went to Nashville to record the new songs and was surprised to find that he had to lie down and rest between songs. He was just running out of breath. He said he would be okay; he just needed a little rest.

"Goddamn, Hank, calm down! Somebody grab him!" Hank was lurching around backstage in Oklahoma City, blood dripping from his cheek, where he'd been trying to shave and sliced himself open.

Webb Pierce finally got him to sit down and wiped the blood off and found a styptic pencil to stanch the flow. Hank was in no shape to play a show or anything else.

"We need a doctor," Perdue shouted, to no one in particular. One of the local booking agents called the doctor's bureau, a central number for doctors available on call.

Hank was incoherent; nobody knew what he was on.

The week before, he had made a quick flight to Havana, had met a man who sold him a package of ups, downs and morphine. Hank took the next plane back. It had all been arranged by a "friend" in Shreveport who had told Hank how easy it was to get whatever he needed in Cuba. Mexico was good for pep pills, but it couldn't touch Havana when a man needed across-the-board drugs.

Hank had just learned that his friend Father Purcell had died in Montgomery and he felt such a loss. And there was nobody he could talk to about it, no one who could understand what the priest's friendship and understanding had meant.

It was another pain he needed to block. And there were a lot of ways to block pain. He had written "I Don't Care if Tomorrow Never Comes" much earlier in his career; he understood its sentiments double by now.

The last time he had played Oklahoma City, Audrey had taken Bocephus away from him. In the hotel restaurant, Hank had suddenly pulled a pistol and fired at a framed painting of the Battleship *Missouri,* there on the wall.

He had kept on eating while waiters and customers knocked each other down on the way out. Hank told the police, "Hell, it drew on me first." He pointed to the battleship's guns.

Backstage in Oklahoma City, a stocky man with a thin, nervous mouth and steel-rimmed glasses walked in, carrying a doctor's satchel. "I'm Dr. Marshall. What seems to be the problem here?" A dozen voices directed him to Hank's dressing room. Dr. Marshall took one look at the sprawled figure wearing the white sequined western suit and understood immediately. Dr. Marshall reached into his bag.

Before everyone could realize it, Hank was up and walking around. He even played the show, although he refused to set foot on stage until he was introduced as "Herman P. Willis."

Dr. Marshall counseled with his patient after the show, and then left town with him as his personal physician, at a salary of $300 a week. Dr. Marshall said he was an expert alcoholic therapist and he seemed to have the drugs to prove it.

Dr. Toby Marshall was better known to prison wardens as Horace R. Marshall. After a term for armed robbery served in San Quentin prison, Marshall had been arrested in Oklahoma for forgery and sent to the state prison at McAlester. He was paroled and bought a doctor's diploma for $35 from the "Chicago School of Applied Science." He turned up addressing the county medical society on the topic, "Medicine Looks at Alcoholics Anonymous." By the time he met Hank, he had talked a real doctor into providing prescriptions and had treated fifty patients.

Hank had never trusted doctors. Now that he had one he trusted, he would no doubt have been disappointed to know that he wasn't really a doctor. Toby felt no need to tell him.

"What's wrong, Hank?"

"I dunno, I feel . . . like I'm *ahead* a myself . . . I dunno . . . I, my heart's thumpin' so but I cain't set still . . ."

"Lay down for a spell, rest."

"Lord, I *cain't*. My mind's way ahead a my body . . ."

"How many a them thangs you take?"

"Aw, shit, just a few. Hep me, my mind's all fuzzy . . . Where's that bottle at?"

"You done drank too much, Harm. Lay down."

"Gimme a taste. I got to get home. That cunt . . .

that damn gash . . . she's all over town with it . . .
I'm gonna kill 'er, I'm gonna kill 'er. Where's my boots
at? Toby, *hep* me. I cain't get my breath, my chest is like
to bust. *Oh . . .*"

"Lay back, Harm. Take this and I'll give you a drank.
That's right, just rest easy."

"I got to get home, Doc, I . . . I . . . Ohhh, God."

The lean figure on the bed finally relaxed. The bottle
slipped from his right hand. His mouth went slack and a
bubble of spit formed at the left corner of his lips. The
phone rang.

"This is Dr. Marshall. No. Cancel the plane. Hank's
decided to stay over. I'll call you when he's ready to
travel."

Toby Marshall hung up the phone and carefully
packed away his syringe. With some difficulty, he slipped
off Hank's brown western-cut jacket, reached into the left
inside breast pocket and removed a roll of bills.

Hank gave Toby an autographed picture. The inscrip-
tion read, "Best wishes to you, Tobey (sic) and thanks for
everything from your friend Hank Williams." Toby gave
Hank fill-in-the-blank medical script that would let him
walk into any pharmacy and buy anything up to and
including morphine.

Usually, Toby preferred to give Hank chloral hydrate,
seven-and-a-half grains at a time, to sedate him and thus
keep him from drinking. Chloral hydrate was better
known as "knockout drops" or "Mickey Finn." He also
had other things on hand; like dextroamphetamine
sulphate, as well as less powerful stimulants that could
get a man up out of bed when he felt he couldn't move
and propel him onto the stage to sing. He might collapse
later, but he had already done the show, after all.

Nudie Cohen was amazed. The man lying there in
front of him in bed in the Jung Hotel in New Orleans, not

the finest hotel Nudie had ever visited, didn't look like the Hank Williams he had known. His face was bloated and unhealthy-looking, he had a pistol tucked into his pajama pants, his eyes had a wild glint to them. "See what I mean, Herman?" he told Nudie. "I bring them in. I haven't been here in weeks. I bring them *in*— people yellin' 'Hank Williams, Hank Williams!' "

Well, if Hank wanted to call everybody 'Herman,' that was okay but this New Orleans wedding was . . . highly unusual.

"All the folks want to see me get married," Hank went on, "and all of them can't get into the auditorium at once."

That explained why the wedding had been rescheduled to happen twice, once at three PM and again at seven PM at the New Orleans Municipal Auditorium, on October 19, 1952.

"I'll do *anything* to spite Ordrey!" That explained it all.

Nudie had seen Hank in a lot of situations, had seen him really pull stunts—that time Nudie was trying to keep him sober and Hank had phoned ahead to a drive-in grocery where a friend of his spiked Cokes with bourbon so Hank could buy guilt-free drinks—but their big wedding on stage was a bit out of hand. He thought Hank was in a daze.

Hank and promoter Oscar Davis had decided to combine the wedding with a show in New Orleans: it would really pull the fans in and would bring in money and Hank needed both. Billie Jean agreed. On October 10, she sent out the engraved invitations: "Miss Billie Jones [although her divorce from Harrison Holland Eshlimar was not final] and Mr. Hank Williams request the honor of the presence of ———— at their solemn wedding ceremony on Sunday afternoon the nineteenth of October at three o'clock, New Orleans Municipal Auditorium. IMMEDIATELY FOLLOWING THE GALA PERFOR-

MANCE AT WHICH PUBLIC OFFICIALS AND
STARS OF STAGE, SCREEN AND RADIO WILL BE
IN ATTENDANCE." Hank enclosed a few handwritten
notes to people he knew, like one to Jimmie Swan over at
radio station WFOR in Hattiesburg, Mississippi: "Jimmie: I want to take this opportunity to personally invite
you to attend my wedding, and to share with me this
happy moment in my life. Please present this invitation at
the Municipal Auditorium at the three o'clock show. You
will be introduced to the people in attendance along with
a few good comments about your D.J. work. Please bring
your wife or a guest. See you at the show & wedding.
Hank."

Things got crowded before the wedding. Toby Marshall was in town, with his black bag. Lilly had come to
town, accompanied, it was widely said, by her own pilot
and a private detective. She was opposed to the marriage.
Hank was regularly calling the Franklin Road house, to
try to talk to Bocephus. Audrey wouldn't let him and he
would weep. Jack Ruby called from Dallas and said he
was on his way. Fred Rose and Jim Denny were disturbed at the spectacle of a stage wedding and decided
not to lend such a "carnival" any dignity with their presence. Hank sent Audrey an invitation. She called him and
said she was coming down to stop the marriage. Hank
told her he would kill her if she did. He chartered a plane
for her to come down.

Hank's moods changed faster than the barometer's
readings. One moment, he was on the phone cursing Audrey. Ten minutes later, he was pleading with her. She
was all he was talking about; her and little Bocephus. He
was determined, though, it seemed, to get a message
through to Audrey, no matter what it took.

After the Hayride show on Saturday, the night before
the wedding, Hank went across the street with Paul
Howard, a songwriter he knew, to get a sandwich.

Hank seemed sober, but his face and hands bore scratches.

"What happened, Hank?"

"What? Oh, this? Ordrey clawed the hell outta me. Her and Mamma don't want me to get married."

"Well, is that thing tomorrow legal?"

"I—it *oughter* be."

"What you oughter do tonight, Hank, if your mamma and Audrey wanta stop you, is just go and get a J.P. wedding right now, this *minute.* You'll be married up; there won't be nothin' they can do."

"They'd *follow* me."

"Hell, take a different car."

"You go with us?"

"Sure."

Howard and his wife and Hank and Billie Jean borrowed Sonny's 1950 Ford and drove out to Minden and woke up Justice of the Peace P. E. Burton and his wife Annie. There was no music, the ceremony took only a few minutes, and the Burtons were not impressed with what they saw. On the way back to town, Billie Jean spilled her makeup and Hank sat in it and got rouge all over the seat of his white pants. They ran out of gas and had to hitch a ride from a soldier. Hank asked him to come on back to the house with them until Howard whispered roughly at him, "This is your wedding night, you damn fool."

Billie Jean clutched the marriage certificate—the "Proces Verbal of Marriage"—which she had signed as "Billie Jean Jones Eshlimar."

He didn't remember the weddings at all; she hardly noticed them, they went by so fast. At the end of the three o'clock and seven o'clock shows, Billie Jean kind of waltzed out on stage in her long white gown and, while Hank peeled back her white veil, the Rev. L. R. Shelton, pastor of the Algiers, Louisiana, First Baptist Church locked them in matrimony. Hank had had so much champagne by the second wedding, he forgot to keep his hat on for the photographers. Fourteen thousand persons attended each concert-wedding, paying from seventy-five cents to a dollar fifty. Some of the crowd rushed to grab some of the lilies-of-the-valley for souvenirs at stage front.

Oscar Davis had gotten some local merchants to donate wedding gifts to the young couple. Billie Jean especially liked a portable sewing machine that she got.

After the weddings, back at the Jung Hotel, she—wearing a negligee—met with reporters and told them that she and Hank had planned a honeymoon in Cuba but that he was "resting" at that moment. What he had done was pass out and piss in his pants.

"You're pissing on me, Hank Williams!" Billie Jean was almost hysterical as she jumped from the bed, her pajamas soaked. Hank couldn't hear her. He was collapsed on his side, snoring with a horrible rattle and still urinating.

Billie Jean called her brother Sonny on the phone to come and get Hank and take him to the "Hut" again, as Hank called it. He was spending a lot of time there, these days, at the North Louisiana Sanitarium in Shreveport.

It was December 11, 1952, and Hank was in atrocious physical shape. Much of the time he lost control over his bladder and his bowels and Billie Jean had had to throw away some of his beautiful Nudie suits because they were so soiled. She and Hank had once been ordered off a commercial airliner before it took off when Hank passed out and shat in his pants.

He had managed an erection twice in two months since their marriage.

Sonny and his brother Al drove to Hank's and Billie's little apartment at 1346 Shamrock and shook Hank awake. Black foam was coming from his mouth. "Aw, gawdamn, boys, not the Hut again. Don't take ole Hank to the Hut." They loaded him into the car—he was too weak to struggle—and drove him to the Hut and Billie signed him in. Dr. J. E. Williams recognized him and made a quick diagnosis: "Alcoholism. Readmit patient in for same complaint. At this admittance patient also had mild contusion of right hand."

As for "same complaint," the doctor was referring to Hank's last stay at the Hut, which had started on November 27; and then there was the admittance of October 31. It seemed like this man Williams came and went with some familiarity at the place.

That admittance of October 31 noted: "This thirty-[sic] year-old man had been admitted for Rx of acute alcoholic intoxication. States he has been on the road for seven weeks playing various stage commitments and has been drinking steadily for the entire period. Complains of chest pain, especially over upper chest regions. States that deep breathing greatly exaggerates pain. Has had almost constant cold and cough for past several weeks. Has taken many kinds of antibiotics in huge quantities."

They hauled him in and put him to bed in Room 127, with its familiar worn fake-tile gray linoleum floor and puke-green walls. He lay there, eyes glazed and mouth slack. First, they dosed him with a grain of sodium amytal. Then came a thousand cc.'s of five percent Vitadex. After that, they stuck a needle in his bony left arm and started an IV of ten cc.'s of adrenal cortical extract. And then came the Empirin and the chloral hydrate and the morphine and the Demerol. He finally rested, the only way he could rest any more, a kind of jagged unconsciousness rather than sleep. He murmured Audrey's name and Bocephus's name. Never Billie Jean's name. He hardly knew her. He had married her to spite Audrey for finally divorcing him. He never thought she would actually go through with it, the lying bitch, *Ordrey.*

At 2:40 on the afternoon of December 11, Hank woke up and—still a bit dazed from the Demerol and the other sedatives—at first didn't realize where he was. When his mind cleared a little and he recognized the puke-green walls, he came out of that bed like a skinny tornado, ripping the IV out of his arm.

"You ain't gonna keep ole Hank in the Hut!" he screamed, to no one in particular. "This is the last damn time I'm stayin' in this shithole." He gathered his pajamas around his bony frame and walked out.

At 4:30, Shreveport police officer H. H. Pittman responded to a citizen's complaint about a drunk wandering around downtown. Hank, who was wearing a blue serge suit and a green hat with a big feather stuck jauntily in the brim, protested bitterly: "I shouldn't have to go to jail." Pittman frisked him and, when he found a .38 pistol, put the handcuffs on and took him to jail.

The police noticed that he was battered up a little around the face and head and was pretty confused. They finally figured things out and delivered him back to the sanitarium at eight PM.

Nurse Gitain summoned Dr. Cassity and they decided that Hank, who lay there with the look of a trapped animal in his eyes, needed more sedation. Seven-and-a-half grains of sodium amytal knocked him out for two hours and then he got seven-and-a-half more. Two hours later, Nurse Aspinall came on duty and found that Hank had defecated and urinated in his bed. He didn't wake up as the attendants cleaned him and the bed and changed the sheets. He awoke at 6:10 AM and was calmed down with seven-and-a-half grains of chloral hydrate, Toby's drug of choice. They kept up doses of sodium amytal and Empirin all morning and, by noon, he was so calm he wouldn't have walked out of there even if he'd been able to get up.

He was so tranquil on the 13th when he was discharged that he went right back out on the road. In Lafayette, Louisiana, at the Civic Auditorium, he became incoherent and belligerent on stage and refused to sing "Lovesick Blues" when the audience kept calling for it. An angry group of men surrounded his Cadillac when he was leaving and tried to turn it over. In Baton Rouge, backstage, someone told him that a "Lonnie Williams" was on the phone and wanted to talk to "his son, Hank."

"Never heard of him," Hank sneered.

Things got so bad that even the Hayride crowd booed him one night when he was too sick to stay on stage. Horace Logan was shaken by that and he went out on stage and lectured that crowd. "You folks have been entertained by this man for hours and weeks and years. You have seen and felt this man's genius and ability. He needs our help and our sympathy, not our hypocrisy. When he's straight you all know how great he is. But when he's having problems, I will not stand for you laughing at this man."

Lilly went with him on a quick swing through Texas, and sometimes she could be seen tucking the gate receipts due Hank into her purse. When Hank played the Skyline Club in Austin on December 19, he played some of his religious songs, which was not like him. He usually preferred to keep the honky-tonk and the church separate.

Hank was tired. He hated to admit it, but his body just wouldn't rally back the way it used to. He was thinking about taking a little rest over the Christmas holidays. He thought he would go back to Montgomery for a while and visit people and just take it easy. Shreveport was starting to wear on him a bit. The Hut—he was not going to go back there. When he couldn't catch his breath and his chest hurt like it was going to break, the doctors told him he had myositis, that his muscles were inflamed in his chest. When his back knocked him to his knees with pain and when he sometimes dragged his right leg because it just wasn't working right, they said he was an alcoholic and then gave him drugs to kill the pain. When

he lost control of his bowels and his bladder, he was told
it was because he was a drunk, not because of a spreading
paralysis caused by his birth defect, the spina bifida occulta that had never been treated. He knew that there
was something wrong with his body but the drugs shut
out the pain and any thought about the pain. [If he could
have had neurosurgery as a child, the defect could have
been corrected. In rural Alabama, as poor white trash, he
had had no glimmer of a chance. Doctors were suspect,
anyway. When Hank had told Hezzy that he had TB of
the spine, he had known that where was something
wrong that was beyond his control.]

Shreveport on the second go-round had just not been
all that he had thought it would be or could be. The last
time Pappy and Wesley Rose talked to Hank, they got the
message from him that he planned to rejoin the Grand
Ole Opry in February and at the same time leave Billie
Jean and remarry Audrey.

Wesley and Pappy had told him to be sure to play all
his scheduled dates, so the Opry would know that he was
serious about coming back. "Jambalaya" was number
one on the country charts: Hank was unstoppable as *the*
country music star. *Cash-Box* had just named "Half as
Much" the number one folk music record of 1952. "Settin' the Woods on Fire" and "I'll Never Get Out of This
World Alive" were shooting up the charts. He was the
horse you had to beat to win the race, he knew that. But
he was tired. If he stayed in Shreveport, Billie Jean would
send him to the Hut. His mamma—his mamma had him
arrested on *stage* in Biloxi and then bundled into a private plane and flown home to her in Montgomery. She
knew how to show that she was in control. Still, his
mamma *was* his mamma, his closest blood. He couldn't
deny that, no matter how much they fought or how many
the times he had cursed her for denying him a father. He
was ashamed that he himself had denied Lonnie when
Lonnie had tried to call him in Baton Rouge. Hank de-

cided to go visit him during the holidays; he would like that. Audrey—Audrey, Audrey, Audrey. Miss Ordrey. She was headstrong, willful, just like his horse Hi-Life was. Sometimes, he had to kick Hi-Life a little to get him to mind Hank. Audrey was the same way. Hank had seen a little notice in *Billboard* that said that Audrey had been out in California trying to line up an all-girl band to back her up on a singing tour. Well, he sure wished her luck with *that*.

Ordrey as a bandleader? And the lead singer? The *star?* She might as well try to drill for oil in the backyard of that fucking mansion on Franklin Road that he had paid for. Sooner or later, she would come to her senses, he knew.

Right now, Hank just wanted to go back home to Alabama, back to his people, and just try to rest easy for a while. They left Shreveport on December 20. Hank and Billie Jean were driving his blue Cadillac convertible; Lilly and Clyde Perdue were in Hank's yellow Cadillac. Hank said little; he told Billie Jean that he wanted to rest up in Montgomery and visit with his family and friends, and run up to Nashville and talk to Mr. Denny about getting back on the Opry; and then play a couple of dates he had up in Ohio and West Virginia. But first, he just wanted to kick back and go see some Alabama home folks who would be *glad* to see him. Who wouldn't be like everybody else he ran into, who automatically *wanted* something from him: money, fame, recording contract, drugs; *everything*. Where in the hell did all those people come from, anyway? Hank himself did not hear from all his Opry mates—former Opry mates—in Nashville and only talked to Pappy and Wesley now and then.

Otherwise, the phone calls were from fans. If Hank had a close friend, he didn't know who it was.

The boarding house on McDonough Street was stifling

to Billie Jean. Lilly was a dictator there. W. W. Stone, Lilly's latest husband, acted like a scared rabbit.

After one supper in the dark, close dining room with Lilly looming above everyone and not one of the boarders daring to say anything except an occasional brief foray about the weather or something, Billie Jean started going out every day and finding a coffee shop or hamburger joint where she could eat. Lilly made her feel like a pariah, without even saying a word. There was a woman staying at Lilly's who made no secret of it that she was carrying Hank's child, and Hank had agreed to provide for the child.

Billie Jean sometimes walked in on Lilly sticking a needle in Hank's arm. Lilly said it was vitamins. Lilly hardly spoke to Billie Jean. Billie Jean sometimes heard Hank and Lilly having shouting and shoving matches over money: Lilly raged at him about his drinking; he railed back about her taking his money. They would physically fight. When Lilly knocked him down, which was when he was drunk or stoned, she and Billie Jean would put him into bed. When Lilly resorted to histrionics, she would slap her right hand over where she thought her heart was and murmur, pitifully, "Oh, my heart,"—just the way she used to do a lot in Shreveport when Billie Jean hinted aloud that it would be better for the marriage if Lilly went home—and Hank would run to get her smelling salts.

Billie Jean was so happy when Hank said he wanted to go and visit kinfolks down in Butler County that she almost slept in the Cadillac so she wouldn't miss the trip. The frost in Lilly's house was getting to her.

Billie Jean had been upset when she spotted Toby Marshall there: she had hated and distrusted him since the first time she had laid eyes on him. Toby and Lilly talked together, without consulting Hank or Billie Jean.

Billie Jean was happy when she and Hank finally got out of town and headed south down Highway 31: if she was just with him, she was happy. Hank was telling jokes, terrible jokes, like he always did: "Baby, did I tell you what a landslide was? I *didn't*? Well, it's a mountain gettin' its rocks off." She just groaned at the punchline and he laughed and squeezed her knee.

"Now, baby, this lady went to the doctor, said she wasn't feelin' too good. Doctor said, 'Now, stick out your tongue and remove your hat.' This lady, she said, 'I'll try, doctor, but I don't think my tongue can reach that high.' "

They laughed.

"Oh, Hank, you're *silly.*"

Taft Skipper was Hank's cousin. He and his wife Erleen had known Hank since he was a little pissant of a kid. They were always ready to welcome him home. They lived outside Georgiana on their farm.

Hank surprised Taft and Erleen when he walked into their house and announced: "Gonna wash up a little bit and go to church with you." Taft lent him his razor. They all went off to the East Chapman Baptist Church and Hank sang along with everyone else.

Taft and Erleen were happy to see Hank. Erleen fixed his favorite dinner; fried chicken and mashed potatoes. Hank sat down in their parlor and crossed his legs and bobbed his knee while he waited for his fried chicken. Billie Jean was demure and didn't say anything. They finally ate fried chicken. Taft and Erleen decided that they liked Billie Jean when, after she'd eaten everything on her plate, she picked up all the plates off the table and stacked them, and offered to wash the dishes. And she thanked Erleen for fixing dinner. Erleen liked to hear that, and she had never heard that from Audrey. Audrey would never, never think of helping with the dishes the way Billie Jean did. Billie Jean seemed to be a sweet girl. Hank didn't say much, but then he never had. He had talked to Taft about the "old days," which were not that old, after all. Hank was twenty-nine years old. He was

not a grandfather yet, even if he did carry a walking cane
—which was not usual in the South for a young man of
twenty-nine years. Hank didn't big-town Taft: he went
out to his big Cadillac now and again to get a bottle of
beer, but he limped when he did so. He was glad to hear
that Taft had gotten them tickets for the Blue-Gray game
the next day in Montgomery. He wasn't so glad when he
found his seat in the upper deck. Taft went up and offered to trade seats, but Hank refused. He was a stubborn
son of a bitch, anyway, everyone knew that. He shook
hands with Taft and told him goodbye and left.

Braxton Schuffert went over to visit Hank on December 23, 1952, at Lilly's boarding house on McDonough
Street. He had long since given up the idea of being a
professional musician and now worked for the Hormel
Meat Company. Every Christmas he would take a Hormel ham over to Lilly's as a gift.

Schuffert still liked to play music occasionally and he
and a thrown-together band were to play that night at the
Hormel plant party and Hank had promised to come.
But when Schuffert got to Lilly's he was shocked by what
he saw.

Hank was laid up in a back bedroom and looked gaunt
and waxy.

"Sorry I cain't get up, Brack," Hank said. "I'm sick."

"Hank, you goin' down there to sing with us tonight?
People just lookin' forward to you comin'. They all
gonna be there."

"I'm just so sorry, Brack. Just tell 'em I cain't be there.
I'm sick. Dr. Stokes has already been over here."

Hank reached under the bed and took a bottle of Jax
out of a paper bag and struggled to open it. "I just cain't
stand up, Brack. I cain't walk around."

"Hank, quit drinkin' all them beers. You'll kill yourself
with it."

"Well, Brack, I done quit drinkin' whiskey. I'm just

drinkin' a little beer along with it. I got off of whiskey now."

"Well, Hank, I sure wisht you'd come tonight. All those people lookin' so much forward for you."

"I'm sorry, Brack, I'm just not able."

The visit was painful for both men. Schuffert hugged him and left. He visited again after Christmas and brought with him a baby picture of Hank that he had. Billie Jean grabbed it and rolled on the floor laughing: "Ole Hank, that's not you, is it?" Schuffert couldn't get a reading on her, he later told his wife; he wasn't sure if there was any love there or not. All he saw was a kid with a big rock of a diamond on her left hand.

The next time he visited, Billie Jean was not there. Lilly told Schuffert this story: Hank and Billie Jean had gone shopping and Hank wanted to buy an electric train and send it to Bocephus, because he hadn't yet gotten him anything for Christmas. Billie Jean told him: "Nope, you're not gonna send him anything," Lilly said. Hank set his jaw and drove her to the airport and put her on a plane and said they were finished and don't come back, thank you very much. He told her he loved Bocephus more than anything in the world, and it was pretty damn obvious she didn't care anything about him, Lilly said.

Schuffert went in to see Hank, who was propped up sipping from a can of beer. Hank didn't mention Billie Jean and Schuffert didn't broach the subject.

After they talked a while, Hank said, "Brack, I know I cain't live without my family, my wife and my children. I'm goin' home. As soon as I get done playin' these shows. I'm booked up ever' night for six months."

"Hank," Schuffert said, "you gonna kill yourself. Come off that road. You can make a livin' writin' songs and recordin'. You stay on the road like that, it'll kill you."

"Brack, I cain't come off the road. I got to keep hittin' that iron while it's hot. I'm on top and people want to hear me and I got to go. Come with me, I want you to be with me."

"I cain't do it, Hank, I got my job here and my family."

"Well, it looks like I'm gonna have to play this show. Then I'm goin' back to Nashville. I'm goin' back on the Opry. I'm goin' back to my family. I know I cain't live in the wrong places. Tell you what, Brack, soon as I'm goin' back to Nashville, you comin' back up there. I wrote some songs and you'll start singin'. I'm gonna give 'em to you and I'm gonna set you up a recordin' contract and you comin' back to Nashville. I want you up there. I want you to come up and record those songs."

"Hank, tell me, where are those songs?"

Hank put his finger up to his temple and said, "They right *here*. Brack, I just wish you'd drive with me on this trip and help take care of me."

"You know I cain't do that, Hank."

"Well. Hand me my gi-tar. I just recorded a new song and it's the best heart song I ever wrote."

"What is it, Hank? You won't never beat 'Cold, Cold Heart.' That's the best you ever did. That's the most beautiful song I ever heard."

"Naw, this is better. This 'un's 'Your Cheatin' Heart.' "

He sang it, soft and low and Schuffert's eyes kind of misted up. Hank's voice could do that.

Billie Jean was getting pretty tired of life at Lilly's, and life with Hank was producing more valleys than peaks. Hank had been obsessed with getting Bocephus an electric train and, right before they'd left Shreveport for Alabama, they had had to run around town until Hank finally found one that he liked at a Western Auto store. In Alabama, when he wasn't sick, he wanted to run around and visit everybody. He went to church, he drove down to McWilliams to see Lonnie and take him Christmas presents. Lonnie hadn't been home. On Christmas Eve, when she had been decorating the tree, the drugstore delivered twenty-four tablets, each containing seven-and-a-half grains of chloral hydrate. Hank didn't drink that night and they made love, for the third time since their marriage in October. Lilly was rude to Billie Jean and came right out and said that she thought they ought to get divorced. Hank and Lilly were having fist fights, even squabbling in public at the local musicians' union show, where Hank sang a few songs the night of the 28th. He would go off alone and sit in churches. He was getting moody again. Monday night, the 29th, the night before he had to go off on tour again, he wouldn't sleep. He was shadow-boxing around the room.

"Come to bed, Hank."

"I can't, baby. Ever' time I close my eyes I see God comin' down the road after me." He smiled and his eyes glinted. "Jesus has told me that I'm gonna die."

"Oh, cut it out, now, and come to bed."

He finally did, after taking four chloral hydrate tablets.

"Hank Williams, you've pissed on me for the last time!" Billie Jean was furious. He was still urinating on her, soaking her negligee. She shook him awake, and he laughed.

In the morning, she told him that she had decided not to go with him on the road and was going home to her mamma and daddy. He got dressed silently. Billie Jean was curling her hair, when she finally noticed him just staring at her. He had walked back into the bedroom, after she thought he was gone.

His intensity made her uneasy.

"Hank, are you sick? Are you feelin' all right?"

"No, baby. Hank ain't sick. I had to say goodbye and look at your face. I just wanted to look at you one more time." He kissed her on the cheek. "Hank will be seein' you."

He called her from the airport to say goodbye again
and she started crying. Lilly gave her a couple of pills and
said they would calm her down. They made Billie Jean
dizzy and she started vomiting.

Lilly was glad to be rid of Billie Jean. She didn't ap-
prove of her. Lilly had already forgotten that she had
threatened Hank when he had wet the bed, had told him
she was going to put diapers on him if he didn't
straighten up and quit messing the bed like a baby. Now
Lilly could take care of her son. She had already called
Toby, who had gone home for Christmas, and told him to
meet Hank in Charleston, West Virginia, on Tuesday
night. She helped Hank pack his bags and got him a
driver—the weather had caused his charter flight to be
canceled—and kissed him goodbye, and his Cadillac
drove away. That's what Lilly remembered.

Hank flew out of Montgomery on Tuesday afternoon,
the 30th, bound for Charleston for his show there the
next night. Bad weather grounded his flight in Knoxville.
He hung around the airport until it was obvious that he
was not going to be able to get a flight to Charleston. He
checked into the Andrew Johnson Hotel and called Lilly
and told her to get a driver to bring his car up from
Montgomery, since it looked like flying was not going to
be possible. Then he called Toby: "Toby, find me a doctor
here."

Toby called the hotel desk and said that he was Hank's
personal physician and that the man needed a doctor.
The desk clerk found one. Hank had a card in his wallet
that said he was a licensed morphine addict.

When Toby called back Wednesday evening, seventeen-
year-old Charles Carr answered the phone. He had
driven Hank's Cadillac convertible up from Montgomery. Hank had just had two morphine injections and was
barely conscious. There was no way he was going to

make the Charleston show that night, but he could get whipped into shape for Thursday night's New Year's Eve show in Canton, Ohio. Toby told Carr to load Hank into the car and head north. Hank had chloral hydrate tablets and a pint of vodka in his jacket pockets, along with his gun.

Hank awoke in the back seat of the car, and washed down a chloral hydrate tablet with a hit of vodka. He found a pencil and a piece of paper in his pockets and started writing.

Highway patrolman Swann Kitts pulled Carr over for speeding, near Rutledge, Tennessee. He looked at Hank, sprawled on the back seat, and said, "Hey, that guy looks dead." Carr told him he was sedated. Carr paid his $25 fine in Rutledge and went on his way.

At about 5:30 in the morning, Carr stopped in Oak Hill, West Virginia, to ask directions. He couldn't tell from the road signs whether to get onto Highway 21 north or to 61 north, so he stopped the Cadillac right on Main Street, across the street from Glen Burdette's twenty-four-hour Pure Oil service station. Hank seemed to be awfully still. Carr felt his hand and it was cold. He ran across the street to get help. Burdette called the police after taking one look at Hank. Patrolman Howard Jamey answered the call and when he looked at Hank, he knew he was dead. There was a piece of paper clutched in the corpse's right hand. It read: "We met, we lived and dear we loved, then comes that fatal day, the love that felt so dear fades far away. Tonight love hathe one alone and lonesome, all that I could sing, I you you [sic] still and always will, but that's the poison we have to pay."

10

PATROLMAN JAMEY drove the Cadillac to the Oak Hill Hospital, where Hank Williams was a Dead on Arrival. There had been another man in the car with Hank and Charles Carr. He told James that his name was "Donald Surface" and that he was a relief driver that Carr had picked up in Bluefield, West Virginia. Donald Surface then vanished.

Jamey decided that this was a big case and called the police chief, O. H. Stamey. Carr told him they had driven through from Montgomery and had stopped in Knoxville to see a doctor friend of Hank's, who had given him a shot for back pain. He said they had stopped again in Bluefield to see a doctor. He said they had also stopped at a bar in Princeton, West Virginia, for sandwiches and beer. Then, he said, Hank had fallen asleep. Carr said he had reached to cover Hank up with a blanket in Oak Hill when he noticed that he seemed to be unconscious. Carr, who was paid $400 for the trip, later elaborated on the story: they had spent Tuesday night at a Birmingham hotel; they had stopped in Fort Payne, Alabama, where Hank bought some whiskey; they had stopped at a diner outside Chattanooga, where Hank had tipped the waiter $50; they stopped in Knoxville and caught a plane which had to return to Knoxville because of bad weather, then Hank had gotten a shot of vitamin B-6 to cure his hiccups, they had stopped somewhere at a coffee shop where Hank played Tony Bennett's version of "Cold, Cold Heart" on the jukebox, and back in the car Hank had sung "Jambalaya" and Red Foley's "Midnight" and then uttered his Last Words: "Well, I'm gonna give ole Red a break and do one of his songs."

By the time the police searched the car, souvenir hunters had picked it clean, even taking Hank's hat. There were a few empty beer bottles on the floor and that was all. No chloral hydrate or guns or anything else.

Carr phoned Lilly and woke her up with the bad news that New Year's morning. She and Audrey flew to Beckley, West Virginia, fiften miles away, and took a taxi to Oak Hill to claim the remains, which had already been embalmed at the Tyree Funeral Home. Lilly, when the mortician asked her about next of kin, said that Hank's father was dead. Lilly demanded an autopsy, so the body was taken back to the hospital. Dr. Ivan Malinin, a recent emigré from the Soviet Union who spoke barely a word of English, conducted the autopsy. He was not looking for drugs and didn't find any. He said that there was some alcohol in the body, but he couldn't tell how much. He wrote that Hank was thirty-seven years old.

He found that Hank's liver was basically normal: he had not drunk himself to death. He found some of the symptoms of spina bifida: kidney damage, hydrocephalus, and ventricular blockage. He also found that Hank had very recently been beaten up and had been hit or kicked very hard in the groin. His conclusion was that "death resulted due to insufficiency of the right ventricle of heart due to the high position of the diaphragm with following external edema of the brain, congestive hyperemia of all the parenchymatous organs and paralysis of the respiratory center with asphyxia (punctate hemorrhages). Small subcutaneous hemorrhages on the back, hemorrhage in the right sterno mastoid muscle, in the aponeurosis, beneath the scab on the forehead, hemorrhage of the end of tongue and dermatorrhagia of scrotum could be regarded as injuries of small vessels due to some trauma."

Heart failure. That's what he was trying to say. It was not the most thorough autopsy ever conducted. Death seldom results from insufficiency of the right ventricle of the heart. An inquest supported Dr. Malinin's findings.

The night of January 1, at the Canton Memorial Auditorium, people wept as a spotlight was shown on the curtain and the musicians behind that curtain sang, "I Saw the Light." The band that Hank had waiting for him there was led by his Drifting Cowboy Don Helms. Hank had called Helms from Montgomery and asked him to get a band together; Helms could take Hank's big seven-passenger tour Cadillac, which he kept stored in a parking garage in downtown Nashville. The Cowboys felt that Hank seemed to have tired of Shreveport and had dropped his Sonny-led Shreveport band and was either going to stay in Montgomery for the time being or else go back to Nashville. He didn't always say what he was going to do until he did it: that was the philosophy of Herman P. Willis.

Billie Jean was with her mamma and daddy in their house on Modica Street. After the phone call, her daddy was struck dumb. He embraced Billie Jean and was weeping. She pulled away from him: "Daddy, how bad's he hurt? He's gone off one of them mountains? How bad's he hurt?"

"Baby, he's dead."

"Nooooooo! He's not! He's not dead. He's just pretending."

The South could not find enough ways to express its grief at Hank's passing. His records sold out in every store, radio stations played him every hour—some of them would play solid Hank Williams for two hours at a time. Even in Troy, New York, listeners to station WPTR —when that station offered copies of "Kaw-liga" and its flip side "Your Cheatin' Heart" in exchange for March of Dimes contributions of $25 or more—flooded the station with letters and money.

Newspaper columns dripped with tears, all about the Shakespeare of the common man and all that, but some of them hit the outer limits: " 'He sho' did write a heap o' songs,' said a Negro woman. 'Sho' did,' said her companion. 'Dat Jambalaya on de Bayou—dat'ns the one I likes bestest.' 'Ain't dat sumpn. Sho' is tuneful.' "

Suddenly it seemed that eveyrone in the world loved Hank Williams, even the people who had known him best and were starting to revise their memories pretty quickly. Everybody was suddenly Hank's best friend.

11

H E WAS dead. No doubt about that. Now he had to be buried. Just how he was to be buried was a tricky question. His widow was Billie Jean Jones Eshlimar Williams, but it had been Lilly and Audrey who went to Oak Hill, West Virginia, to claim the remains. Lilly had been named administratrix of Hank's Alabama estate. Audrey laid claim to the Nashville estate. Billie Jean was welcome to whatever was left in Louisiana, if there *was* anything there. Audrey and Lilly wanted her out of the picture.

That he would be buried in Montgomery went without saying. He once again belonged to Lilly. Audrey had divorced him and Lilly was sure his marriage to the girl from Louisiana was invalid, certainly so in her eyes if not in the eyes of the law. So Lilly brought him home to Montgomery, from whence she had launched his career.

He would be lain to rest at home, to wait for the day when his mother could join him.

She laid him out in a silver casket in the living room of her boarding house at 318 North McDonough Street. An unending stream of visitors came to call at the two-story white frame house that still had a hand-lettered "Room and Board" sign on the front, next to the long front porch shaded by a metal awning. Police kept an honor guard outside.

The grief-stricken mother, in a new black dress, held up well under the new cross to bear. W. W. Stone, her current husband, was relegated to serving coffee and iced tea to the visitors. Irene, Hank's sister, hovered at her mother's side, along with Lilly's brother Bob Skipper and her sisters Alice and Mattie and W.W.'s daughter Kathy. Lilly hadn't bothered to call Lonnie.

W.W. couldn't be trusted to manage a funeral on the grand scale that Hank deserved. ("He could screw up a two-car nigger funeral," Lilly once said scornfully of W.W. to Hank.)

Audrey certainly couldn't handle the funeral and it wouldn't be seemly for Lilly herself to roll up the sleeves of her black mourning dress and plunge into booking Hank's last appearance. Although she could have done a hell of a job of it.

Finally, a workable solution was arrived at: A. V. Bamford, the genial old promoter who had booked Hank into the Canton show and the canceled Charleston show the night before that, would book the funeral. He was respected and furthermore knew his business; he could handle an affair of this importance. Also his wife Maxine was close to Audrey and the two of them had had New Year's Eve dinner together at the Plantation Club in Nashville while Hank was dying in the back seat of his Cadillac and A.V. was waiting for him in Canton.

So A.V., along with Maxine and Audrey, drove to Montgomery and he set in motion the wheels of a grand

Southern funeral. He reserved the City Auditorium (the
city gave it free) for the services, for he knew that any
church or funeral home would be hopelessly overrun
with mourners. Also two preachers, numerous music acts
to pay homage, and the entire Montgomery police force
and fire department to keep order. All this was easy for
A.V. but painful too, for he had genuinely liked Hank
even if he didn't understand him.

Lilly had called on her friend Leaborne L. Eads of the
Henley Memorial Company to aid her in her time of
need. Eads was flat on his back ill but he got up out of
that sickbed to help Lilly. He sent to Atlanta for the best
vault possible: a Wilbert Continental vault, reinforced
with steel and lined with asphalt and copper. "That's
what preserved King Tut," he told Lilly.

All day Saturday, thousands of people tracked through
Lilly's living room to look at the thin body in the elegant
casket and to press Lilly's hands and murmur words of
comfort to the brave, bereaved mother. "It was his heart,
I understand. But he never was a strong boy, kinda sickly
and frail. Thank God he went quickly and didn't suffer.
What a burden that would have been to you, Miz Stone."
She smiled bravely.

Sunday morning, January 4, 1953, it was cold but
clear. Lilly refused any food. Shortly before one o'clock
the long black 1952 Cadillac hearse finally came for
Hank's body, to take him to the Auditorium where he'd
performed many times. Police had roped off Perry Street
around the colonnaded auditorium. Thousands were already waiting. The roads leading into Montgomery were
hopelessly choked with traffic.

Seldom did a man have more grieving women at his
funeral. Hank had thousands, some weeping in the street
outside Montgomery's Municipal Auditorium because
they couldn't get into the service and had to settle for
hearing it on the loudspeakers thoughtfully installed to

pipe the laying-away out to the 20,000 or so mourners and merely curious who were thronged on Perry Street.

But up there on the front oak pew there was a very interesting group of women with some intense private thoughts as they attended the corpse of the country music legend Hank Williams, laid out there—without his cowboy hat for once, for he had always worn it to conceal his balding head.

There was Lilly. Jessie Lillybelle Skipper Dean Williams Stone, Hank's mother, still a veritable rock of a woman at six feet and about 200 pounds. She sat red-eyed and tight-lipped, with the dignity befitting her role as crown mother of the king of country music. Hank's natural father, Lon Williams, sat some thirty rows back. W. W. Stone sat meekly beside Lilly.

Then there was Audrey, the lovely high-cheeked blonde who had married Hank some nine years before. The divorce was slipping from her memory and she considered herself the rightful widow of the king. That reasoning would keep many a lawyer well-paid for the next twenty-five years.

And there was Billie Jean, the absolutely stunning nineteen-year-old redhead whom Hank married two months before his death. Billie Jean of course considered herself to be the real widow. She and Audrey were not speaking and she and Lilly were barely speaking.

There had been a little bit of ugliness earlier at Lilly's boarding house, where they held the wake. Billie Jean—who horrified everyone by wearing *slacks* to the wake—and her folks stayed in one part of the house and Audrey and Lilly were together in another room. The two factions were kept apart by the undertaker, who allowed each side 30 minutes at a time with the body. There was a lot of ugliness to come, when Billie Jean and Audrey would each hit the concert trail, each billing herself as "Mrs. Hank Williams." But for the moment they sat side by side on that pew in a weird, silent truce.

And there was Irene, Hank's sister, who had received an ESP bulletin about his death while Hank was dying in the back seat of his powder blue 1952 Cadillac en route to the concert in Canton. Irene would continue to receive messages from Hank in the years to come, even while she was in prison just a few miles from where he was pronounced dead in Oak Hill, West Virginia, on January 1, 1953.

Right at one PM, the casket was slowly carried to the foot of the stage, which was almost completely covered with flowers.

At 1:15, the top half of the casket was opened and the mourners began to file past, many sobbing, a few to faint. One woman screamed, "He's gone" and keeled over. The 3,000-seat auditorium would clearly not hold the thousands lined up outside. Assistant Police Chief Marvin Stanley and Fire chief R. L. Lampley ordered the doors closed at 2:30 and the crowd surged against the six white columns surrounding the front door. Fortunately, Bamford had had the presence of mind to have loudspeakers outside to carry the service to those in the street, and two local radio stations were broadcasting the whole thing.

Dr. Henry Lyon, pastor of the Highland Avenue Baptist Church, got things under way a little after 2:30. He was a stocky, energetic man known as a peppery preacher and a fine southern orator. His voice rose and fell like a mighty ocean and he could talk forever without any prepared notes whatsoever.

"My friends," he boomed, "as we begin this service this afternoon, Ernest Tubb will bring us close to the Lord as he sings 'Beyond the Sunset.' "

Tubb sang it slowly, mournfully.

Dr. Lyon sprang to the microphone, his worn King James Bible already open to Psalms. He began to read, that sepulchral voice rising and falling: "The Lord is my shepherd; I shall not want . . . and I will dwell in the house of the Lord forever."

He paused dramatically. "Among the friends of Hank Williams we have the members of this colored quartet, the Southwind Singers, who will bring this message to us: 'My Record Will Be There.' "

They sang beautifully, *a capella:* "Oh, my Lord, oh my record will be there, oh my Lord, will be there, singing way down yonder, oh my record will be there, will be there." The entire balcony of the auditorium, which was segregated, was full of Negroes.

Dr. Lyon went back to his Bible: "Oh death, where is thy sting, Oh grave, where is thy victory?" He read on and on.

He paused again and there were a few coughs in the audience: "One of Hank's own compositions, 'I Saw the Light' will be brought to us by Roy Acuff."

Acuff, a deeply religious man if not a profound one, was uncomfortable. He knew he had been one of Hank's musical inspirations and he also knew that he, like most of Nashville, had not really been there to help when Hank needed help. Still, duty called, and he was not a man to shirk duty.

He began uncertainly: "Thank you, Reverend, very much. Friends and neighbors, several years ago I came here to visit with you in this city and stood on this stage with this fine young gentleman that we're here to pay our respects to. No finer boy has ever come or gone as far as we're concerned." A baby started crying loudly and its cries echoed throughout the cavernous auditorium. Acuff continued: "Several of us came down by plane, you know, to make it. We had to be on the Grand Ole Opry show last night. We flew down here in order that we might be here to pay our last respects to young Hank and his fine family. Uh, quite a few years ago, I appeared here with him and this is one of the numbers, as the Reverend just told you, that he introduced to me and asked me if I would sing it. This meant a whole lot and the kind words expressing, that Hank Williams expressed. I want you to meet all the boys that came down. They're gonna all sing with me. We're gonna do it just in the style that Hank asked me to do it. Will you boys gather 'round me here and I can see Bill Monroe coming in and Jimmie Dickens and Carl Smith, Red Foley, uhm and uhm, my old and uh I can't think of the names that fast. And Webb Pierce and Eddie Hill and then over there on the right is uh my good friend and down in uh, uh, Lew Childre, been with him a long time. I'm not gonna try any further 'cause I'm kinda choked up a little bit and uh . . . Let's do this as Hank would want it done. I'd like to try it. Will you boys take it away?"

Jerry Rivers started his fiddle softly and Acuff sang lead: it sounded like a mournful field chant, a cotton-field blues.

Hank had sung it sad but not this sad. More handkerchiefs appeared throughout the auditorium and men and women wept. The baby kept crying. Roy and the boys cut the song short and Roy said in a choked voice, "Goodbye neighbors." Jimmie Dickens began weeping and didn't stop.

Good southern preachers are used to emotional moments like this and know just how to handle them, how to keep the emotion flowing without kindling breakdowns from the women and without making the men, who didn't like to be seen crying, too uncomfortable.

After regaining the microphone, Dr. Lyon assumed his sternest, most authoritative voice: "Now we'll come to God from a grace in prayer as the Reverend Talmadge Smith, pastor of the Ramer Baptist Church in Ramer, Alabama, a warm personal friend of Hank, leads us to God in prayer."

Reverend Smith, in an almost impenetrable Alabama accent got his prayers out of the way quickly: "Let us pray. Our Father, we thank Thee for the Savior that God gave us, we thank Thee our Father for Jesus Christ. But, our Father, He said that He would be with us even to the end of the world. We ask now that his spirit would come and give comfort, spirit, and encouragement to our hearts. We ask, our Father, thy blessings upon his mother, we pray our Father, that thou would give her strength to bear her cross." Lilly sat up a little straighter. People around her touched her shoulder and whispered "amen."

Reverend Smith pressed on: "We ask, Oh God, that especially in this hour and the years ahead, to his wife and his child and the mother of his child, we pray our Father that Thou would give them the strength and the courage to carry on." Neither Billie Jean nor Audrey liked that too much and they squirmed a little bit; it was a bit disgraceful to refer to them that way, women who had loved him and tried to save him, after all, from himself. Even Lilly winced at the phrasing: as far as she was concerned Hank wasn't married at all.

Reverend Smith hurried to a finish: "Speak to those here and to his many friends and those listening in. And, last, our Father, through it all may we still give Thy Son Jesus the praise, the honor, and glory for all that is done. Speak to us Lord, we know not what to say but we ask for Thy comforting hand and for Thy comforting presence with us. Speak to our hearts. In Jesus's name we ask it. Amen."

There followed much coughing and shuffling of feet and shifting of seating positions.

Dr. Lyon rushed back: "My friends, even since the coming to this world of Jesus, there has been *peace in the valley* for those of us who would seek that peace. And so at this time Red Foley comes to bring us a message of peace in the valley."

Foley had tears streaming down his cheeks before he got to the microphone. Hank had once made him swear on a pact that whichever went first, the other had to sing

"Peace in the Valley" at his funeral. Red never thought it would come to this.

He started the song slowly, still weeping. The Southwind Singers rose behind him and Red gratefully let them take the chorus: "There will be peace in the valley for me some day."

Even Lilly wiped a tear away and thought, "Lord, those niggers can sing."

More handkerchiefs came out.

Dr. Lyon solemnly looked out over his congregation. *"Hank Williams,"* he said and paused. Three thousand faces looked up at him. "The singing idol of millions of Americans has just answered the call of the last roundup. *Even so,"* his voice rose to the roof, "if this world should last a *thousand years,* Hank shall remain dear to *millions* of hearts. I cannot preach the funeral of Hank Williams."

With that said, he began to preach the funeral of Hank Williams.

"It has already been preached in music and song, on the radio, listened to by millions of admiring Americans, since the sad message of his death was announced Thursday. The preacher of the message on the radio —*Hank Williams.* The congregation—the *American people.* His life is a real personification of what can happen in this country to one little insignificant speck of humanity.

"Upon hearing of Hank's death the other day, one of our good people of Montgomery has been quoted as saying amid his tears, 'Why, this young man, Hank, as a boy used to shine my shoes.' Yes, Hank *shined* this man's shoes and thousands of other shoes. Even then he was singing with every snap and every pop of his shoe brush."

Lonnie, whom Lilly seldom allowed to speak, much less think, thought an independent thought for once, one that he would repeat to anyone who would listen: "I shined shoes, too, and I never heard a shoe brush snap or pop. It's the cloth that you make pop." He remembered that to his grave.

Dr. Lyon rose to his tiptoes and pointed heavenward: "We shall ever remember the man who climbed from the shoeshine stand to the heights of *immortal glory* in the hearts of all the people who loved Hank's special brand of folk music. We thank God for our great American country which gives us the privilege to sing like we *want* to sing, to sing *fast*, to sing . . . *slow*, to sing *low*, to sing *high*, to sing—or not to sing at all—is the God-given privilege that America gives us to sing like we *want* to sing. And to *listen* when we want to listen."

He stopped and mopped his sweating brow. He was clearly out on a limb here and on the radio as well and had to find a way to crawl back off that shaky limb to the solid trunk of gospel.

"*Enjoying* it with the entirety of our being. Millions and millions never tire of the genuine heart appeal of Hank's songs. As long as we shall have America with its freedom for individuals to succeed, we will have our Hank Williams to inspire us in the midst of life's hardships. Hank Williams was a great American, a great Alabamian. *What* was the secret of his greatness? Listen, I'll tell you what it was. He had a *message*. It was a *swelling* in his bosom like a great body of water behind a great massive dam. It was a message of the heart, Hank Williams' heart. *Deep down* in the citadel of his inner being, there was *desire, burdens, fear, ambition, reverse after reverse, bitter disappointment, joy, success, everything*— and above all *love* for *people*. It was *all* there in Hank's heart. The break *had* to come; it did come. It came with Hank Williams playing his guitar, singing only as a freeborn American can sing. When Hank played on his guitar, he played on the heartstrings of millions of Americans. They listened to Hank over the radio, in their *homes*, in the *bus stations*, in the *cars* driving along the highways, in the *prisons*, in the *office*. They listened ev-a-ree-wheah! Whites and colored, rich and poor, the illiterate and the educated, the young and the old. Yes, we *all* listened, and we will still listen. Why? *Hank had a message.* This message was written in the language of all the people, it was the message of things that *everyone* feels, *life itself.* Years ago, one of America's foremost doctors said, 'If you have something which represents a genuine need of humanity, though you live in a cottage *deep* in the forest, mankind will beat a trail to your door.' Hank Williams did have something humanity universally needs: a song with a heartfelt message."

Dr. Lyon paused and wiped his brow again.

He was getting ready to move off uneasy ground—the burial of a worldly singer who, even though he wrote some credible spirituals, still had a taint about him—and onto solid rock: salvation and sin. Guilt and redemption. This was a sermon Dr. Lyon could deliver in his sleep and sometimes did, to the distress of Mrs. Lyon. He was getting ready to *preach,* to reach those thousands of sinners listening in on the radio who knew Hank Williams only from the honky-tonks. It was time to thump the Bible, to use the airwaves to humble the sinners. Dr. Lyon had a keen sense of history and he determined to make certain that future preachers knew exactly who had preached the South's grandest funeral and just how grandly it was preached. He wiped the sweat off his rimless glasses and raised his voice. "Now, my friends, I come to the message of *all* messages; the message of Jesus Christ." Lonnie in his seat groaned at that. He knew what was coming, and he wanted to go outside and have a cigarette.

Dr. Lyon was now in high gear: "Let not your heart be troubled. Ye believe in God, believe also in me. This is God's message to every troubled soul. To the loved ones of Hank and his family and his many friends I wish to recommend Jesus Christ. Jesus came to this world saying that I am the way and I am the truth and the light and no man cometh unto the Father but by Me. To you loved ones, to you friends with your hearts grieved this afternoon, you'll find unfailing strength and comfort for your bereaved hearts *only* in Jesus Christ. I say again to the millions of friends of Hank Williams, I recommend to you Jesus Christ for salvation and for peace, for inward security and eternal rest. My friends, this afternoon as you've gathered here in the heart of Dixie in this City Auditorium and out there yonder on the streets by the thousands and all over this state and elsewhere listening in your homes and on the highway by means of radio, we are living in a troubled world.

"If you appreciated Hank Williams and want to show that appreciation, I believe that this man had one desire. It was to make us *happy* inside. We will show our appreciation by atoning for our sinfulness and all of our shortcomings as members of the church and the great host of people who do not know Jesus Christ as personal savior."

Dr. Lyon paused for a glass of water and gave Reverend Talmadge Smith a sidelong glance to see if his fellow preacher appreciated the dazzling trick he had just pulled off: if you liked Hank Williams, you'd better like Jesus Christ. Reverend Smith gave Dr. Lyon a nod of respect.

Dr. Lyon surged ahead: "Yes, we will turn to Jesus Christ, the only hope for this life. Do you know, my friends, in these troubled days, that people, not only the people of America, but the people of the entire world must make a decision. We are either going to plunge again in another bloody war or we're going to *evangelize* this world. And give our heart to Christ, rededicating ourselves to Him as Christians and if we'll unfailingly begin to surrender our hearts to Jesus Christ as personal savior. I'm not preaching a denomination this afternoon. I haven't even mentioned what church I belong to. That's not important. The thing that's important is that I'm a Christian, I'm redeemed, I'm *saved*. And one day God called me to preach and it's my commission, it's my responsibility to say to every man living here under the sound of my voice: don't wait till it's too late to give your heart to Christ. You have only this afternoon."

If Hank were indeed listening as his sister Irene insisted he was, he must have been laughing with irony. "Listen, preacher, I've heard that one enough times."

Dr. Lyon moved into his best revival thunder: "You can go to a *thousand* churches for a thousand *years* but you'll never have salvation for your heart until you repent of your sins and put your faith in Jesus Christ. I'm *hoping and praying* that among the great host of people listening to my voice this afternoon, that you'll forget about this preacher and listen to the still, small voice of Jesus Christ as He says 'Come to me.' *Who* did He invite to come? Whosoever will, let him come, whosoever thirsts deep in his heart and soul, let him come and let him drink. He said, 'I am the bread of life and behold I stand at the door and knock.' And right now as I bring this message to a close may I say to you, where you're *standing,* where you're *seated,* won't you slip your hand into the unseen hand of Jesus Christ and then *one of these days,* whether it be *suddenly* without *warning* or whether it be after a long, lingering illness God shall call you away from this world in which we live now, you shall be able to meet your God without fear and without trembling. Remember the words of Jesus Christ. Let not your heart be troubled, ye believe in God, believe also in Me. I'm the way, I'm the truth, I'm the light. No man cometh," he paused dramatically and pointed his finger heavenward, "unto the Father," another pause and now both arms were stretched up to heaven, "but by Me."

He paused again and said, *"Precious Memories.* The Statesmen Quartet." He sat down bathed in sweat but with the comforting knowledge of a job well done. Reverend Smith shook his hand.

The Statesmen, wearing identical gray double-breasted suits and matching striped ties, lifted their voices.

Dr. Lyon got back to round things out.

"My friends, before we have our benediction, I know without my saying it, that you want, in the name of your friend and my friend Hank Williams, to show our appreciation in just a moment after this benediction. When we stand, will you remain standing with your heads reverently bowed until the procession has left the auditorium. And then when we as a congregation shall leave, because we're in great number, we're in the hands of our friends, our police officers and the firemen, we're going to be careful and obey their every wish in leaving this building and going yonder to the cemetery.

"Our heavenly Father, into Thy hands we put our hands. We are weak, we are frail, children of Thine. We throw ourselves prostrate before Thy throne. If we know our hearts, we love Christ. We love Him with all the entirety of our being. God bless our homes. God bless our families of America, around the fireside of our great nation today. Be with us, lead us and guide us. Amen."

There was a fresh outburst of weeping as the pallbearers—A. V. Bamford, Jim Denny, Jack Anglin, Johnnie Wright, Bill Smith, W. Louis King, Bob Helton and Braxton Schuffert—carried the ornate coffin down the aisle, the family following. Lilly walked proudly, as the mother of a fallen king should bear herself. People pressed forward to touch the coffin, to touch the Bible Dr. Lyon was carrying.

The crowd outside parted for them. Lilly saw a young boy, maybe seven or eight years old, selling peanuts outside and the sight brought fresh tears to her eyes.

Thousands more mourners waited at Oakwood Cemetery Annex, where Hank was lowered into the ground and Dr. Lyon gave rosebuds to the family members. Police tried to keep people from carrying away all the flowers.

At the graveyard, Jim Denny turned to Horace Logan.

"Horace," he said, "If Hank was here, he'd say, 'See, I

told you boys I could draw better dead than you could living.' "

Horace nodded. He knew it was the truth.

Hank had used to call Horace on the phone in the middle of the night if he had nothing better to do. Horace remembered one of the happier phone calls.

"Horace, hoss, did I wake you up?"

"Naw, Hank, I had to get up to answer the phone, anyway."

"What's new?"

"Not much. What's new with you?"

"I got me a lady wrestler here and she's teachin' me some new holds."

Fred Rose was stopped by Joe Azbell, the city editor of the Montgomery *Advertiser,* who asked him if the well was dry. Rose knew exactly what he meant. "Hank wrote, recorded and sang a lot of songs we haven't released yet. I can't say how many. It's a trade secret, but you'll be hearing Hank right along for some time."

12

WHEN HANK was laid away in 1953, they discovered that the plot was too small, so they disinterred the remains of some French aviation cadets who'd been killed in training at Maxwell Air Force Base, outside town, and picked Hank up and moved him about 300 yards.

Even Hank's monument remains a matter of dispute. Leaborne L. Eads of the Henley Memorial Company remembered that he and Lilly sat down and drew up a rough design, which they then gave to Willie Gayle, one of Henley's "artists" who did the final rendering. Willie Gayle, who now runs a self-help firm called Willie Gayle's Swiftsuccess System and writes self-improvement books like *Seven Seconds to Success,* remembered that he created the monument. Willie and Lilly supposedly sat up till three AM in the old Pickwick Cafe drinking coffee and talking monument design. He remembered that the inspiration for the monolith came to him when Lilly told him the story of how Hank came to write "I Saw the Light."

"Willie," she said, "we was driving back from doin' a show in Georgiana and I was drivin' and Hank had his head in my lap and he said, 'Oh, Mamma, I'm tired, so tired, but I know we're almost home because I saw the light.'" What Hank had seen—although how he saw it while lying down with his head in Lilly's lap is a neat optical trick—was the tower beacon at the airport. Never mind. Lilly and Willie both knew that what he had seen was of heavenly origin. So Willie went to work with that and created a white Georgia marble monolith. At the top, it says "Praise the Lord, I Saw the Light." Beneath that is a bronze plaque with Hank's picture and lovely billowy clouds with sunbeams breaking through them. Next he and Lilly worked on the idea of having Hank's hat at the base of the monolith. Lilly said that whenever Hank came home he would take off his hat and sail it across the room and announce, "Mamma, I'm home." Willie took one of Hank's hats and threw it about thirty times before he got what he thought was a perfect replica in stone. A low stone slab across the top of Hank's plot has etched in it the titled of some of Hank's songs: "Mansion on the Hill," "Your Cheatin' Heart," "I Can't Help It if I'm Still in Love with You," "I'll Never Get Out of This World Alive," "Kaw-liga," "Jambalaya," and so on.

Audrey wanted some say about the monument, so Lilly and Willie finally gave her the back of the monolith to keep her quiet. She composed a poem for it:

"Thank you for all the love you gave me.
There could be no one stronger.
Thank you for the many beautiful songs you left me.
They will live long and longer.
Thank you for being a wonderful father to Lycrecia
She loved you more than you knew

Thank you for our precious son
And thank God he looks so much like you
And now I can say there are no words in the dictionary
That can express my love for you
Someday beyond the blue . . ."

—Audrey

There are two marble vases on either side of the monolith and Audrey used to send fresh flowers every week till
she died. Now they contain artificial red flowers of an
unrecognizable nature. The ledger—the marble slab atop
the actual grave has a drawing of Hank's guitar and one
of his fancy, initialed boots engraved in it. There are two
white marble benches to either side of Hank's feet for
visitors to sit on and contemplate what lies before them.
Visitors long ago trampled the grass into dust so they laid
green Astroturf down. Lilly is buried to Hank's immediate left. Her grave is marked only by a marble ledger,
adorned with the five-pointed Eastern Star emblem and
the words: "Lillian Skipper Williams (what happened
to Stone?), August 12, 1898, February 26, 1955,
MOTHER." She has plastic white roses in a tinfoil-cov-
ered Folger's coffee can at her feet. Audrey is probably
not resting easy knowing that Lilly once again came between her and Hank. Audrey had wanted to be buried at
Hank's feet but the cemetery people refused. They said
that not even Lilly could get through the concrete that
protects Hank.

13: Coda

LILLY SAT at the massive oak dining table, leafing through a mass of legal papers. She sat silently for a long time, her huge shoulders finally sagging.

Abruptly, she began reading aloud, in a flat grating monotone. Audrey got up to put on a fresh pot of coffee. The two uneasy allies in the battle for possession of Hank's legacy had both visibly aged since his death. Lilly read: "Item: Royalty contract between Hank Williams and Acuff-Rose Publications, dated the 14th day of April, 1951, Item: Royalty contract between Hank Williams and M-G-M Records, a division of Loews Incorporated, dated the 5th day of July, 1951. Item: Stage Costumes: one white with red and blue piping, value $125. One white with costume trim, value $300. One white and brown buckskin jacket, value $450. One blue double-breasted check with red piping, $300. One blue double-breasted with red piping, $325. One black and white hand-embroidered shirt, $50. One brown striped double-breasted with red piping, $300. One gray-tan striped double-breasted with green piping, $325. One light blue double-breasted with maroon stripe and maroon piping, $225. One black, white and gray striped with black piping, $275. One medium-tan white-striped double-breasted with green piping, $300. One gray wool shirt with red suede fringe trimmed in rhinestones and piped in royal blue, $100. One black double-breasted piped in red, white and green with shirt to match trimmed in green suede, $500. One medium-tan self-striped single-breasted with leather buttons, $125. One teal blue western slack suit, $125. One white gabardine with blue music notes, $500. One cowhide vest with zipper front, $75."

Audrey was getting nervous. She had never seen Lilly like this. "How about some coffee?"

"Shut up," Lilly said without even looking up. "Don't you want to hear what he left?"

She continued reading: "Item: civilian clothes. One tan tick weave double-breasted suit, value $45. One western-style slacks, $15. One navy blue topcoat, $75. One brown double-breasted suit, $75. One gray and blue striped double-breasted suit, $85. One gray double-breasted, Hart Schaffner and Marx, $65. One gray double-breasted, Featherspun, $55. One tan double-breasted, Hart, Schaffner and Marx, $85. One tan striped double-breasted, Kingsridge, $55. One navy blue self-striped double-breasted, $55. One brown over plaid double-breasted, $75. One light tan sharkskin double-breasted, $45. One gray striped double-breasted, Curlee, $60. One brown double-breasted, Kenilworth, $75. One rust flannel double-breasted, $65. One navy blue double-breasted, Kingsridge, $65. One off-white rayon gabardine sport shirt with pearl loop buttons, $12.50. One civilian topcoat, blue-gray, $75. Four white dress shirts with pearl buttons, $8.95 each, $35.70. Two striped western dress shirts, $8.95 each, $17.90."

Audrey began to pace nervously. Lilly read on, her voice getting harsher and louder.

"Item: hats. One 3X beaver, Charles P. Shipley, white, $15. One 2X Resistol, Working Man's Store, rust, $12.50. One 4X Truval, Nudie's Rodeo Tailors, white, $25. One Alboum, Wolf Brothers, gray, $12.50. One Florey hat, white, $12.50. One Dobbs, Hank and Audrey's Corral, black, $20. One Stetson Open Road, medium almond, $10. One Dobbs, suede, navy, hand-stitched edge, $20. One Caxton, gray, $15. One Stetson Open Road, 3X, Beaver, Silver Bally, $15.

"Item: jewelry. One pioneer tie and cuff set, Compass, $4.95. One pair maroon and gold cuff links, $3.50. One white-gold dueling-pistol cuff-link set, $10. One pair yellow gold cuff links, flat, $3.50. One pair tan and white Hickok cuff links, $2.50. One pair yellow gold Swank cuff links, weave pattern, $2.50. One pair yellow gold and leather Swank cuff links, $3.50.

"Item: ties. Seven western ties, $3.50 each, $24.50. Sixteen Foulard ties, $2.50 each, $40.

"Item: wallets. One handmade pocket secretary, Hank, $40. One western billfold, $6.

"Item: belts. One leather hand-tooled belt with 14-karat gold buckle, Hank, $75. One leather hat strap, no buckle, $2.50. One leather guitar strap, 10-karat gold buckle, $35. One leather designed belt without buckle, $2.50.

"Item: musical instruments. One D-18 Martin Guitar with pearl inlay with case, $322.50. One Gibson S.J. Guitar and case, $162. One Martin D-28 Guitar and case, $258. One hand tooled black belt with double holsters trimmed in white with 'Hank' tooled on both holsters, $200. One nickel plated .45 caliber Frontier revolver with stag handles, Number 202124, Colt, $125. One nickel plated .44 caliber Frontier revolver with stag handles,

Number 328891, Colt, $125. One nickel plated Smith and Wesson revolver, .45 caliber with pearl handles, $75. One nickel plated Colt revolver, .45 caliber with pearl handles, Number 325446, $75. One German Luger, blue steel, stag handles, Number 317, $75. One 16-gauge single barrel shotgun, Number 708937, $25. One 16-gauge Remington Automatic shotgun, Number 3505811, $100. One 16-gauge Winchester Pump, Number 1234540, $100. Eight pair of boots, $500. One saddle, $500. Two pieces of hand luggage, $75.

"Item: jewelry. One watch, G493321, case W493, $200. One wedding ring, 14K, $25. One Bulova watch, 5031887, $50. One Gruen watch, movement number 19548, case number 0418266, $50.

"Item: cash. Cash on deposit in the First National Bank of Montgomery, $4,394.80."

"The total, Miss Audrey," Lilly continued in her monotone, "is $13,329.35." She laughed bitterly. "$13,329.35. My son, Miss Audrey, earned a million dollars. Where did it go, I wonder? Did Miss Audrey clean him out?"

"You got your share," Audrey stood up to her former mother-in-law for once. "He signed over those two Cadillacs to you last year."

"What about *your* two Cadillacs, Miss? What about your great fine house out there on Franklin Road? What about that divorce settlement? You get half the royalties, you get the store, you cleaned him out. I made that boy what he became and you tore him down."

"What about you? You used to roll him, I know you did. You got plenty money out of his pockets."

Lilly's voice turned to pure scorn. "And I guess you didn't, Miss? Oh, I know all about you. You should be down on your knees thanking me for keeping that Louisiana girl out of the estate. At least now it'll go to my grandson."

Audrey jumped up, knocking over her coffee, and

raced out of the boarding house, got in her yellow Cadillac convertible and fled for Nashville.

Lilly didn't even look up from her stacks of legal papers.

Billie Jean Jones Eshlimar Williams was a bit nervous but she returned Toby Marshall's hostile gaze as they faced each other in a crowded hearing room of the state capital in Oklahoma City on Tuesday, March 17, 1953. Hank was just over two months in his grave. Billie Jean was out on the road singing as "Mrs. Hank Williams," as was Audrey. The legal problems were only beginning. The day before, Billie Jean had been in Houston for a show at the Western Jamboree club when she'd gotten the call to fly to Oklahoma City to testify before the House narcotics panel, which had just stumbled across H. R. "Dr. Toby" Marshall and which was very interested in learning more about him.

Billie Jean took the witness stand and more than one young legislator fell in love at the sight of her. State Rep. Robert O. Cunningham, the panel's chairman, asked her if she knew who Toby Marshall was.

"Yes sir," she said evenly. "Every time my husband went to fill a singing date and got away from me, that guy with the bag would meet him and administer to him. I destroyed all the drugs he brought home. One time when he was in Oklahoma City with the Grand Ole Opry, he made three thousand dollars and returned home with three hundred dollars. He said he spent some money for expenses and other money for treatment."

She talked on, describing Toby and his little black bag following Hank around.

Toby took off his steel-rimmed glasses, wiped the sweat from around his eyes, and blinked nervously. Toby, at age forty-three, was facing his toughest dilemma. He had always lived by his wits and now he had to find—to conjure up—new depths to his wits that would keep him out of prison. Five years in San Quentin prison and a year in the Oklahoma State Penitentiary at McAlester had been enough for him of life behind the walls.

He had committed two bad mistakes after Hank Williams's death. First, he had sent Billie Jean a bill for $736.39 for services rendered to Hank. That had angered Billie Jean no little bit. Secondly, he had continued his charade as a doctor and kept on prescribing drugs. One prescription in particular, for chloral hydrate, had gone to his wife Fay. On March 3, 1953, she had died suddenly of a cerebral hemorrhage. Police found in her possession a letter from Toby that referred to a "deal" he had made with Hank Williams.

The Oklahoma legislature had not known any of that when it had decided to try to combat what seemed to be a drug epidemic. Police, led by Rep. Cunningham, had swept down on Toby's apartment at 133A Northeast 19th and arrested Toby and seized his files and some barbiturates. At first, Toby insisted that he was a doctor and refused to say anything else. He finally agreed to give Cunningham a list of his "patients." Hank Williams was on the list.

It didn't take long to expose him as a fake doctor; as an ex-convict who had discovered that therapy was the best con game. He tried to defend his phony medical practice. He made immediate headlines when he claimed to have information that Hank Williams may have killed himself. He said that Hank had told him that he had decided to "destroy the Hank Williams that was making the money they were getting."

Toby said that the "they" Hank referred to was everyone who was making a living off of Hank Williams. Said Toby: "Although he had a multiplicity of emotional problems, basically he was a very lonely person and couldn't stand being alone. This was expressed in his music. This, in spite of the fact he had a host of fair-weather friends, most of whom were parasites who fawned on him, played up to him, kept him supplied with liquor. . . . I can't overlook the fact that . . . he had been on a rapid decline. Most of his bookings were of the honky-tonk beer joint variety that he simply hated. If he came to this conclusion (of suicide), he still had enough prestige left as a star to make a first-class production out of it . . . whereas, six months from now, unless he pulled himself back up into some high-class bookings, he might have been playing for nickels and dimes on skid row." Toby wiped a tear from his eye. Billie Jean had already gone back on the road.

Toby was sent back to prison. The committee tried to find out what had killed Hank Williams. It had no luck. Dr. Ivan Malinin, who spoke little English, was not able to elaborate upon his sketchy autopsy. No one pressed him.

Toby, amid such local headlines as "Singer Given Leopard Drug" and "Was Singer a Suicide?", still hinted that Hank had killed himself. He denied a suggestion from the panel that he might have been part of a conspiracy to murder Hank Williams. The panel did not pursue the question.

If Hank had thought he had troubles while he was alive, he should have been around to watch the excitement his death caused. Montgomery, especially, was a long time getting over the spectacle of his funeral and the unveiling ceremony the next year, in the football stadium, of his tombstone. The letters-to-the-editor columns in the *Journal* and *Advertiser* brimmed over with lamentations and controversy as well: was Hank Williams a "hillbilly" songwriter or a "folk music" genius? Feelings ran pretty high for a long while there and all you had to do to get yourself punched out in any honky-tonk in most parts of the South was to say something wrong when one of Hank's songs was played on the jukebox. And they were played often. M-G-M's pressing plant in Bloomfield, New Jersey, had to go to around-the-clock operations to meet the demand for Hank's records, especially the newest: "Kaw-liga" and "Your Cheatin' Heart." Besides Williams's recordings of these, M-G-M also released versions of "Kaw-liga" by Bill Farrell and "Your Cheatin' Heart" by Joni James, for the pop markets. Columbia Records readied "Kaw-liga" by Champ Butler and "Heart" by Frankie Lane. M-G-M was also throwing together collections of older songs for two quick "memorial" albums; one of Luke the Drifter material and the other of Hank. The latter carried on the back of it M-G-M president Frank Walker's celebrated "Letter to Williams." Each year that Hank had been with M-G-M, walker wrote him a little letter recapping the year's events. He saw no need to pass up one last missive to Hank, for, wherever he was, Hank would be certain to appreciate it.

It was addressed to Hank, care of "Songwriter's Paradise." "Dear Hank: You see, it was my intention to write to you today as has been my custom for many years past. . . . An hour or so ago I received a phone call from Nashville. It was rather a sad call, too, Hank, for it told me that you had died early this morning. I don't know much about the circumstances and it really doesn't matter, does it? What does matter though is that the world is ever so much better for the fact that you have lived with us, even for such a short time. . . . Remember the time the newspaperman asked you how you wrote a song? I'll never forget your answer—'I just sit down for a few minutes, do a little thinking about things, and God writes them for me.' You were so right, Hank, and do you know I think HE wanted to have you just a bit closer to him; Nashville's pretty far away, so HE just sent word this morning Hank that HE wanted you with him. You're going to be kept busy, too, there's lots of work to be done way up there, for we aren't improving too much here on earth. You'll be writing for the greatest singers too, the

Angels, they're so wonderful—I know they'll want you to join them . . . I guess that's all I have to write about on this New Year's Day, Hank. Thanks so much for being with us, and until I see you again, HAPPY NEW YEAR HANK. Your pal, Frank."

With Hank—uncooperative, hard-drinking, stubborn, drug-ingesting, unmanageable—safely out of the way, the Hank Williams industry was really gearing up.

Tribute records proliferated like crabgrass. Three of them were on jukeboxes before Hank was in the ground a month: "The Death of Hank Williams" by Jack Cardwell, "Hank Williams Will Live Forever (in People's Hearts)" by Johnnie and Jack, and "Tribute to Hank Williams" by Joe Rumore. They kept coming, reaching the maudlin saturation point with Little Barbara's "(I Would Like to Have Been) Hank's Little Flower Girl." Jimmie Swan, a disc jockey at radio station WFOR in Hattiesburg, Mississippi, wrote and recorded "The Last Letter" based on the Frank Walker letter to Hank.

Fred Rose casually announced that the words to about ninety unpublished songs had been found in Hank's effects. Rose also announced that persons trying to sell tape recordings of the funeral would be "prosecuted to the fullest extent of the law. This company holds publishing and recording rights to a song that was sung during the services and we will not allow these rights to be violated."

Rose also, when asked by *Country Song Roundup* magazine for a few remarks for a memorial issue on Hank, spoke out in public for really the first time about his feelings for Hank: "Gentlemen: It is written that "AS A MAN THINKETH, SO IS HE" so I would like to tell you what I think in my heart regarding a very dear friend of mine, Hank Williams. I hope you will not think I am lost in a maze of superficial religion before you read all of what I have to say, as I think I am too practical to delve into the transcendental, beyond the realm of reason. I believe that Hank Williams is just as much alive today as he ever was, and if you will just listen to some of the great songs he has written and recorded, plus the GOOD deeds he has done (that are just now coming to the front) I'm sure you will agree with me. Hank's life was, and is, in his great love for country music and I intend to do all in my power to keep his songs alive eternally because I believe that is the way Hank wants it to be. I cannot spare any sympathy for death because I do not know whether it is good or bad and I don't think anyone else does either. I feel that we will all have to wait until we go through the actual experience of what is called death before we do know what it is. Therefore, I refuse to believe that Hank has migrated to a locality called heaven, or been consigned to a state of oblivion. So I intend to see, hear and enjoy the living of Hank Williams in his music. If you feel the same as I do about the life of Hank Williams, then you will not only be preserving Hank's great love for country music, but the loved ones who are depending on him for their livelihood. What Hank gave to the world will never die! It will live longer than you or me. Excuse me for being so practical about my friend's welfare and I am, Sincerely, Fred Rose."

While Hank in death started to be bigger money than Hank ever was in life, undreamt-of complications and entanglements began to draw "the loved ones" into wrangles that would keep lawyers and judges busy for the next two decades and longer.

After the funeral, Billie Jean, shunned by Lilly and all, went back to Louisiana and hired a lawyer. Lonnie Williams, ignored by Lilly and all, went back to McWilliams, where he would live quietly until his death in 1970, of uremia, at the age of 78. Lilly, Audrey and Irene initially joined forces, drew up the wagons to protect the legend and its estate. No one could find a last will or testament; apparently Hank had not been planning to die. Nor was

there an insurance policy. It would take Lilly almost a
year to figure out exactly what was left of an estate, other
than what was going to Audrey as a result of her divorce
settlement. Of Hank's fleet of five Cadillacs, only the
powder blue convertible in which he died had belonged to
him, and Audrey had it driven from Oak Hill to be stored
in the garage of the Franklin Road house.

Lilly's lawyer, Robert Stewart, petitioned two days after her son was buried for her to be named administratrix
of Hank's estate. In the petition, filed in Probate Court,
Lilly described Billie Jean as "stating she is his widow."
Lilly contended that Hank's three marriages to Billie
Jean, a Justice of the Peace wedding on October 18, 1952,
and two on-stage ceremonies in New Orleans October 19,
were invalid since her divorce from her first husband under Louisiana law was not final until October 28. Audrey
agreed, conveniently forgetting that her own marriage to
Hank had probably been invalid because *her* divorce
from *her* first husband was fifty days short of Alabama's
waiting period of sixty days for final divorce decree when
she and Hank were married.

Audrey also seemed to be forgetting that she had divorced Hank at all. Four days after the funeral, she was
granting long interviews in the Montgomery newspapers
at Lilly's house and claiming that she and Hank had
planned to remarry in February, right after the Grand
Ole Opry took him back.

Lilly had already turned Hank's room in her boarding
house into a Hank Shrine, with mementos scattered
around. She would often sit alone in there.

Neither Audrey nor Lilly nor Irene would comment
about Billie Jean.

Audrey said that, as an initial tribute to Hank, she
would form an all-girl band, "The Drifting Cowgirls,"
and take it out on the road. She would, of course, be the
lead singer.

A reporter asked her which of Hank's songs he had

written for her. Before she could answer, Lilly jumped in: "Just about all of them."

Audrey found time the next week to write an article for the *Advertiser* about her marriage with Hank. It didn't mention that they had been divorced. She did acknowledge that his best "suffering songs" were written during the times they were separated. "I always went back. I went back because I knew that the heart of Hank Williams was great. He was genius if ever there was genius. I knew he would never hurt me or anyone else knowingly. He was often misunderstood because his emotions and his thinking and his feelings were so much deeper than the average person. . . . Everything I ever wanted or could desire, I found in Hank Williams. The heights of joy could not be told, or even imagined, of the happiness I have known as his wife. Nothing can ever take that away from me. Since he is gone, his memory is still like the beautiful dream he made come true for me. I will try to carry on where he left off. The world of music was his —I am making it mine. My band will be the Drifting Cowgirls in memory of his Drifting Cowboys. And I will try to find happiness in the world in which he found it and gave it to me."

Not to be outdone at the writing game, Lilly also wrote a story for the *Advertiser* and dictated a two-thousand word biography of Hank to Allan Rankin, a Montgomery columnist, and sold the pamphlet for a dollar as "Our Hank Williams." She didn't mention Billie Jean at all, but she was careful to point out that "Hank's Mother was always his first girl and he never forgot it."

Meanwhile, the inquest that Lilly had requested in Oak Hill was delivered: official cause of death—a "severe heart condition and hemorrhages in the heart and neck. No evidence was found of foul play." Magistrate Virgil Lyons said alcohol was found in Hank's bloodstream but no drugs were. The coroner's jury based its finding on State Police laboratory tests and on Dr. Malinin's autopsy report that had concluded Hank died of "insufficiency of the right ventricle," an odd cause of death. Only Billie Jean spoke up about that: "I will never believe Hank died of a heart attack." She also replied to Audrey's claim that Hank was going to remarry *her*. She said that while Hank was on the road, she had gone back to Shreveport to sell their furniture and then she and Hank were going to meet in Nashville on January 3. "There, we planned to rent a house until we could build one of our own. Hank never had any intention of remarrying Audrey." Billie Jean also fired a salvo at Lilly: "She is trying to cheat me out of everything. But I think she will fail."

Lilly, finally, although she herself was convinced that Hank's marriages to Billie Jean were not valid, offered Billie Jean a $30,000 settlement if she would just remove herself from the Hank arena. Billie Jean agreed. No one ever wondered where Lilly got the $30,000. Hank's Alabama estate, which Lilly controlled, was worth little: just about forty-three hundred dollars in a bank in Montgomery. Lilly had two of Hank's Cadillacs and much of his personal effects, but not $30,000 worth. After the weddings on stage in New Orleans, Hank had bragged to everybody who would listen that he had made $30,000 getting married and that he just might by gum do it again the next week. But by the time he got to Alabama just before Christmas, he had shown his cousin Taft Skipper a $4,000 check and had told Taft that that was all he had left that women hadn't tied up. He was virtually broke.

In April 1954, Lilly signed a deal with M-G-M Pictures for an authorized movie about Hank. Lilly got $2,000 to option the rights to M-G-M, with an agreement that she would eventually get $20,000 once the movie was completed. The agreement said that M-G-M desired "the consent of yourself, individually and as administratrix of the estate of the said Hiram 'Hank' Williams, and

of the other members of his family, including his first
wife, Mrs. Audrey Williams, and his sister, Mrs. Irene
Smith. We would agree not to refer to the divorce of
Hiram 'Hank' Williams, or to his second wife."

Then Lilly died and the movie was tabled.

M-G-M cranked the idea up again in 1964, with Audrey as technical adviser. Anthony Perkins was first mentioned as the perfect actor to portray Hank; then
Bocephus was. Finally, George Hamilton was picked,
and Bocephus—Hank Jr,. that is—sang the sound track.
Press releases for the movie, titled *Your Cheatin' Heart,*
did not mention Billie Jean. They did mention Audrey, at
great length. "The remarkable story of Audrey Williams,
attractive widow of the famous country singer-composer
Hank Williams, is a fascinating version of the classic Cin-
derella tale," read one release. "Born in the small town of
Banks, Alabama, Mrs. Williams married into show business and with no previous experience became one of the
most successful personal managers in a highly competi-
tive field. . . . Audrey's chore was taking admission at
the door. However, soon she began putting her common
sense to work ('You can't learn personal managing in
school') and made bookings and deals for Williams that
led him to the top. She held conferences with agents and
confounded them with her knowledgeable handling of
her husband's career. . . . When Hank Williams died
suddenly and tragically on January 1, 1953, his wife completely withdrew from business life for more than a year.
Then the pressure of Williams' varied projects—his
records, song publishing and myriad other concerns—
forced her into the music world again. . . . 'Hank and I
had a lot of sayings,' she recalled, 'but I think this was his
best. He believed that phonies don't last. They may be
successful in the beginning, but the veneer soon chips
away. First you have to have talent. Then you have to
work on it to make it shine.' "

Well. Audrey wrote her divorce—all her divorces—

right out of history. There was another woman in the movie, who might have been identified by some as resembling Billie Jean.

Billie Jean sued for libel, charging that the film portrayed her as a lewd woman. She eventually won the suit, after a judge ruled that she was Hank's lawful widow. The movie was withdrawn from circulation.

Billie Jean sued Acuff-Rose for control of some of Hank's copyrights. Audrey and Hank Jr. sued Irene, after Irene successfully had herself named administratrix of the estate following Lilly's death, to try to recover "certain items of personal property, records of business transactions, monies, and assets." The suit also claimed that Irene had managed to be named Hank Jr.'s guardian, even while Hank Jr. was living with Audrey. Irene sued M-G-M for allegedly failing to uphold its contracts. She charged that M-G-M, among other things, had "repeatedly dubbed additional music, voices, and new musical arrangements upon the [old] records, [thus creating] entirely new recordings, in violation of contractorial agreements." Records cited included *Hank Williams With Strings, More Hank Williams and Strings,* and a duet album that Hank Jr. recorded with old Hank tapes. Audrey charged that Fred Rose Music was "conspiring to conceal the hitherto unpublished lyrics and to sell them at an artificially low price" and that Hank's unrecorded songs were worth between half a million and a million dollars and that Irene had sold the material to Fred Rose Music for $25,000 without notifying Audrey or Hank Jr. The lawsuits continued.

Billie Jean married country singer Johnny Horton in 1954. He was killed in 1960 in a car wreck.

Horton had left hundreds of songs that he had recorded at home. Billie Jean became a businesswoman and took those tapes to Nashville and hired musicians to play behind his vocals and she kept the late Johnny Horton on the record charts.

She married an insurance man and then divorced him and stayed active in the music business. She wrote a magazine article in which she said that Lilly had prevented her from recovering the wedding ring she had given Hank. In the article Billie Jean talked about how Hank in death was taken from her: "Hank was gone—the buzzards had started to pick at his leavin's. All I really wanted was some of his personal belongings and the weddin' ring I gave him. I never got them—possession is nine-tenths of the law, and just about everything we owned was in his mother's house, since that's where we were staying when he died. . . . By 'buzzards,' I mean Mrs. Stone, his mother, and Audrey, his ex-wife. Hank's mother, of whose love we didn't share for each other naturally, died in a year, so she didn't reap the wealth she took. Irene, Hank's sister, harvested a better crop as administratrix of the Alabama estate and went into the real estate business in Dallas—that is, until peddling cocaine got to paying better. Right after that girl was voted Woman of the Year, she got herself caught carrying a few million dollars worth of goodies over the border at Laredo. The feds frowned on that. She got eight years. . . . [Audrey] died—in hock to the IRS. In self-defense, Junior had moved to Alabama. Surely, by now, he must know why Hank Sr. was running—you can never keep up with what you're supposed to be."

Wesley, who might have known better, took Audrey into the studio in 1956 to make a record. He had convinced M-G-M Records that Audrey might still retain enough of the Hank legend to sell records. "Parakeet Polka" and "Let Me Sit Alone (and Think)" showed Audrey to be in her usual vocal form.

Although the record was a stiff, Audrey took the occasion to counter the Nashville rumors about her tomcat-

ting around town with a different man every night. She
granted the Nashville *Banner* an interview that was
astonishing in its scope: not only did it not mention Billie
Jean, it did not mention any of Audrey's divorces. "Audrey Williams—all-loving mother worshipped by her two
children; spic-and-span housekeeper; a stately beauty
with silvery blonde hair; an interior decorator of rare
artistry—has expressed in the Hank Williams Den
[where her Hank shrine was located; that is, in the den of
the Franklin Road house] much of the pent-up feeling of
devotion she often had little opportunity to show the
'great traveling man of country music . . . the strange,
wonderful, somewhat terrifying genius who loved to be
sad. . . . This rare specimen of creativeness enjoyed life
most when he was melancholy and mourning over some
real or fancied trouble. . . . His greatest songs were
written in such moments of self-torture.' "

It seemed as if Audrey and Lilly could not buy enough
black mourning cloth. After Lilly published her little
book about Hank, Audrey started publishing "Hank Williams Family Photo Albums" and put them on sale for
$1.25 each, "No checks or C.O.D. accepted." She had
already sold Hank and Audrey's Corral. Audrey had not
advertised the fact that when Hank had moved out, she
had kept a number of his things, such as his Stradivarius
violin.

She started writing yearly poems to Hank. This was
1954's poem:

You know, honey, it's been a year now
Since we got together for a little talk
I was sitting here thinking of how
We first met for that first walk.
That's how I started my life with you.
Yes, Hank, I remember when we first met
You were working on a medicine show

In my hometown, I'll never forget
I happened to drive by and we said hello
That's how I started my life with you.
I acted foolish and played hard-to-get
I had never heard of you then, little did I know
You were singing me love songs and playing a part
Soon on the strings of your guitar you won my heart.
'Twas in Andalusia, Alabama, December 15, year of '44
I became your bride, remember how I cried?
Couldn't find a preacher, so we married in a store
Without a honeymoon to run away and hide
That's how I started my life with you.
The next few years a little rough—not too long
We worked hard and waited for that day
Then you began to sing a certain song
The lovesick blues paved the way
That's how I started my life with you.
About the time that fame had just begun
The Grand Ole Opry in Nashville called you
That was the year of '49, God gave us a son
Life was complete, a girl like me, a boy like you
That's how I started my life with you.
But our happiness didn't last too long
People began to wagging their tongues
And you and I just couldn't seem to get along
So you began to writing more and more songs
That's how I started my life with you.
Along about then everything went wrong
Little did we know it wouldn't be long
'Till you'd be in heaven, no more to be blue
It's hard to go on without my life with you.
Well, honey, it's time for me to go
I can see a bright star shining
It's you to guide me, I know
To that gold and silver lining
Then I can go on with my life with you.

Until then, she tried the concert trail and taught little Bocephus—now "Hank Jr."—how to imitate his daddy. Audrey had once gone to Ernest Tubb to ask his advice about what to do. She was desperate; she was feeling remorse; she was alone and she knew what the Nashville gossips said about her. Ernest, as serious as ever, told her to open up a little "tea parlor" and sell souvenirs of Hank. But she wouldn't listen to Ernest. She told him she was going crazy sitting at home and wanted to go out on the road and sing. She had never accepted the notion that she was not a star-quality singer. As Hank's legend grew after his death, she—who had bitterly resented his success while he was alive—still thought she was part of that legend. She went out on the road with a "talent search." Her billboards read: "Tomorrow's Stars hit the Road Today. America's No. 1 Rockabilly Bombshell!! Audrey Williams, Mrs. Hank Williams, presents her Country Music Talent Show with · A stage full of radio, TV, and recording stars of tomorrow in competition for fame and fortune · Jimmy Hinkle and His Western Swing Band · Many other special features. Empty seats are the enemy of profits. With this attraction playing, no auditorium is large enough." Governor Frank Clement gave her the state's "Official Blessings" for her talent search. That didn't help much. She limped home tour after tour with a ledger full of red ink—"Battlecreek: gross receipts of $2,607 less expenses of $3,162; Toledo: gross receipts of $2,224 less expenses of $2,726.11"—and looked to the young men of Nashville for solace. She turned the Franklin Road house into a big party; she became the scandal of Nashville.

In November 1974, Audrey put a hand-lettered sign out in her front yard: "Garage Sale. Tour Buses Welcome. Souvenirs." She was finally selling off her treasure chest of Hank souvenirs. She also charged $2 admission.

"I was married to a legend," Audrey said. "What else am I going to do?"

The next year, Billie Jean finally won her court fight and was adjudged to have been Hank's wife at the time of his death. The Internal Revenue Service moved to seize some of Audrey's holdings. She died, at age 52, within two weeks after Billie Jean had beaten her in court. "Natural causes" was ruled in her death.

Audrey had two funeral services. The first was in Troy, so that Audrey's mother, who was too ill to travel, could attend. The service, at the McGee-Dillard Funeral Home, lasted only sixteen minutes and she was never mentioned by name. Elder Gilbert Walker, pastor of the Ramah Primitive Baptist Church, said he did not know Audrey at all but had been asked to officiate by her parents. "This was an unusual service," Walker said. "In fact, I was in a quandary as to what to say. I was kind of surprised at the funeral home. There were not as many people as I expected."

Audrey's second service was in Montgomery. Her oft-stated wish to be buried at Hank's feet was not honored. First she lay in state at White Chapel Funeral Home, in her silver casket, in her fringed beige and purple cowgirl outfit with pearl snap buttons and a large initial "A" in purple design, set off by rhinestones.

At Oakwood Annex cemetery, there were few mourners for the graveside service. George and Cornelia Wallace were two; Wesley Rose was another; Big Jim Folsom's sister Ruby was another.

Bob Harrington, who had been variously known as "The Chaplain of Waikiki" and "The Chaplain of Bourbon Street," had, he said, gotten close to Audrey in her waning months and said she had told him that "I've got the faith I need not only to live with, but to die with." Harrington's funeral rites were casual: "There will be no more cold, cold heart, no more parting, no more heartache, no more lonely nights. Audrey will never be alone again." Audrey had asked that the hymn "Beyond the

Sunset" be sung at her funeral. Instead, Harrington just recited it. "I'm no singer," he said.

He turned toward her casket and recited part of Hank's "Hey Good Lookin'."

Audrey was lowered away; even in death she was separated from Hank by Lilly's grave.

Hank's songs, these many years after his death in the first few moments of the year 1953, are still on every country jukebox in the land. He is imitated in every honky-tonk there is; tourists come from all over the world to view (and vandalize) his tombstone in Montgomery, Alabama (officials there once seriously planned to exhume his remains and entomb them in a giant boot as a tourist attraction); country singers still try to emulate his enormous breakthrough in being the first country writer to tear down the walls between the worlds of country music and pop music. All of country music's essential elements were compressed into his few years: sudden success, depths of despair, spending sprees, awesome fan loyalty, total dissipation mixed incongruously with homemade fundamental religion, breakup of the old South and diffusion of southern verities in the sprawl of urban centers, the pain of unfulfilled overreaching, the instilled inferiority of being southern and poor and uneducated and much, much more. Williams, as a writer and singer from the heart, always understood more than he knew and yet seemed to know more than he understood. Physically wounded and thrashing about like an injured buffalo, he was never really able to reach out and touch anyone; only the great mass of his audience ever made him whatever man he was—when he was sober enough to stand up and sing, he affected audiences the way few public performers have ever been able to do.

Hank the Legend bears little resemblance to Hank the Man. The former was a colossus who intuitively sensed the needs of the common man and answered those needs in songs that he himself said came from God; the latter was a weak man who found temporary salvation from his pain only when he was inside a song, a bottle, or a woman. Was he driven by demons or by raw, pure genius? Or was he only another hillbilly who accidentally possessed the skill to articulate the unarticulated yearnings of his peers? He never would say and those who knew him at all never really knew him well enough to know what the hell was going on in his brain.

The man wrote hardly any letters, read nothing but comic books, and revealed his inner self only through his songs. Those who did know him revise his history to sweeten their own. Plain facts and dates and cities do not explain him or his extraordinary impact on American music and particularly on whole generations in the South.

As with many dead musicians, Williams is attributed powers of premonition. When he died, his hit in the *Billboard* charts was "I'll Never Get Out of This World Alive."

Index

Exciting Lives—
Memorable People
from St. Martin's Press!

MAN OF THE HOUSE
"Tip" O'Neill with William Novak
_____ 91191-2 $4.95 U.S.   _____ 91192-0 $5.95 Can.

CRISTY LANE: ONE DAY AT A TIME
Lee Stoller with Peter Chaney
_____ 90415-0 $4.50 U.S.   _____ 90416-9 $5.50 Can.

THE MAN FROM LAKE WOBEGON
Michael Fedo
_____ 91295-1 $3.95 U.S.   _____ 91297-8 $4.95 Can.

FROM THE HEART
June Carter Cash
_____ 91148-3 $3.50 U.S.   _____ 91149-1 $4.50 Can.

DON JOHNSON
David Hershkovits
_____ 90165-8 $3.50 U.S.   _____ 90166-6 $3.95 Can.

ISAK DINESEN
Judith Thurman
_____ 90202-6 $4.95 U.S.   _____ 90203-4 $5.95 Can.

DENNIS QUAID
Gail Birnbaum
_____ 91247-1 $3.50 U.S.   _____ 91249-8 $4.50 Can.

Publishers Book and Audio Mailing Service
P.O. Box 120159, Staten Island, NY 10312-0004

Please send me the book(s) I have checked above. I am enclosing
$ _____ (please add $1.25 for the first book, and $.25 for each
additional book to cover postage and handling. Send check or
money order only—no CODs.)

Name _____

Address _____

City _____ State/Zip _____

Please allow six weeks for delivery. Prices subject to change
without notice.   MP 1/89